WHY KNOCK ROCK?

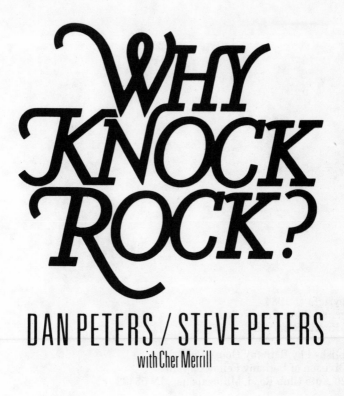

WHY KNOCK ROCK?

DAN PETERS / STEVE PETERS
with Cher Merrill

BETHANY HOUSE PUBLISHERS
MINNEAPOLIS, MINNESOTA 55438
A Division of Bethany Fellowship, Inc.

Published by Bethany House Publishers
A Division of Bethany Fellowship, Inc.
6820 Auto Club Road, Minneapolis, MN 55438

Printed in the United States of America

Library of Congress Cataloging in Publication Data

Peters, Dan.
  Why knock rock?

  Summary: Examines the spiritual effects of rock music, presenting
evidence that the lyrics, the paraphernalia, and the musicians' lifestyles
may be harmful for teenagers.
  1. Rock music—Religious aspects—Christianity—Juvenile literature.
[1. Rock music—Religious aspects—Christianity]
I. Peters, Steve. II. Merrill, Cher. III. Title.
ML3534.P47 1984   784.5'4   84-12515
ISBN 0-87123-440-8

Acknowledgments

This book is a milestone. It is our first book produced by an established publisher, in contrast to the books we have written and published ourselves. And in launching the project we have come to realize more fully the influence and blessing many people have been to our Truth About Rock Ministry. We would therefore like to thank the following:

Our wives, Julie Huisman Peters (Steve) and Renae Gjovik Peters (Dan), for inspiration, encouragement and criticism.

Mom and Dad Peters, for a solid, Christian upbringing and godly influence.

Our younger brother Jim, our older brother Lee, Zion Christian Center, and our entire church family, for patiently fasting and praying as we followed God's leading.

Lorie Kaeser, Ruth Johnson, and Janet Devine Schmidt, for thousands of hours of selfless service, including the organizing and documenting of our manuscripts.

Gary Atchison and Al Loquasto, for their expertise in photography and special effects slides.

Don Kastner and his family, and Pastor Jeff Johnson and his family, for constant encouragement.

Gaylen Erickson, for helping us clarify our goals and Don Kooy for giving us the big vision.

Minnehaha Academy and North Central Bible College, for tolerating the Peters brothers while educating their minds and hearts. The Reverend Gordon Peterson of Soul's Harbor, and the leaders of Jesus People Church, all beacons in the darkness of downtown Minneapolis.

Bob Larson, the grandaddy of rock music seminars.

The hundreds of pastors and lay people who have sponsored our seminars, and the growing army of people who regularly support us with funds and prayers.

Cher Merrill, for beautifully organizing, researching, writing, and putting it all together. With the patience of Job she worked with two guys who were often too busy to talk when she called. We look forward to her articles in our monthly magazine.

Bethany Missionary Church and Bethany Fellowship, for teaching Mom and Dad Peters the incomparable message of the Cross.

Bethany House Publishers, for believing in our ministry enough to publish this book.

Our readers—skeptics, agnostics, atheists, and Christians—who will discover in these pages the truth about rock.

Dan and Steve Peters
St. Paul, Minnesota

Contents

A Note to Parents

Some of the information and documented incidents in this book may shock you. They of course were not included for their sensationalism but to give you a true understanding of the current rock scene. You may wish to use this material as background for discussion with your teenager or the book could be read firsthand by young people, depending on their familiarity with rock music.

You might be surprised at the extent of your children's familiarity—a youngster simply walking into a record store can see and hear in graphic detail some of the immorality referred to in this book. Walkman® headsets and car radios can fill teenagers' minds and hearts with some of rock's suggestive concepts without their parents even realizing it.

This book has been written to provide you, and others who are responsible for guiding young people in Christian values, with a neutral meeting ground for dealing with this emotional issue—some place beyond the usual, "It's way too loud and the beat is too strong!"—"You just don't understand it, Dad!" exchange. This book will help "both sides" evaluate the main issues:

1. What are the lyrics saying?
2. What kind of lifestyles have the musicians chosen?
3. What do the graphics on the album covers indicate?
4. What are the goals of the songs and the performers?

Introduction

Did you know that a civil war has been raging in America for nearly 30 years? The war is spiritual, but nonetheless real, and the hostilities began back in the early fifties.

Who Threw the First Rock?

Of course, it's ancient history now, but some will contend it was Elvis Presley, the hillbilly cat from Memphis who unwittingly fired the first shot—straight from his gyrating hip—which ignited this war. Others allege the baggy-trousered bopper Bill Haley, and his Comets, as the source for the round-the-clock conflict. Still others would like to blame the battle on hysterical parents or witch-hunting preachers, who, while possibly well-intentioned, have sometimes made a big deal out of nothing. What is all the hassle about? Rock music.

Is there something wrong with rock music? Is it harmful? Have people actually experienced problems in their lives because they listened to rock and roll? Can the alleged evil effects be proved?

These questions and more have fueled the continuing clash that began in the infancy of rock music. Sometimes the battle has been evidenced by cold-war name-calling, and other times it has flared into open confrontation. Despite the state of war, however, the rock music phenomenon has boomed, spawning a multi-billion-dollar industry that has produced everything from records and video cassettes to posters and belt buckles—all designed to promote the latest hit group.

The Giant Killers

In 1979, three brothers from St. Paul, Minnesota—Dan, Steve and Jim Peters—joined forces to present a small seminar for the youth group at the church they co-pastor. The agenda included a discussion of some of the effects of rock music, and an opportunity for the teenagers to discard and burn their questionable records, tapes and music memorabilia. Little did the Peters brothers know, however, as the small seminar and subsequent record-burning caught the attention of the media, they would be engulfed in a full-scale war.

Suddenly, in a scene reminiscent of young David's faith-filled, gutsy challenge to Goliath, the Peters brothers were hurled into national prominence for throwing stones at the giant rock music industry. Since then, they have appeared nationwide on *ABC Nightline* with Ted Koppel, *CBS News* with Dan Rather, *PM Magazine*, and hundreds of other television and radio programs. The battle has taken them coast to coast, presenting carefully-documented evidence of the harmful effects of rock music—and the entire rock mystique. Over ten million dollars worth of rock music paraphernalia has been destroyed by people who, after attending a Truth About Rock seminar, have decided to set themselves free from rock music's damaging influence.

On which side are you? Do you know the issues? Or are you one of the casualties in this hotly contested battle? Before you clutch your precious rock records tightly in your arms and vow never to give them up, remember, it's *your* future that is at stake. Keep an open mind as you read this book. It's nice to know what you stand for, but such knowing can only come after an honest, open search for the truth.

So, come along with the Peters brothers as they chronicle this war and its causes. They will discuss the issues fairly; investigate the controversies involved; interview current and former rock stars, and those who love and hate rock music. Then they'll suggest some solutions to the problem and offer you some powerful alternatives.

Now, take a look at the musical war and see if you can discover the truth about rock.

Credit to Whom Credit Is Due

The information in this book was compiled to be *used*, so we hope you'll do more with it than just read the book and set it on a shelf. Tell other parents, your friends, your kids, or your youth group charges about what you've discovered. Conduct your own mini-seminar. But whatever you do, please acknowledge your source: the Peters brothers and Cher Merrill. We've spent thousands of hours researching the facts in order to document the truth about rock and roll. So when you present this documentation, please tell your audience we provided it. Thanks.

Dan and Steve Peters
and Cher Merrill

PART ONE

From the Big Bopper to Big Bucks: The History of Rock Music

1

Happy Days Are Here Again

In 1947, the same year the term "teenager" was coined, a rhythm-and-blues singer named "Wild Bill" Moore wrote and sang a rinky-tink tune that went, "We're gonna rock, We're gonna roll." While that bawdy line of lyric, actually sexual metaphor, was set to a catchy melody, there was nothing particularly memorable about it.

Several years later, however, a Cleveland deejay named Alan Freed made those words unforgettable. Freed borrowed that short bit of lyric to describe a "new sound" of music he had been playing on his late afternoon Cleveland radio program. The music, a combination of boogie-woogie and jazz, hillbilly and blues, had emerged from dark city streets and bleak, back-country roads—places the "happy days" of the Eisenhower years hadn't seemed to touch with their magic wand.

The music was sensual and rhythmic, doused with humor but also steeped in rebellion. Alan Freed, on his *Moondog Matinee* show, lifted the line from Moore's boogie-woogie number and christened the new music "rock and roll." A new music genre was born.

Although just an average deejay, Freed was a promoter's promoter, and knew a money-maker when he saw one. In 1952, the 30-year-old "Moondog" decided to capitalize on the growing popularity of rock and roll by staging a dance, featuring live music of hometown artists. The "Moondog Ball," as it was dubbed, brought to the 10,000-capacity Cleveland arena an unexpected turnout of some 25,000 fans—many from as far away as Toledo. The ensuing free-for-all resulted in the arrest of five people, and at least one stabbing. This first rock concert made Freed famous and gave the *enfant terrible,* rock and roll, an early reputation as a spoiled, rebellious brat.

Within a few years, however, Freed's raucous, rockin' radio program moved on to the Big Apple—New York City—where he was the first to let fly the rapid-fire delivery now synonymous with disc jockeying. Soon Freed was hosting dance-show sellouts along the entire eastern seaboard. From 1956 to 1959, he appeared in three rock and roll films, hosted a TV disc show—the *Big Beat*—and co-authored a number of hit tunes.

At the height of his success, Freed boasted, "Anyone who says rock 'n' roll is a passing fad or a flash in the pan trend along the music roads has rocks in the head, dad."[1] He was right.

Rock *was* here to stay, but Freed wasn't. In 1959, his career came to an abrupt halt when he was indicted on "payola" charges—taking kickbacks for giving airplay to specified records. It was right in the middle of "Shimmy Shimmy Ko-Ko-Bop," by Little Anthony and the Imperials—a group Freed had helped name—that he burst on the air, sobbing. Quickly, he blurted that, as of that moment, he had officially resigned from WABC. It was the first sign all was not just youthful fun and games in the budding rock music industry, even in its infancy.

Overnight, the atmosphere turned smoggy as the payola investigations unveiled the rotting foundation on which rock was built—greed. The public was incensed. Parents wrote indignant letters to the editors of their newspapers and called the managers of their local radio stations. Fearful of repercussions (loss of revenue), the industry looked for, and found, a fall guy in Freed.

Only five years after his career had been blown to pieces by the scandal, Freed died in a Florida hospital—drunk, broke, and all but forgotten at the age of 42. The man who named rock and roll had become its first victim.

It's Bigger Than All of Us

In happier days, Freed had once remarked, "Let's face it—rock 'n' roll is bigger than all of us."[2] That line became his epitaph. As quickly as he stepped aside, rock rolled on. Names such as Bill Haley, Little Richard, and Chuck Berry became regulars on the new pop music charts, along with the unforgettable Jerry Lee Lewis and the mythical Buddy Holly.

Bill Haley had been a country singer in his early years, but the pudgy balladeer was impressed by the energy of the kids he met while playing at local school dances. In order to match that energy, he began to include a number of jivey, rhythm-and-blues tunes in his act. Depending on teen slang for his lyrics—phrases like "Crazy Man, Crazy," and "Rock The Joint"—he quickly gained recognition. Then his tune, "Shake, Rattle and Roll," bolted up the charts to become a million-seller.

In April of 1954, Haley and his Comets produced "Rock Around the Clock," a "cover" tune of a previously recorded rhythm-and-blues piece. The jumping ditty was initially a flop, but it sailed to the top when it became the theme song for a popular teenage rebel movie called *Blackboard Jungle*. Now, the song is better known as the theme song of TV's *Happy Days*.

After *Blackboard Jungle,* the chubby-cheeked singer with a spit curl was elevated to stardom. It's hard to believe today that the middle-aged bopster actually caused riots wherever he went, but when Haley's own movie, *Rock Around the Clock*, was released, theater seats were torn to shreds by fans in San Francisco and elsewhere; and when Haley toured Great Britain in 1957, thousands of screaming fans turned out to greet him, producing near-riot conditions.

Incredibly, the numerous incidents of mayhem were labeled kiddish pranks by parents and authorities refusing to recognize the impact rock was having on its youthful fans. Haley confessed bewilderment at both the adulation and the bedlam, and seemed almost relieved when his careening career was derailed by more "hip" up-and-comers.

Little Richard (Penniman) was one of those up-and-comers. He pranced boldly onto the early rock scene proclaiming, "My music, it makes the blind see, the lame walk, and the dumb and the deaf hear and talk."[3]

Yet for all his biblical parody, Little Richard's early fifties songs contained such lines as: "Good golly Miss Molly/Sure like to ball." (He was quick to explain those lyrics referred to dancing. He neglected to mention, however, that "dancing" was also street jargon for sexual activity.)

In 1955, Little Richard's recording of "Tutti Frutti" was a million-seller, to which he quickly added a half-dozen more gold records. A flamboyant character, given to self-deification and bizarre dress, it's not surprising that he proclaimed—often, in fact—that he was the greatest.

Then in 1957, at the peak of his success, the pompadoured rocker "gave up rock 'n' roll for the Rock of Ages."[4] Having thrown all his gaudy jewelry into the Sydney, Australia, harbor, he reportedly dumped show business for the life of an evangelist. His previously recorded songs, however, continued to be released and promoted. Top 40 hits, and top earnings, kept coming for Little Richard as if nothing had happened and he has shifted in and out of the rock scene several times.

During one of his "in" periods, Little Richard proudly boasted, "I gave the Beatles their first tour—I took them to Hamburg before they ever made a record. I gave Mick Jagger his first tour in this country. James Brown was with me. I put Joe Tex in business."[5]

One early rock star Little Richard neglected to claim in his litany of musical achievements is Chuck Berry. Berry, however, is his own best promoter. Often hailed as the greatest of all rock and roll poets, he once described the rock composers' motivation in far less profound terms: "The dollar dictates what music is written."[6] In other words, Berry was wiley enough to perceive that even in the fledgling rock-music business, money dictated the content of the message—that is, *if* he wanted his music to sell. And sell it did.

"Maybellene," his first big hit, was released in July, 1955. It was a car/woman, sex-and-driving masterpiece of sexual innuendo. Though the lyrics could be interpreted more than one way, the real meaning was not lost on the teens of the day. Berry followed "Maybellene" with hit after hit for the next several years. Some of the most successful were: "Johnny B. Goode," "Sweet Little Sixteen," and "Brown-Eyed Handsome Man." Berry also chalked up four movies during that time: *Rock Rock Rock, Mr. Rock and Roll, Go Johnny Go,* and *Jazz on a Summer's Day*. Certain that he'd found the key to success in the music business, it appeared that Berry would rock on forever with his salty, caustic themes of sex and rebellion. However, a trial and imprisonment which lasted over three years took the momentum out of his career.

Some say he was singled out because he was black and successful—and Berry once claimed he had been framed by a competitor. He was indicted, however, and convicted on charges of statutory rape under the Mann Act. After a notorious trial which stretched out over two years, Berry spent nearly two more years in prison—all the while protesting his innocence.

Nonetheless, Berry's influence on rock music cannot be overstated. *The Harmony Illustrated Encyclopedia of Rock* says:

> Berry was rock's single most influential figure. . . . There is no doubt that his contribution to the history of rock music has been unique; even in recent years, his old songs have continued to prove ready-made hit material.[7]

Though his previous fame has diminished over the years, he has accumulated wealth and acclaim through his live concerts.

Famous for his stage show "duck walk," and lauded as the teenagers' poet laureate, Berry could perhaps be more appropriately remembered as the Pied Piper of rock—singing songs that lead teens down a perilous path.

Another early rocker, who has had a lasting effect on the genre's style and content, is Jerry Lee Lewis. Like Berry, Lewis' promising career rocketed upward with bawdy tunes such as, "Whole Lot of Shakin' Goin' On" and "Great Balls of Fire." Unlike Berry, however, Lewis wrestled with his conscience over the obvious sexual overtones in his lyrics—at one time even refusing to record a tune he labeled blasphemous. Once he had overcome his misgivings, however, Lewis proceeded to play rock and roll with religious fervor.

His crazy stage antics—throwing chairs, pounding the ivories with his feet, and various other parts of the anatomy (even burning his piano)—quickly came to an end, however, when the public discovered Lewis, 23, had married his 13-year-old second cousin. This marriage, though legal, was Lewis' third, and the scandal of a "child bride" caused his career to take a tailspin. (Those were the days when that sort of thing could cause a public scandal. Therefore, both Elvis Presley and Buddy Holly kept their relationships with younger women closely guarded secrets.)

A heavy drinker in his early teens, Lewis renewed the old habit with the same passion he had once applied to music, and resorted to heavy drug use.[8] In time, his child bride sued Lewis for divorce. "The Killer" has rocked on, however, through a life filled with tragedy—the deaths of two sons, the break-up of a fourth marriage, the death of his fifth wife, and the burden of poor health—and a career marked by financial ups and downs and IRS merry-go-rounds.

"I'll never get tired of playing this music," says early rock's wildest performer. "I'm never gonna stop playing it. I'll go on playing just as long as there are people to listen."[9] Lewis is a survivor, and in recent years has received some recognition for his showmanship, but one has to wonder—has it all been worth it, just to be able to "keep on playing"?

Buddy Holly was not so (for lack of a better word) lucky. He survived the rock scene just two years. Born Charles Harden Holley—he eventually dropped the "e"—in Lubbock, Texas, in 1936, he started out, as many early stars had, in country and western, recording demo songs and playing at high school hops.

Then in 1956, with a newly formed group called the Crickets, Holly recorded "That'll Be the Day." The song had a rollicking beat, and innocent-sounding lyrics. A closer look, however, reveals a tune that actually taunts and jeers at the woman to which it's addressed. Though perhaps mildly stated, by today's standards, it is still I-double-dare-you macho stuff. Despite the attitude it portrayed, the platter quickly climbed the top 40 charts.

Between 1956 and 1958, Holly racked up a succession of hits still being re-recorded today, including "Maybe Baby," "Peggy Sue," and "Reminiscing." Given his preppie looks—toothy smile, horn-rimmed glasses, suit and tie—rather like Superman in disguise—it's hard to picture Holly's hits as being anything but Mom and apple pie. Close attention to the lyrics, however, reveals a casual attitude toward sex that exposes the beginning of moral deterioration. Until Holly, rock musicians simply weren't given airplay if the lyrics were the least bit lurid (ironically, many rhythm-and-blues and country singers were able to get by with sexual innuendo).

Holly, at 22, enjoyed a popularity surpassed perhaps only by the soon-to-come first rock sex symbol, Elvis Presley. However, Holly's music died when his chartered plane crash-landed near Mason City, Iowa. The accident killed all passengers, including two other well-known early rollers—the Big Bopper (Jiles Perry Richardson) and Ritchie Valens.

The impact of Holly's unprecedented success, and his influence on countless other rock stars, combined with the shock of his sudden death, has no doubt exalted the Holly legend, which inspired the melodramatic line, "the day the music died," in Don McLean's 1971 hit, "American Pie." Still, rock did seem to suffer many life-threatening blows at that time. Freed was axed, Little Richard dropped out of sight and into a seminary, Buddy Holly died, and Jerry Lee Lewis was as good as dead. Frantically, teens searched for a new king to rule the realm of rock and roll.

The King

Though Little Richard often called himself the greatest, and Jerry Lee Lewis said he was the best, it was Elvis Presley who earned—and died still wearing—the undisputed crown of "The King of Rock and Roll."

Born in poverty in East Tupelo, Mississippi, in 1935, Presley was raised on gospel, country, and rhythm-and-blues music in Memphis, Tennessee. After his first major hit in 1956, "Heartbreak Hotel," he became the most potent symbol rock music has ever produced.

Arnold Shaw, author of the *Dictionary of American Pop/Rock*, describes Presley's arrival on the music scene as a "pop explosion." He writes:

> Presley represented not only a new sound, but a new look (sideburns and duck-tail haircut), new dress (blue suedes), new sensibility (the sneer), new mores (a more sensual approach to love), new speech ("all shook up"), and new dances. His hysterical acceptance was the expression of a young generation in conflict with and in rebellion against the older generation.[10]

Certainly, the fifties had its share of problems—the Korean conflict had already proven that the "war to end all wars" was not; civil rights were, as yet, unknown for most blacks; and the bomb shelter was suburbia's newest status symbol. It was inevitable that the eggshell of domestic tranquillity would crack.

Suddenly, Elvis "the Pelvis" came twisting and shouting onto the scene, the symbol and king of a growing teenage subculture. Within one year of the release of "Heartbreak Hotel," Presley had received six gold records.

The "older generation," who had been lulled to sleep by the hidden meanings of earlier rock and roll hits, suddenly woke up as they heard this snarling anti-hero ask their daughters if they were "lonesome tonight," and tell their young sons that "it's now or never." Presley further agitated adults with his tease-me-please-me stage performances. He had a charismatic appeal—an animalistic sexual allure—and the uncanny ability to draw out of his audiences (made up mostly of young girls) a spontaneous, sexual response.

Pinpointing the secret of Presley's legendary, overnight success is difficult. His talent seems hard to identify; his vacillating personality remains a puzzle; and the mythic quality that surrounded him makes it impossible to separate the stage-show seducer from the self-professed Christian.

Presley was, at once, the angelic choir boy and the riotous, rebellious prodigal punk. "God gave me a voice," he once said. "If I turned against God I'd be ruined." And yet, as Gary Herman points out in *Rock 'n' Roll Babylon*, "He also recognized the devil's part in his success, saying that 'my voice is ordinary; if I stand still while I'm singing, I'm a dead man.' "[11]

When Presley's suggestive stage antics ("like a stamping stallion,"[12] as biographer Goldman describes him) started drawing flak from the press, parents and the pulpit, a change of *modus operandi* was needed. Colonel Tom Parker, Presley's crafty manager, staged a coup that served to guarantee the king's longevity on the throne. In a brilliant move, the Colonel advised Presley to report for a preinduction draft physical. The action promptly quieted Presley's critics; he was reclassified by the press as a patriotic, home-lovin' boy that every couple would be proud to see date their daughter.

Unfortunately for Presley, he was also reclassified 1-A, and on March 24, 1958, was inducted. Following bootcamp days shared with an army of photographers, he was dispatched to Germany for two years. Though shorn of his famous sideburns, Presley's enlistment did not cut his profits. His existing movies and recordings continued to keep him in the limelight, and in the bucks. By the time he came stateside again, a well-planned metamorphosis had occurred. Gone were the swivel-hipped antics, the snarling smile and the rockabilly records. Presley donned, instead, the mystique of the Hollywood star and the Vegas showman.

Undoubtedly one of the best live entertainers in the country, Presley possibly would have enjoyed the lifelong success of pop singers like Frank Sinatra and Bing Crosby had he not begun to believe in the mythic, fantasy illusion of Elvis instead of the real person.

Gary Herman says, "Elvis' attempt to cope with the illusion of sexual omnipotence fostered by rock 'n' roll stardom was to try and become divine— an attempt whose very audacity was only possible because Elvis, as his early friends and colleagues remember, was a colorless youth with little in his life but his burning ambition to succeed. And his success was not based on any extraordinary ability to be everything, but on his need to be nothing but the passive instrument of his own myth. The truth about Elvis is that this myth was the realest thing about him."[13]

The King Is Dead

Swallowed up by his own phenomenal success until there was nothing left of the real Presley, he began to retreat physically from reality, through drugs. It is not known precisely when he became addicted, but in the last five years before his death, Presley was in a constant drug-induced state, swallowing a rainbow of pills. His drastic efforts to control his weight, while at the same time binging on mountains of junk food, caused dramatic physical deterioration. During that time he was hospitalized at least five times. Then, in August of 1977, paramedics were called to the Presley mansion to find him face down on his bathroom floor, dead for perhaps an hour or more.

The *official* cause of death was heart failure, but the coroner's report states that at the time of his death, Presley's body contained 14 different drugs. Incredibly, this was not an unusual amount of drugs for him to have ingested. Following Presley's death, it was discovered he had purchased over 10,000 stimulants, sedatives, and pain-killers in the 20 months before his death.[14] It has been well-documented that Presley used the drug-prescribing services of several doctors around the country.

Unparalleled scenes of mourning followed the death of the king, but the man who knew best what had killed Presley—Colonel Parker—seemed to have no time for public mourning. Minutes after hearing of Presley's death, Parker remarked coolly, "Nothing has changed. This won't change a thing."[15] And certainly for Parker, it didn't. The heavily promoted "deification" of Presley brought in posthumous earnings during the next few years far greater than Elvis had made in any other year of his wasted life.[16] The Colonel's career must have become much easier, now that he no longer had to deal with the inconvenience of a drugged-up paper doll rock star.

Through theatrics and promotional skill, the Colonel was able to project the Elvis Presley image, as rock's biggest, most glittering star, to a world full of willing suckers. The saddest fact, though, is that Presley was the biggest sucker of them all.

2

Takin' Care of Business

On hearing about the death of Elvis, John Lennon remarked somewhat callously, "Elvis died when he went into the Army."[1] Lennon was referring to the exchange of Presley's rock and roll style for a more adult, more lucrative pop image. Although true to some extent, Presley's army stint didn't bring the end of rock and roll, even if it did mean Presley's abdication of rock's throne. In fact, eager Elvis forgeries were anxiously waiting in the wings, ready to pick up the dropped scepter.

Rock music had become a mega-bucks money-maker, and for every aspiring Elvis clone, there was a conspiring manager, record mogul, or groupie. Though the music of this period—the late fifties and early sixties—was not nearly as offensive as some of the earlier material, the commercialism of rock was particularly ugly. Image-makers such as *American Bandstand*, first seen nationally in 1957, at the most popular weekday viewing hours for teenagers (3 to 5 p.m.), made baby starlets from mediocre Elvis imitators.

Shlock Rock

David Pichaske, in his book *A Generation In Motion,* describes the product as "shlock rock." "In fact," he says, "it was an almost incredible parade of one South Philadelphia mediocrity after another, many of them reprocessed especially for the occasion: voice lessons, makeup, new clothes, new accents, new teeth, maybe even a good song (although this was incidental—witness Fabiano Forte, Fabian, who went the whole hundred yards on pure image, and nobody ever guessed)."[2]

Many adults will doubtless recall the late fifties and early sixties with a nostalgic sigh—ah, the days of the "golden oldies." Rock was golden, all right. Music critic Michael Lydon put it this way: "Rock is the surest way to the hearts and wallets of millions of Americans between 8 and 35—the richest, most extravagant children in the history of the world."[3]

Apparently, what interested the promoters most, then, was not lofty business principles, nor even quality talent, but what could make the most money. Dick Clark, *American Bandstand's* slick super-entrepeneur and host, was a good example. A consummate promoter who expressed his mercenary motives very bluntly,[4] Clark was quoted as saying, "I don't make culture. I sell it."[5] Not your average deejay, Clark at one time held interest in 33 recording and publishing companies and on his show plugged over half the records released by those companies.[6]

Clark was already a millionaire when, in the early sixties, a widely-publicized House investigation of payola schemes subpoenaed him to testify with Alan Freed and others. Though many came to question the ethics of the music industry because of the hearings, Clark was eventually cleared of wrongdoing and the scandal did little to stymie the growth of rock and roll.

When the dust had settled, backers and promoters pushed goody-goody-kid teenagerism to the limits, exploiting a rash of young stars with names like Bobby, Frankie, Ricky, Tab or Fab, and ensnaring teens with the joys of consumerism.

By 1973, mild-mannered Clark, Philadelphia's superboy, was grossing over $5 million a year; so others, hoping to get on the *Bandstand's* wagon, began producing lookalikes. First on the scene was *Where the Action Is*, pro-duced by—surprise—Dick Clark. Then followed *Shindig; Ready, Steady Go!; Hullabaloo; Top of the Pops; The Old Grey Whistle Test; Soul Train; Holly-wood a Go Go; The Lloyd Thaxton Show; Malibu U.;* and more recently, shows like *Dance Fever* and *Solid Gold*.[7] The combined impact of rock music and television's double-whammy is just beginning to be studied (and Chapter 3 will offer some interesting facts on the subject), but the impetus behind their promotion is obvious: money makes the music go 'round.

Songwriter Linton Kwesi Johnson probably stated it best: "The music business is one of the nastiest, dirtiest businesses in the world. It seems to be very fertile ground for conmen and tricksters, all kinds of ruthless and un-scrupulous people. I suppose because there's so much money to be picked up. It's a dirty, stinking business."[8]

Although entrepeneurs were doing their best to give rock the business in the late fifties and early sixties, by 1963, a new movement was blowin' in the wind, and folk music gave it a voice. It was a time for truth, justice and the "American Way," and rock rose up out of the money-making mire to become a sort of musical superman.

Soon, names such as Pete Seeger (on his banjo was written: "This machine surrounds hate and forces it to surrender");[9] Peter, Paul and Mary; Bob Dylan; the Kingston Trio; Simon and Garfunkel; and Joan Baez were playing in coffeehouses like the Purple Onion and the Hungry i.

Predecessors of the hippie, peace-and-love radicals yet to come, they at-tempted, as Dave Guard of the Kingston Trio put it, to make "folk music more palatable to the masses, not the downtrodden masses, but the upscale, striped-shirt, rep-tie, clip-on-pen middle class."[10] In other words, the masses with money.

By 1966, folk music had broadened somewhat in scope, and, without a doubt, approached some subjects that had needed discussing for a long time.

The answers offered by these troubadours to the impressionable youth of the day were, unfortunately, increasingly devoid of hope. In fact, there were far more questions raised than answers given. The answers, they were told, were blowin' in the wind. Folk music took on a quality of desperation and an element of hypocrisy. Critic Michael Lydon wrote:

> Bob Dylan has described with a fiendish accuracy the pain of growing up in America, and millions have responded passionately to his vision. His song, "Maggie's Farm," contains the lines, "He gives me a nickel, he gives me a dime/ he asks me with a grin if I'm having a good time/and he fines me everytime I slam the door/oh, I ain't gonna work on Maggie's farm no more." But along with Walter Cronkite and the New York Yankees, Dylan works for one of Maggie's biggest farms, the Columbia Broadcasting System.[11]

Though diversity came into the folk style of music, producing folk/rock, soul, hard rock, and country/rock, by 1967 the folk protest movement had taken a turn down the bitterly hopeless "Bleeker Street," where "Voices leaking from a sad cafe/smiling faces try to understand/I saw a shadow touch a shadow's hand. . . ."

In Paul Simon's own words ("the poet writes his crooked rhyme"), many songwriters had "sold out" for the thirty pieces of silver needed to pay the rent. Empty, aching and not knowing why, the folk protest movement died out by 1968, or, more appropriately, committed suicide.

British Invasion

After the revolutionary refrain of "The Times They Are A-Changin'," the strains of "Love, Love Me Do" came breezing across the Atlantic like clouds of cotton candy. By the time the Liverpool mop tops arrived in North America in April 1964, they had blitzed the first five spots on the top 40 list, and the Fab Four had won the hearts of American youth and adults alike. The Beatles had become a rock phenomenon—the first rock group, and perhaps the only, to ever have bridged the generation gap.

Beatlemania was everywhere, causing Lennon to quip, to many a raised eyebrow, "We're more popular than Jesus now."[12] The Beatles had already made a fortune selling their records—prior to 1968, every Beatles album had sold more than one million copies[13]—and anything and everything else that could have their names or pictures stamped on it. In fact, even the stage of the Cavern Club, where they had often performed before they were famous, was hacked up and sold piece by piece. "This is the most sought after wood in the world," the club owner had announced gleefully.[14]

That kind of adulation cannot go on for long without having a profound effect. As early as 1966, the Beatles' music began to reflect their jaded, cynical outlook on life. Instead of eternal, hand-holding bliss, there appeared despair, bitterness, futility, and—of greatest consequence—drugs.

Drugs had almost always been a part of the Beatles' private scene (Lennon said he began taking pills at age 17).[15] Uppers and downers are an occupational hazard in the rock industry—a field that makes tremendous demands on its drones. Quiet Riot's drummer once bemoaned, "There are only two guarantees in the music business, and those are failure and exhaustion."[16]

It was not until another well-known singer introduced the Beatles to the mind-numbing qualities of marijuana in 1964, that they began to flaunt and promote drug use. Living in an unreal world, where drugs and sex flowed freely, and possessions were easily attainable, it is no wonder that the Beatles suffered from the effects of lives filled with illusions.

Still, they "had eyes, yet could not see." Lennon later boasted, "We were kings. We were all just at the prime . . . it was like a men's smoking club, just a very good scene." Their tours, he said, were like the Fellini film *Satyricon* (named for an archaic, satirical novel describing the vices and extravagances of ancient Rome). "They were Satyricon, all right." He boasted that his manager's and press agent's rooms were "always full of junk [drugs]."[17] By 1967, they were up to their heads in LSD as well. Lennon claimed he had dropped acid a thousand times—all the while taking speed to help survive the recording sessions.[18] The Beatles had become psychedelic sellouts, and so had their music.

Time magazine's review of the Beatles' *Sergeant Pepper's Lonely Hearts Club Band* album said it was "drenched in drugs."[19] The album, which spoke cynically and despairingly of modern society's emptiness, was significant because it was designed to give the listener something complex and vivid to focus on while getting stoned.

Remarkably few adults were aware of the content and impact of the Beatles' music, but then, on the surface at least, it did appear, as media expert Wilson Key put it, "gay, light, and even humorous." Key asserts that most teenagers, as well, perceived the largest portion of the Beatles' message only at subliminal levels.[20]

Compounding the confusion was the smokescreen with which the press hid the Beatles' true lifestyles and intentions. Lennon admitted later that the scrubbed-face, mop-haired image of the Beatles was only a myth maintained by the press, in return for favors (particularly entrance into the cushy life of the "smoking club," with all the free drinks and prostitutes within).

Although it is impossible to judge how much the Beatles innovated the drug scene and how much they simply latched onto a developing trend, it is certain their pro-drug message had a profound effect on the youth culture. In the book *The Love You Make: An Insider's Story of the Beatles,* by Peter Brown and Steven Gaines, the authors said the Beatles certainly didn't invent LSD or marijuana, and they weren't the first to take it, but they always managed to be on the forefront of a trend and then popularize it to an international level.[21]

Key, well-known for his exposés of media exploitation, says he has examined song titles and lyrics of rock music before, during, and after the Beatles' public career. He has concluded that the Beatles' main contribution to western society was to make the use of hallucinatory drugs commonplace and culturally legitimate among teenagers throughout the world. "The Beatles became the super drug culture prophets . . . of all time," Key maintains.[22]

Perhaps unwittingly, the Beatles became prophets in another sense as well. In an effort to find some meaning in the plastic world show business had created around them, they began to explore the spiritual dimension for answers.

George Harrison was the religious mystic of the group. It was he who penned "My Sweet Lord" ("I really want to know you/I really want to go with you"). Although the song was sung about "Lord Krishna," not the Lord Jesus, it struck a familiar chord in the minds and hearts of a great many who were searching at that time. In fact, Lennon eventually complained that "My Sweet Lord" was everywhere. "Everytime I put the radio on, it's 'oh my Lord'! I'm beginning to think there must be a God!" [23] It is unfortunate the Beatles' jaded view of life made it so difficult for them to give Christianity's claims serious consideration.

In late 1966, Harrison and his wife Patti went to India, apparently to study the sitar with musician Ravi Shankar. However, upset with rumblings of a Beatle breakup and confused by LSD-inspired magical mystical tours, he was ripe for the simple, pacifist Hindu philosophy as taught by Guru Maharishi Mahesh Yogi. Patti was first to join the Maharishi's Spiritual Regeneration Movement, but soon, all four rubber souls were bouncing to the guru's advice to "be happy."

Sixties generation chronicler, David Pichaske, described the scene: "When the Maharishi Mahesh Yogi and Transcendental Meditation came bouncing into England, and into the consciousnesses of the Beatles, and into the consciousness of the world, older people who had been doing the religious thing for many years found him suspect, simplistic, maybe even slick and commercial. . . . The Maharishi was, however, perfectly attuned to the popular, romantic religiosity of the times and achieved instant assimilation into the artifice of the sixties." [24]

"Media coverage soon guaranteed the Maharishi a solid reputation as someone who mattered to the Beatles," author Gary Herman recalls in *Rock 'n' Roll Babylon*, "and the group members sang his praises and lauded meditation to the skies." [25]

Eventually, the cynical Lennon called the yogi's meditation techniques just "colored water," and finally all but Harrison gave up the practice, but the unprecedented exposure the Beatles had given TM lent it an air of credibility. Their deceptive endorsement made it possible for TM to develop a stronghold in the Western world that has developed into big business and done incalculable damage to young people's spirits.

Ultimately, the Beatles broke up, and all of rock's promoters and all of rock's producers couldn't put them back together again. Still, in the six short years since their original assault on the American public, they had become a mythic institution.

Of their pervasive influence, Key writes:

> No one today questions the Beatles' impact upon Western society. . . . The mythology follows each of the four young multi-millionaires as they grow older and journey from wife to wife and from one misadventure to another. They are viewed as the initiators of an important epoch in history, the founders of popular culture, and the beginning of an entire army of popular music heroes who exploited their tradition.[26]

The Stones Roll into North America

The Rolling Stones, who took their name from an old Muddy Waters blues song, hit it big in 1965 with "I Can't Get No Satisfaction." *Time* magazine (April 28, 1967) described it as a song "about 'trying to make some girl,' with supposedly coded allusions to menstruation, marijuana and birth control pills."[27] Actually the song can be experienced on many levels as explained in *The Rolling Stones—The First Twenty Years,* ". . . from ambiguous vulgarity embodiment to lewdness to eroticism."[28] It's an accurate description of the band as well.

Their hard and angry image, enhanced by media coverage of their urinating in public, grew to legendary proportions. Their first visit to the West Coast was greeted by the following radical welcome:

> Greetings and welcome Rolling Stones, our comrades in the desperate battle against the maniacs who hold power. The revolutionary youth of the world hears your music and is inspired to even more deadly acts. . . .
> We will play your music in rock-'n'-roll marching bands as we tear down the jails and free the prisoners, as we tear down the State schools and free the students, as we tear down the military bases and arm the poor. . . .[29]

In 1967, the group continued to stir up controversy, first with their release of "Let's Spend the Night Together"—gone were the days of sexual innuendo!—then with drug-related scandals.

Drugs were particularly destructive in the life of guitarist Brian Jones. Eventually the angelic-looking towhead was hardly included on their records, and spent most of the group's recording sessions sitting in the corner getting high. As former Stones member Ian Stewart reminisced, "Brian loved it in that he was a Rolling Stone . . . but forgot every so often that he was supposed to be playing guitar. Brian just got himself incredibly messed up very quickly."[30] At one time the driving inspiration for the Stones, Jones tragically retreated into his own drug-filled world. In 1969, when he died in his swimming pool as a direct result of an overdose, rock music had claimed another victim.

The Stones were determined to gather no moss, however; and with their comrade not yet in the grave, they gave a concert in London, then jetted away to Australia.

In December of that same year, another concert forced the Stones to be thrown again into the limelight of infamy. It was at the festival at Altamont, where the Hell's Angels had been hired to keep the peace. As Mick Jagger went through his diabolical routine—prancing around for "Jumping Jack Flash" and "Sympathy For The Devil," the violence that had surfaced frequently throughout the festival broke loose. As Jagger watched, first in stunned silence and then while singing fearfully, a man was clubbed to death with pool cues, fists and chains, and stabbed five times—all within reach of the stage. Later Jagger said of the hellish atmosphere that day, "If Jesus had been there, he would have been crucified."[31]

Though Altamont was the ultimate mistake for the Stones ("Sympathy For The Devil" was not performed again on stage for six years), the violence that spills out of the frenetic scene that is a Rolling Stones concert apparently is no accident—but is a natural result of the music and the way it is played. At a Berlin concert, where crowds ran wild, setting fire to the stadium and vandalizing the shops outside, Jagger smoothly commented afterward, "I entice the audience. Of course I do."[32] Despite the openness with which they expressed their intentions, the Stones have been allowed to roll on, quite successfully, producing 20 years' worth of music sotted with drugs, sexual debauchery, violence and Satanism.

Flower Power and Metal Mashers

While the Stones were performing their brand of raunch and roll, the mainstream of rock had dissolved into a commercialism similar to that of the late fifties. As the country began to come undone at the seams—the Bay of Pigs, Kennedy's assassination, Vietnam—the music unraveled as well. Songs began to spoof protest and the insanity of the times. In Dylan's words, "I was much older then; I'm younger than that now."[33] The sixties generation was saying, "That's cool. I can dig that. Peace, brother." Personal freedom was "in" and love was found to be the answer. The scene in 1967, at the first "Be-In"—the Monterrey Festival in San Francisco—personified the times. Later, Gary Herman would describe it this way: "A banner across the stage read 'Music, Love, Flowers'—a slogan which seemed, at the time, both reasonable and radical. Later it would look merely naive."[34]

Their lyrics overflowing with dreams and drugs, flower power groups such as Buffalo Springfield, the Mamas and the Papas, the Doors, Grateful Dead, and Jefferson Airplane preached love and freedom through their songs; and weekend hippies followed their waterpipe dreams. Sadly, neither singer nor listener seemed to notice that the whole picture was a media hype, carefully cultivated by the rock industry.

Music critic Michael Lydon states:

Rock and roll is a lovely playground and within it kids have more power than they have anywhere else in society, but the playground's walls are carefully maintained and guarded by the corporate elite that set it up in the first place. While the White Panthers talk of "total assault upon culture by any means necessary, including rock and roll," *Billboard,* the music trade paper, announces with pride that in 1968 the record industry became a billion-dollar business.[35]

Though the Mamas and Papas sent people "California Dreamin'," Mama Cass Elliot was more realistic when she said, "Pop music is just long hours, hard work, and lots of drugs. . . ."[36]

There were dozens more—groups which sang their songs about the "freedom" that could come from droppin' out, lovin' in and gettin' high. But soon the phoniness of it all became evident. Lost in a world of excesses—excess drugs, excess sex, excess violence—flower power faded in the pot while rock bands searched anxiously for new direction.

The early seventies saw the beginnings of the careers of many individual stars whose success has continued into the eighties, although they often play a game of musical chairs—sitting in on many rock groups. The majority, however, moved away from pop sounds to something called heavy metal.

West Coast bands Blue Cheer and Iron Butterfly were two of the first bands to take off, amps blasting away, toward a sound that made lyric listening nearly impossible. Metal mashers such as MC5, Grand Funk Railroad, Black Pearl, Amboy Dukes, Queen, and Bad Company thundered onto the rock scene.

"Wild Man" Ted Nugent of Dukes remembered, "We were mad, Jack. We don't know why, and we don't care. We just know that pluggin' in a guitar and crankin' it up as loud as it would go made the world seem a whole lot better."[37]

In Britain, groups such as Led Zeppelin, Deep Purple, Uriah Heep, and Black Sabbath brought the macabre into metal music—satanic rock. Black Sabbath was introduced to the British press at a "party" featuring the mock sacrifice of a semi-nude girl, and although they now claim the black magic routine was a sales gimmick, they still produce albums with references to demons, witches, suicide and the like on the covers and in the lyrics. It was not a "jolly band," admitted vocalist Ronnie James Dio.

That kind of theatrics—glitter rock—gave rise to a number of groups in the early seventies, as metal searched for a look as outrageous as its sound. It didn't have to look very far.

Enter four New York musicians named KISS. These fire-breathing, blood-spurting "entertainers," with their copyrighted demonic facial designs and bizarre costumes, would almost be comical—were their music not promoting the devil himself. Although the group was not photographed or seen in public without full makeup for the first ten years of its existence, the members have now "unmasked." The facelift has little significance, however.

"Taking the makeup off has meant nothing but taking the makeup off," assured the group's Gene Simmons, lest anyone think they had changed their tune as well. "The change in us goes no farther than that."[38] For KISS, that means more of the same—songs about sadomasochism, satanic messages, and plenty of volume. "You can turn it up and get a musical lobotomy," guitarist Paul Stanley said.[39]

Metallic rock has made a devastating impact on teens, and the audience seems to be expanding. Late in 1983, *Newsweek* reported that one of the hottest metal groups, Quiet Riot, a Los Angeles-based band that "played concerts for four years in California without getting a record contract, has sold more copies of its debut album . . . than any heavy-metal band ever in America. . . . Def Leppard has been on the record charts for 40 weeks . . . and AC/DC is currently in the Top 20 in *Billboard*."[40]

The fans are mostly male, *Newsweek* went on to explain, and mostly under 20. The music appeals to the frustrated working-class—and to the electronic gadgetry buff. Most certainly its barbarism appeals to the baser nature common to all people. Says David Lee Roth, of another successful group, Van Halen, "We've taken everything that's gone down in the last million years, thrown it in a huge blender and ended up with the loudest, wildest, craziest music in the history of mankind."[41]

The same theatrics that spawned heavy metal and monster rock influenced the development of two other "mutants": the explicit and outrageous sex rock and the violent, aggressive style of punk rock.

David Bowie is perhaps the best-known and longest-lasting star of the first variety. The carrot-topped, painted-up Frankenstein brought to rock music a new meaning for the word decadence. Like Jagger of the Rolling Stones, Bowie took on drag-queen characteristics, after claiming to be androgynous, a move that was to bring out of the closet imitators like sexually overt Prince (Rodgers Nelson); provocative Rick James; the swishy swashbuckler Adam Ant; and Culture Club's Boy George (real name O'Dowd), whose dolls, hairstyles and clothing put America in rags and the British group's front man in riches.

Over the years, Bowie has demonstrated the anything-for-a-buck crass commercialism of rock with his chameleon-like changes. More recently, he has switched to a Las Vegas crooner image, as well as tried his hand at Broadway and films. In 1983, his LP *Let's Dance* was one of the five best-selling albums. His real claim to fame, however, is that he is the only rock star ever to be voted Great Britain's number-one male star *and* number-three female star at the same time!

Rock has been known for its rebellion throughout its sordid history, and many a rock group has disintegrated due to in-fighting, just as it began to taste success.

Punk rock, a development of the late seventies, has taken that rebellion one step further: not only do punkers rebel against upper-class society, and against the rock establishment itself—they even attack their fans! At a punk rock festival, staged at London's 100 Club, several people were badly cut, and one fan's eyesight was severely endangered during a bottle-throwing ruckus.[42] That incident occurred in 1976, and should have been a signal to parents and fans that punk rock is hazardous to one's health.

But violence and aggression, and provocation of outrage by being outrageous, are punk rock's key attributes, and offstage incidents of violence seem to enhance rather than detract from its popularity.

In the St. Paul (MN) *Pioneer Press*, under the headline, "Punk Rock Bands Seen Inspiring New Wave of Violent Behavior," the following appeared:

> The punk tradition, with its disrespect for life and property, has always been violent. British Skinheads, gangs of working class youths who prowl London in steel-heeled boots, have long been the model for would-be punks here. . . . Band leaders are in on the violence, too, and many are blamed for encouraging the brutal behavior. Punk gangs also are seizing on slam dancing as an excuse for violence. In this latest craze, dancers hurl themselves at each other in a frenzy. With the gangs involved, the number of dancers piled on the floor when the music stops is getting higher—and bloodier."[43]

On stage, the anarchistic punkers appear in dirty, torn clothes, sporting orange, purple and/or green hair—or perhaps no hair at all. They exhibit self-abusive practices, such as sticking safety pins through their skin, and express hostility toward the audience with foul language, vomiting and spitting. Rock contortionist, Iggy Pop (then Iggy and the Stooges), performed acts of violence and self-mutilation on stage (in July 1973, Pop slit open his chest); the Sex Pistols—whom *Newsweek* described as paragons of late seventies blood-and-guts[44]—used four-letter words in their performances (even on television); and James Chance went beyond both self- and verbal-abuse—he took to slapping fans in the audience.[45]

The earliest progenitors of punk, however, were American. There were the cartoonish Television, the Talking Heads, Patti Smith, the Plasmatics, and five non-female, non-musicians—the New York Dolls. Earliest of all, though, was Lou Reed (and the Velvet Underground), whose songs unleashed a whole closet full of unhealthy subjects: ". . . smack, speed, homosexuality, lesbianism, transvestitism, masochism, misogyny [hatred of women], murder, suicide and death."[46]

In 1976, when several punk groups toured England, punk began to emerge there as well, with groups such as the Sex Pistols, Eddie and the Hot Rods, Elvis Costello, the Clash, BowWowWow, and the Boomtown Rats. Gay political activist and punk rocker, Tom Robinson, said with glee, "After ten years of bland, brilliant music, we were back to what Rock 'n' Roll should be— nasty, crude, rebellious people's music."[47]

David Bowie agreed. "I hated the whole togetherness, peace, love thing," he told *Newsweek*, describing with disdain the sixties hippie, counter-culture scene. "It was conceited, flabby, *suffocating*—and didn't mean what it said."[48]

Punk rock, on the other hand, is in deadly earnest. Johnny Rotten Lydon, formerly head punk of the mis-fired Sex Pistols, who currently sports Public Image, Ltd., says he is Antichrist, and an anarchist who desires to kill and "bring anarchy in the U.K." (the title of his chart-topping 1976 LP).[49]

That attitude nearly toppled American politics as well! According to David A. Noebel, in *The Legacy of John Lennon*, unsuccessful assassin John W. Hinckley, Jr., was a punk rock advocate who had attended a concert by his favorite punk group, the Kamikaze Klones, just days before his attack on President Ronald Reagan. At the show, the Klones played such songs as "Death Can Be Fun" and "Psycho Killer."[50]

The whole punk scene seemed to peak about 1977, but just when it seemed to be gasping its last breath, waves of new British bands and "new" music moved on the scene, providing a shot in the arm to the floundering music industry.

While no one style of music seems to predominate, a common look prevails, a look that *Newsweek* magazine calls "outlandish." Most of the proponents of the "new" sound—really a plagiarism of lots of old sounds—are from England, and they run the gamut from the gender-bender Eurythmics' synthesizer-rock, to the Irish soul of Dexy's Midnight Runners; from the rockabilly-Afro beat of King Lurt, to the Jamaican-flavored reggae rock of UB40. Even bagpipes and fiddles are heard when the Scottish group, Big Country, plays.

Though the look of new music is decidedly British, the groups' roots are worldwide: INXS from Australia; Juluka from South Africa; Alarm from Wales; Yello from Switzerland; Aztec Camera from Scotland; Peter Schilling from Germany; and several American groups—REM, Rank & File, B-52s, The Violent Femmes, and Oxo, to name a few.

Still, it is Britannia who rules the New Waves; and tops on the scene are Culture Club, the Eurythmics and Duran Duran, all of whom owe to MTV their meteoric rise to top-40 status—the rock-video cable network which, for rock and roll, was the best thing to come along since the jukebox.

Where rock music goes next is anyone's guess. No matter what the style or trend, however, rock music has always had a tremendous effect on its listeners, and will continue to do so. It has become one of the twentieth century's most powerful mediums for a message.

3

The Medium with a Message

We have explored the relatively recent history of rock music and have touched on its impact on young people throughout its 30-year history, but we haven't pinpointed why rock music—in fact, all modern music—has had such a profound effect on today's society.

To appreciate music as an important modern force, we need to view it in the context of the technological revolution of the last 40 years. Before this century, and the ingenious inventions of such men as Edison (phonograph) and Marconi (radio), music was always "on location"; to enjoy music one had to be in the same place as the musician. So unless Uncle Charlie could play a fiddle, or Sister Kate could carry a tune, music was a pleasure reserved only for others—usually the elite. And of course, one heard a tune repeated only if the musician was in the mood.

Not until the 1900s, through the use of the phonograph, radio, and finally television, did music acquire its "pop" attributes—it became accessible to everyone. In *Windstorm* magazine, we read:

> Musicians, the good and the bad, had found their Valhalla, a century that belonged to them. As truly as the nineteenth century had belonged to authors and philosophers because of the printing press, so the twentieth belongs to the musician because of records and radio.[1]

While popular music perhaps emerged from innocent beginnings, it had grown from a mischievous twenties toddler, through its romantic adolescence in the thirties and forties, into a full-fledged, unruly adulthood by the fifties. Although it was noted long ago by English dramatist William Congreve that music has the wherewithal to "soothe the savage beast," in recent times mass media has given music even more muscle. Music has power, says Dr. Howard Hanson, former director of the Eastman School of Music at the University of Rochester (NY): "It can be soothing or invigorating, ennobling or vulgarizing, philosophical or orgiastic. It has powers of evil as well as for good."[2] And living as we do in an age of wrap-around sound, that power has swelled to powderkeg proportions since Hanson penned those words back in 1942!

Bob Pittman, a 29-year-old executive at Warner Amex Satellite Entertainment Corporation—the company that daily brings the nation 24 hours of rock music on cable TV—says, "When you're dealing with a music culture—say, people aged 12 to 30—music serves as something beyond entertainment. It's really a peg they use to identify themselves. *It's representative of their values and their culture* [authors' italics]."[3] We no longer have music just for music's sake, but for the message's sake, and music is a powerful medium for a message.

The medium has carried "political messages, moral messages, anger, rebellion," *Windstorm*'s Kenneth Parker points out. "It was music of a revolution and they told us that it was. Music had become the language of a culture."[4] As a language of a culture in the age of communication, popular music—rock music in particular—has today become the most influential of the arts in people's lives.

As a language, however, music has the capability to communicate only to the culture which produces it. It often confuses outsiders, even as people with different languages sometimes fall prey to misunderstandings and frustrations due to communication failure. This occurs with music of different generations. Simply ask a 10-year-old to explain the meaning of the song, "Mademoiselle From Ärmentierés," or a grandmother to translate the lyric, "Tutti frutti, all rutti/ A-wop-bob-a-loom-op-a-lop-bam-boom," and you'll see the similarity.

For those who do understand a particular style of music, there is a sense of belonging, a sense of shared identity and purpose. That is why it is so important to critique the style of music toward which you gravitate, to discover its hidden meanings and explore its purposes, and to find out what philosophies you would be promoting if that music became a part of your life and identity.

If you are a concerned parent, strive to understand the music to which your children listen, so that you can "bridge the generation gap" and give sound, credible guidance.

Rolling Stone, the leading rock newspaper in the U.S., has advertised:

> If you are a corporate executive trying to understand what is happening to youth today, you cannot afford to be without *Rolling Stone.* If you are a student, a professor, a parent, this is your life because you already know that rock and roll is more than just music; it is the energy center of the new culture and your revolution.[5]

While it may not be necessary to read *Rolling Stone*, it is necessary to be acquainted with and understand rock music, for it is without a doubt a powerful force affecting the lives of not just teens, but all of society.

Rock and roll, as today's most popular music, receives unprecedented exposure. Its impact is magnified by the cumulative effect of mass media—there is simply no escaping rock's message. AM and FM radios fill our ears as we walk, run or drive; records, tapes and laser discs allow us to own music; television and films bombard us with visual images; and now, videocassette recorders and disc players give permanence to those images. As we shop, as we wait "on hold" on the telephone, even as we allow the Novocain to numb our gums at the dentist's office, music is piped to us, incessantly conveying its messages.

That is why awareness of the music and the message, of what we hear and how we hear it, has become so important. As the ancient maxim goes, "We become like that with which we surround ourselves." And, like it or not, we are surrounded with rock music.

Mass Media: Rock's Conveyor Belt

There are, today, more radios in the United States than people. When 1,500 teens were asked how much time they thought they spent listening to the radio, they offered the conservative estimate of a little over 12.5 hours per week.[6] A university study shows, however, that the average young person actually listens to radio about 6 hours per *day* and even the average adult listens to radio 3 hours and 20 minutes of every day![7] Originally a forum for news, drama, comedy and documentary, with music simply used as a filler, radio stations now increasingly opt for a musical format, and rock music programming outnumbers all the rest.

By the time Elvis Presley had checked into the Heartbreak Hotel, in the early fifties, radio had already become tremendously important as a conveyor of rock and roll's message. Suddenly, 17 million teenagers were virtually putty in the hands of the country's 1,700 deejays. Albert Goldman, Presley's biographer, noted:

> As these kids got up in the morning, or came home from school, as they rode in cars or lay on the beach with their portables, as they did their homework in the evening or snuggled in their beds at night with the lights out and their minds open in the most suggestible condition, the DJs enjoyed an incomparable opportunity to mold the imagination of an entire generation.[8]

Radio's influence alone is enough to promote the pervasive effects of rock music on young and old alike, but it isn't the sole source of musical proliferation. In fact, in many ways, it has been drowned out by more recent visual media forms.

The motion picture is one of the visual forms now heightening music's impact on society. Teenagers, as America's most-frequent moviegoers, average more than 2.5 hours a week watching movies—that's more than one motion picture each week. Since a cult often develops around a particularly popular production—or one that is cunningly marketed for teens—a show may remain in circulation for years, as fans see the picture five, six or more times. Music scores tied to these motion pictures often outgross the film in sales profits, and many movies impact everything from hairstyles to lunchbox designs. It didn't take the music industry long to realize that the less stringent decency codes of the motion picture field provided a wide open avenue to promote rock's raw image, and had the added benefit of bringing rock and roller's performances to the hinterlands where live concerts weren't feasible.

The success of *Blackboard Jungle*, the popular rebel film which launched Bill Haley's tune, "Rock Around the Clock," proved the-bigger-than-life movie screen was the perfect vehicle to promote rock's fantasy images. Sales of records following the release of the movie sparked the production of scores of made-for-teens movies designed specifically to commercialize and sell rock stars and records.

Bill Haley starred in a number of money-makers, as did Chuck Berry and rock's grandaddy, Alan Freed, but it was Elvis Presley who showed the music world how best to milk a movie. The king virtually held court on the sound stage, producing an astounding total of 33 movies. They all had three common characteristics: low budget, poor quality, and phenomenal record sales. The records reciprocated and hyped the movies, some among the highest grossing rock films ever made.

Goldman said that in 1964, Presley's profit-conscious Colonel Parker decreed that Presley would record nothing more but movie soundtrack albums. "After all, there's no sense in competing with yourself!" Goldman said.

> Elvis despised these songs and would often explode in the studio. Eventually, he grew so dejected that he relinquished the last bit of control he held over his career, the supervision of his recording sessions, and bowed his neck to the same yoke borne by the paid by the hour jinglemakers.[9]

The Presley/Parker musical movie merry-go-round was an astounding success. Naturally, it produced a tidal wave of imitators. The formula was always the same: combine a band, a beach party, blankets, bopping, beautiful girls, bikinis and—bingo!—they had a hit movie (and hopefully some hit records).

Then came the British invasion of the early sixties, and with it, the innovation of Beatle psychedelia. Always eager to stretch the imagination, and their pocketbooks, the Beatles departed from pop-film tradition with *A Hard Day's Night*. The movie was an immediate hit, with U.S. ticket sales topping 5.5 million dollars. Steering clear of the overdone, Elvis-style stereotyped situations, the film documented the actual lifestyle of the Beatles, combined with surrealistic episodes and offbeat wit.

Each successive Beatles' film, however, also tracked their lifestyle—one that had become more and more self-indulgent and introspective. *Help!*, *Magical Mystery Tour*, and *Yellow Submarine* each relied heavily on sarcastic humor, symbolic psychedelics and trick photography.

Tide magazine, the journal of merchandisers, explains the Beatles' heavy use of symbols this way: ". . . all popular movements, from Christianity's cross to the Nazi's swastika, have their distinctive symbols."[10] The Beatles' expert use of allegory and symbolism was a device used to draw the line between "us" and "them," to widen the gap and thwart communication between the "rock" generation and all previous generations. As a unifying force for youth, the Beatles' use of visual symbols, combined with their music's powerful impact, was an unqualified success.

By 1970, that gap had stretched to unparalleled proportions. It became no longer necessary to couch hidden meanings in careful phrases and allegory. It was the time to "tell it like it is—to let it all hang out."

Already a veteran of 10 films, Mick Jagger of the Rolling Stones did just that. In his infamous *Gimme Shelter*, cameras boldly recorded a rock concert in stark realism. The violent nature of rock was hung out like dirty laundry as Hell's Angels battered the life out of Meredith Hunter while the band played on.

With appearances in about 20 films to date, the Stones have excelled at the combined documentary/concert flick, despite the bad press stirred up by *Gimme Shelter*. With usual "hop on the bandwagon" mentality, a slew of rock groups have produced their own rock documentaries, among them Jimi Hendrix, Rod Steward, David Bowie, the Grateful Dead and the Sex Pistols.

Rock and the Boogie Man

As monster rock stalked the concert stages of the middle seventies, motion pictures followed suit with the avant-garde rock musical. The earliest example—and one that has maintained a cult following for nearly a decade—is the *Rocky Horror Picture Show*. This macabre musical is actually a spoof on horror movies and glitter rock. The movie tells the perverse tale of Dr. Frank N. Furter, a "transvestite from transsexual Transylvania."[11] The punk production continues to draw new fans into its power, maintaining steady ticket, poster and trivia sales.

In 1978, KISS repeated the horror theme with their $2 million multimedia assault on the nation's senses. The full-length feature film entitled *KISS Meets the Phantom of the Park* featured the costumed crusaders of monster rock endowed with super-hero powers: Gene Simmons breathed fire and flew effortlessly; Ace Frehley blasted death rays from the palms of his hands; Peter Criss crawled catlike over hill and dale; and Paul Stanley portrayed a man with X-ray eyes.[12]

After KISS's makeup had disappeared in 1983, it appeared that monster rock had died a natural death, but Alice Cooper (a.k.a., Vincent Furnier) attempted to revive the monster with his gory song-and-dance, *Welcome to My Nightmare*. The movie was released for home video just in time for Halloween, 1983. The film, which co-starred Vincent Price, received ghoulish reviews and probably won't get a chance to cause too many bad dreams.

Just as depressing, though, is the punk play, *Pink Floyd—The Wall*. The film version of this off-beat production is showing signs of becoming another cult movie. It's a fictitious musical story about Pink Floyd, schoolboy-turned-rock-star. Floyd clambers his way to stardom balanced precariously on the edge of sanity (or is it insanity?), as 26 songs tell his life's sorry story.

Floyd's philosophy of the uselessness of life enshrouds the show in a sarcophagus of despair. It's a far cry from the "my pop's got a barn" gee-whiz showbiz stuff of the thirties and forties. *The Wall* leaves the viewer with the suicidal notion that life is just a bowl of prune pits. Nevertheless, attendance figures show the movie is attracting a young, impressionable crowd which ingests pessimism with its popcorn. Evidence also suggests several members of that impressionable crowd, some as young as 13, have committed suicide at the suggestion of *The Wall's* nihilistic, punkish pap (see Chapter 11).

Several rock stars, in an attempt to make the quantum leap from rock and roll to theatrical roles, have landed parts in full-length feature films sans music. David Bowie has plied his acting talents in several productions, as has the Police's vocalist/writer Sting (Gordon Sumner), and Prince has penned his own juicy plot, supposedly based on his life, for the film *Purple Rain*. Though some have become quite successful in carrying their rock star image onto the silver screen, it is the promotion of rock music itself that most interests the music industry, which hopes to produce top-grossers such as those listed below:[13]

Saturday Night Fever, 1977	$74,100,000
American Graffiti, 1973	55,886,000
Woodstock, 1970 (Documentary/Concert)	16,200,000
Tommy, 1975 (Rock Opera)	16,000,000
Sgt. Pepper's Lonely Hearts Club Band, 1978 (Beatles)	12,958,000
Fame, 1980	7,000,000
The Buddy Holly Story, 1978	5,900,000
A Hard Day's Night, 1964 (Beatles)	5,655,000
Help!, 1965 (Beatles)	5,335,000
Viva Las Vegas, 1965 (Elvis)	5,152,000
Blue Hawaii, 1961 (Elvis)	4,700,000
G.I. Blues, 1960 (Elvis)	4,300,000
Love Me Tender, 1956 (Elvis)	4,200,000

The millions of dollars earned by these rock films are from domestic theater rentals only, and don't include foreign distribution, television rights, paraphernalia sales, record and tapes sales, or multimedia mergers, such as those seen with increasing frequency on MTV (Music Television—a cable network). The box office smash *Flashdance* is a good example of such a merger.

Producers of *Flashdance* hope to top its older sister, *Saturday Night Fever*, in both ticket and album sales. Jack Kierman, executive president of Polygram Records, told *Time*, "A dealer in Chicago just told me, 'It feels like 1978 all over again.' " That was the year *Fever* grossed $258 million worldwide and sold more than 30 million double albums.[14] *Flashdance*, however, has an added sales gimmick going for it—it was designed and filmed specifically with MTV in mind. In May of 1983, MTV began airing two *Flashdance* videos featuring sexy 19-year-old Jennifer Beals, dancing her way through an erotic fantasy of smoke, strobe lights and hazy camera shots.

A successful video, especially when shown in heavy rotation on MTV, can sell millions of records, as well as theater tickets. Though their clips may be filled with fantasies and illusions, MTV executives harbor none—they know that video clips such as *Flashdance's* "Maniac" are nothing more than movie trailers. Simon Fields, the producer of over 200 clips, readily admitted to *Rolling Stone* that "the purpose of the video clip is to sell the soundtrack."[15]

With the kind of promotion that spews from the 24-hour-a-day mouth of MTV, *Flashdance* producers expect a lucrative future. In fact, in the first two weeks after its release the movie earned $11.3 million, and had improved its earnings the second week. The movie, with little plot but lots of music, became one of 1983's top box office draws. In addition, the *Flashdance* LP moved off the shelves at the rate of 50,000 to 100,000 per day, and by the end of 1983 had sold nearly 4.5 million copies (as well as spawned two number one singles).[16] All this while the music and theater businesses claimed they were still in a slump. Ironically, both the slumps and the successes have to thank America's love affair with television.

Television: The American Pastime Turned Passion

Americans set an all-time high in 1980, by daily, watching an average of 6 hours and 36 minutes of television per household—eight minutes more than the record set in 1979.[17] And according to *USA Today*, kids, ages 12 to 17, watch 22.5 hours of TV weekly.[18] It's no wonder that TV can have such a profound influence on buying habits, attitudes and even mores. That sort of promotional power has not been overlooked by rock's pushers.

As early as 1954, an unknown singer, Joan Weber, appeared in a television drama singing "Let Me Go, Lover." The show, which dealt with the story of a disc jockey, was part of the old *Studio One* series. Though Weber's recording of "Let Me Go, Lover" had been released weeks before the television exposure, it had enjoyed little sales and displayed all the earmarks of a flop. On the day after the television show, however, the record began to sell. Rock music chronicler Carl Belz says, "It literally became an overnight sensation; it reached the top of the Pop charts, and it was covered by numerous Pop vocalists, including Peggy Lee, Patti Page, Teresa Brewer, and Sunny Gale.[19]

Though Joan Weber never issued another hit record, "Let Me Go, Lover" did much to convince the music business that TV was a valuable ally.

Two weeks after Elvis Presley had made his first RCA recording, he was scheduled for his television debut on Jackie Gleason's *Stage Show*. In the year following, Presley crooned tunes at least once on every major TV variety show on the air, including his now famous waist-up performance on the *Ed Sullivan Show*. According to Goldman:

> That famous incident—which has come to symbolize more than anything else the moral tone of the fifties—occurred on the last show [of the three in which Elvis appeared]. And it had nothing to do with morality. It was, in fact, the very opposite of censorship, being a deliberate tease intended to suggest that there was a lot more going on "down there" than in truth there was.[20]

Television did much to promote the sultry singer's sexy image—and his tour.

While television promotion of rock music has spiralled, television's standards have nose-dived. In 1956, the Presley incident on Sullivan's show had scandalized the nation, but less than two decades later, Alice Cooper was on the screen schlepping his way through a creepy top-hat-and-guillotine routine. When a 14-year-old boy in Calgary, Alberta, Canada, died while attempting to imitate Cooper's mock hanging, a coroner's jury called for "definite and immediate steps to ban these programs of violence."[21] Predictably, however, nothing has changed—except, perhaps, to get worse.

While program content deteriorates, TV viewership increases, most recently given a boost by the spread of cable television now available to 40% of the nation's homes. And the fastest growing cable channel is none other than rockin' MTV. As of May 1983, MTV was beaming 300 video segments a day through about 1,650 cable systems to more than 21 million homes.[22]

Launched in 1980, MTV has displaced radio listening for many of its 12- to 35-year-old target audience. The cable channel, which is signing on at least half a million new subscribers a month, "has given us a phenomenal new way to expose music and has changed the record industry dramatically," according to Elektra/Asylum board chairman Bob Krasnow.[23]

Research has shown that people in MTV's target audience watch it almost fanatically, averaging well over an hour a day, nearly five days a week.[24] And of those who watch MTV daily, it's the younger ones who stay tuned for the longest periods of time.[25]

But why is the recording industry willing to spend anywhere from $40,000 to almost $1 million on each 3-to-5-minute musical clip that they in turn donate to the MTV channel? Once again, the musical motivation is money. MTV impacts the buying habits of its viewers in a way that radio can't touch. Says *Rolling Stone*:

> From the start, MTV had promised the record companies they would see benefits from airing their promo clips on the channel. . . . [Bob Pittman, the driving force behind MTV], promised results would be clear within a couple of years. As it turned out, *six weeks* after MTV went on the air, record sales of certain artists in heavy rotation started to rise in places saturated by MTV. . . ."[26]

Those artists include veterans like Paul McCartney, Def Leppard, Michael Jackson, David Bowie and Barry Manilow, and relative newcomers such as Duran Duran, The Stray Cats, Eurythmics, Culture Club, Yes and U2. A Nielson survey further solidified MTV's success when it found that of the nine album purchases MTV viewers averaged per year, four were influenced by what they saw on the channel.[27]

Even more awesome is the mass of competitors MTV's prosperity has generated—some of which already enjoy larger shares of the market—such as Atlanta's late Friday and Saturday night's *Night Tracks*; USA Cable Network's weekend *Night Flight*; as well as the weeknightly *Radio 1990*; and recently, with a potential audience of nearly the entire U.S., *Friday Night Videos*, which has *SCTV*'s former time slot on NBC.

Rolling Stone says "the increased exposure of these promo clips will only make video an even more powerful force in the music business," a force it already describes as an "obsession."[28]

The real power of video rock, however, is not its high saturation level, but its mood and emotion synthesis. "Our core audience is the television babies who grew up on TV and rock & roll," says Pittman. "The strongest appeal you can make [to these TV and rock babies] is emotionally. If you can get their emotions going, [make them] forget their logic, you've got 'em."[29]

MTV does that by creating a world of its own—a world of fantasy where taboos are outlawed and the rule is, the more bizarre the better. The idea is to keep the viewer's attention with the glut of visuals. Video clip producers talk in terms of IMP's—ideas per minute—and they keep them rolling. "The surest shortcut to memorable videos seems to be a liberal dose of sex, violence, or both," *Rolling Stone* says.[30] Those themes are, of course, the easiest to conjure up quickly, and according to the National Coalition on Television Violence, the video clips of many rock songs add "violent imagery that [isn't] even present in the lyrics."[31]

The resulting product is a mini-cinema such as Duran Duran's "Hungry Like the Wolf" jungle adventure, featuring a brief wrestling match—not with the wolf, but with a skimpily clad native girl; or the Rolling Stones' controversial video, "Undercover of the Night," which was banned in Britain for its violence, but has received heavy rotation here; or J. Geils Band's high-stepping "Centerfold," with its titillating shots of would-be pin-ups in flimsy nightgowns; or John Cougar Mellencamp's "Hurts So Good," with its ballad sung to a leather-clad woman in chains who dances and writhes through the tune; or Bryan Adams' macho clip, "Cuts Like a Knife"; *ad nauseam*. The idea is to plant in the viewer's mind a hot and lasting visual image of the song's message, and the producers are succeeding.

Video producers and broadcasters excuse the violence, sadism and sexual fantasy as mere farce—poking fun. Pittman was a bit more honest when he called the clips a reflection of what rock and roll is all about. "It's not the Barry Manilow channel. Some songs are unhappy. Some have a dark message. It's the essence of rock."[32] But NCTV's findings indicate that of the average 18 violent incidences depicted per hour on MTV, less than half (8.5) involve the lyrics. In other words, the visual images more than double the violence (usually sexual in nature) the song's lyrics suggest.

As if this video pollution from cable TV were not enough, home video recorder-players are providing yet another market for music producers. It's a booming industry, with 50,000 home video units being sold nationwide each week.[34] Since problems of good sound reproduction and simplified contract negotiations have been ironed out, visual music for home VCR's and disc players threatens to soon offer stiff competition to the record and tape markets.

Video has already created a large following for rock groups adept at musical mini-films. This was dramatically pointed out when 4,000 excited fans lined up at a Manhattan Video Shack store for a video autograph party promoting Duran Duran's "Hungry Like the Wolf," as well as the uncut R-rated antics of "Girls on Film." Two hundred videos were snatched up that day, many by young fans. As *Hit Parader* magazine described it: "Young girls climbed metal bars protecting the display windows for a glimpse inside. Policemen on horseback tried to keep the crowd in order." A store employee recalled, "Our concern shifted from a successful promotion to kids getting hurt."[35]

The problem with the accessibility of home videos is that young, suggestible minds are free to view, repeatedly, themes that would be flatly rejected for album covers as too suggestive; denied air play on radio for their violence; censored by regular television channels; and given a rating requiring parental supervision at theaters. Granted, these censorship possibilities are often pushed to the limits or ignored, but at least they are there—at least there is an attempt to establish some guidelines. However, it appears the video producers are free to grind out trash with no holds barred.

The video producers defend their freedom with the argument that the consumer performs the "censorship" at the time of purchase. However video-cassettes are showing up in public places, where just a few years ago only mild-mannered Muzak was heard and not seen.

Ed Steinburg, president of Rockamerica, a New York City-based subscription service that supplies video tapes to more than 380 outlets—including rock clubs, record stores and TV programs—says that music videos are aired not just in smoky after-hours clubs or on adult-oriented cable television,[36] but also in hotels (Holiday Inns are their biggest customers), theaters (some 500 movie theaters are now showing video mini-concerts before feature films),[37] roller rinks, restaurants and, most recently, even schools!

A former language teacher at the University of Texas, Dr. J. Michael Bell, is using the music and videos of current teenybopper heartthrobs such as Michael Jackson and Paul McCartney and the New Wave idols, Culture Club, to teach two of the three R's—reading and 'riting. Research has shown that people will watch a video 70% more intently than regular television programming.[38] Why not use that long attention span to teach kids phonics or grammar, Bell proposed, and PBS television agreed. Of course, the idea is not entirely new. "For many years," Bell says, "people around the world have used music as a means of teaching their children language acquisition."[39]

Then, too, children's programs such as *Sesame Street* and *Electric Company* have been utilizing the talents of popular celebrities for years to teach language concepts. The difference here is the format.

Dr. Bell explained to *USA Today* how the program works : "On the front end of a video, it says 'adverb search' in magenta letters. Every time you come to an adverb in the lyrics, that adverb will be seen in magenta. After a while, the kids will know what an adverb is."[40]

Since September 1983, Bell's videos have been broadcast every month to PBS stations nationwide, and are seen in at least 45 cities. Beginning in September 1984, Bell's *Colorsounds* program will air in a 30-minute weekly version as well as a 15-minute daytime version for school use, according to the *USA* article. Not only are the students given lyrics sheets (for home practice), but the recording artists and companies supply participating schools with posters and concert tickets to use as prizes to honor students, and a monthly magazine, complete with interviews with the rock stars! So now, instead of the *Sesame Street* approach, which was to sometimes invite guest celebrities such as the Pointer Sisters, and utilize their talents to sing a rocking, Motown version of "Now I Know My ABC's," kids in grades three through twelve are treated to the real thing!

Michael Jackson is teaching grade school grammar with his song "Beat It," and lyrics that go, "This ain't no truth or dare/They'll kick you then they beat you/Then they'll tell you it's fair/ . . . It doesn't matter who's wrong or right/Just beat it."

Lionel Ritchie promotes reading—that is, if you can keep your eyes open after partying "All Night Long": "Everybody sing. Everybody dance/Lose yourself in wild romance/We're going to party . . . forever . . . all night long. . . ." The videos used are supposedly carefully screened, but have already included such performers as Donna Summer, Genesis, Diana Ross, the Stray Cats, Kool & the Gang, David Bowie, Kenny Rogers, and Alabama, as well as the aforementioned Jackson, McCartney and Ritchie.

Thanks to the miracle of modern television and the ingenuity of *Colorsounds*, our children will be able, during school time, to memorize the lyrics to the latest rock hits—a genre that conservative *Newsweek* magazine once called "the music of rebellion—against parents, against the establishment, against social restraints"[41]—right along with their grammar lessons. School will no doubt become the place to learn the five R's: readin', 'ritin', 'rithmetic, and rock and roll.

Visual music is perfect for today's generation which was never completely weaned from television, because it erases the line between reality and fantasy. Consequently, it has changed the face of the music industry, for as one video producer told the *New York Times* magazine, "There's going to be an entire generation of rock music fans whose first exposure to the music is going to be visual."[42]

The fear in George Orwell's futuristic novel, *1984*, was that soon Big

Brother would be always watching us and our children. Thanks to the re-cording and broadcasting industries, Big Brother won't need to have his eye on the lookout for us—we'll all be sitting in our media rooms, mesmerized by video muses.

4

Light My Fire

It was during the turbulence of the late sixties that Dan, the second of four Peters brothers (Lee, Dan, Steve and Jim), was a teenager.

Mom and Dad Peters had become Christians before their sons were born, so the brothers were raised in a committed Christian environment. Dad Peters operated a very successful heating and air-conditioning company. From the time he had become a Christian, though, he had rooted himself in the Word of God, and his life showed it. He was no phony, for he practiced what he preached. The four boys had to admit, therefore, he was a man to be respected, and obeyed—he meant what he said.

As far back as they could remember, Mom Peters had always shown a special love for young people. While the boys were still preschoolers, she had organized a children's Bible club, the Sunshine Club. Soon it grew to over one hundred kids. (That group was eventually to become the nucleus of the youth fellowship and church that the Peters family would form.) Mom was a strict adherent of the Scriptures and ran a tight ship. Unfortunately, she presided over a mutinous crew!

A Christian home doesn't guarantee immunity to problems, pressures or temptations. The Peters family was no different from any other family. Each person had to deal with relationships that weren't always loving and attitudes that sometimes detoured God's laws. Even though all the boys had given their lives to the Lord, and even experienced some of the deeper blessings of God, the Peters brothers were still typical kids. They had strong wills and their own ideas for the future—ideas that didn't include any plans of the ministry— or a crusade against rock and roll!

Mama Don't Allow No Rock 'n' Roll 'Round Here

As a junior high schooler, Dan learned to play several instruments, including the guitar, and even formed a junior-version rock band, destined to live a short but raucous life. Jim loved music too. His favorite instrument was the drums, and he eventually pursued a music major in college.

Mom Peters, however, was adamant about secular music—it was a "threat to the Christian lifestyle," she had said, and refused to let it be brought into

44

or played in her home. She ferreted out record albums that Dan and Jim had hoarded but that didn't stop the Peters brothers. In fact, Dan even used false bottoms in his dresser drawers as secret repositories for rock records.

Dan, weary of his parents' pious lifestyle, rebelled against Mom Peters' authority for a short time. He actually came to resent her, often deceiving her just to be nasty.

Jim's struggle was even harder, and went beyond battles over rock records. His life centered around his music and car, and, at first, he had little time for his parents' religious bent.

Steve, although not such a burden for his parents, caused problems of another sort—problems for rebellious Dan and Jim. He was obedient (that was undeniable), but he was also compulsively honest. He would hang around the scene long enough to get the full scoop, then report to Mom or Dad the wayward deeds of his prodigal brothers.

The boys' problems, though, were just a part of growing and maturing. They learned how to live, learned how to love, and learned how to say, "I'm sorry."

Watch That First Step

For Dan, a turnabout came during his freshman year at North Central Bible College. Although at a Bible college, Dan was seeking little involvement with "the Lord's work."

Then he took a step that quite literally caused him to fall into God's plan for his life. Near midnight, the day before New Year's Eve, 1969, he took an accidental step straight down an old elevator shaft. As he waited alone in dark, semi-consciousness for help to arrive, a scripture came back to him: "And we know that all things work together for good to them that love God, to them who are the called according to his purpose" (Rom. 8:28).

How can any good possibly come from this? Dan wondered at the time. As it turned out, he had many long recovery hours to listen for an answer, and it wasn't an easy one to accept.

"Look what it took to get you to listen," Dan heard the Lord say. "I'm not interested in changing your situation. I want to change *you* through your situation." God made it clear to Dan (not vocally but in his heart) that He had a plan for Dan's life—a life of leadership and ministry. Finally, Dan was rescued by friends and rushed to the nearest hospital where the doctors diagnosed a shattered heel bone, a broken wrist, and two hairline fractures of the vertebrae. Flat on his back, waiting to hear from the doctors whether he would fully recover, Dan knew there could be no more running away. He committed his whole life to God. Although Dan was not instantly healed, he knew he had been visited by God. Within a month was he back to normal, at least physically. Spiritually, however, he would never be the same.

Dan sealed his commitment by offering to start a youth group, utilizing a piece of property Dad Peters owned—Camp Zion. Though the small group gradually grew in number and maturity as the Spirit fanned the flames, the real fireworks were yet to come.

Meanwhile, Steve was fast becoming a star basketball player. As a freshman on North Central's varsity team, he was named All-Tourney and All-Conference. That same season, Dan left home to spend his ministerial internship in Chicago, entrusting Zion's small youth group to Steve's reluctant hands. As the summer waned, Steve began to feel the tug of the Lord on his life as well. Slowly he recognized God's call to play a different game—by God's rules.

By the start of his sophomore year, Steve had decided he should drop his heavy involvement in basketball and make a greater commitment to the ministry, especially his youth group. It was a difficult decision and brought the criticism of faculty and friends. Undaunted, Steve pursued *God's* approval, not man's. With determination, he not only excelled scholastically, he also kept the youth group growing and, with Dad's assistance, soon formed it into a church.

In the meantime, Jim, in his last year of high school, was spending most of his spare time working at a gas station to pay for his beloved 1969 Roadrunner. Soon, however, his natural tendency toward eczema began to plague him as he pumped gas and washed windshields. Without warning, a staph infection developed and within days Jim's temperature soared, plunging him in and out of delirium. Painful, oozing sores soon had encased his face, scalp, eyes, nostrils, and even his tongue, in an ugly yellowish glaze. Jim's eyes swelled shut and the doctor feared for his eyesight as the infection invaded the eyeballs.

Through his days of misery, Jim grew sullen, then bitter. Certain that God had done this to him, but unable to understand why, he could easily relate to Job, of the Old Testament, who also had been afflicted with a repulsive skin disease. In the midst of his troubles, Job had cried out to the Lord, "Night after night brings me grief. . . . I toss all night and long for dawn. My body is . . . covered with scabs; pus runs out of my sores" (Job 7:3–5, GNB).

Jim cried out, just as Job had done: "Why?"

In the Old Testament, and sometimes even in the New, we read of cases where God spoke audibly to men. That can still happen, but more often God speaks either in our hearts, through others, or through circumstances. When God speaks like that, we must be ready to listen or we won't get the message.

Physically unable to read or write, Jim finally had the time and the desire to hear what God had to say. God spoke to him about life goals—something he hadn't bothered to consider before. It was a step in the right direction, but God had a longer walk in mind. Jim's fever continued to climb. Finally, Jim released his will to God's design. With determination, he gave his life totally to God for whatever goal He had in mind.

And God accepted.

The fever broke and, day by day, Jim's healing progressed. The sores dried, the scabs fell away. Although the doctors' prognosis had been possible blindness and permanent scarring, Jim's eyes returned to normal and his skin grew back in baby-like softness.

During Jim's struggles with the Lord over his future plans, Dad Peters had been in the throes of a similar debate. In fact, he had been wrestling with the Lord over this issue for quite a while. It seems God wanted Dad Peters to enter the ministry also. Of more stubborn constitution than his four sons, however, Dad had over the years been able to resist the call with fairly good excuses.

Now the familiar urging seemed absurd to Dad—he was close to retirement age and had never received any formal ministerial training. Nonetheless, Dad's resistance finally wore down as his arguments grew more and more feeble. Eventually, like his sons had done before him, Dad Peters, too, stepped out in faith to answer the call. Soon after, Dan came home to roost, and Zion Christian Center became a family affair.

War Clouds

All was quiet on the home front. The church was increasing, but there were no bugles blowing—nothing to indicate a battle was looming. Then, in the fall of 1979, Steve encountered a tape by a local preacher—one that, for the Peters brothers, would become a summons to report for duty, a call to war.

The message of the tape was designed to persuade the listener to avoid rock music. It quoted certain public statements made by rock stars, and listed examples of some rather foul lyric lines. It caused Steve to wonder—was rock and roll a bigger influence in the lives of its listeners than anyone suspected? Intrigued, he later asked Jim to review the tape, thinking it would make a good subject for the coming Friday night's youth meeting. After hearing the tape, Jim agreed, and offered to photograph some album covers to enhance the talk.

The slides, however, could not be developed in time for Friday night. Not a big deal, they figured, and postponed the presentation for two weeks—until Thanksgiving weekend. In its place, Steve and Jim scheduled a "mini" rock seminar—something to whet the kids' appetites and excite them to come back for more information. The idea proved a winner—far beyond their wildest expectations!

A few days before the first meeting, Steve sat alone, paging through the Scriptures, not looking for anything in particular. Suddenly, an account of a two-thousand-year-old event leaped off the page at him, fresh as today's news. The event had taken place among the believers at Ephesus:

Many of them also which used curious arts [also translated "occult practices"] brought their books together, and burned them before all men: and they counted the price of them, and found it fifty thousand pieces of silver. So mightily grew the word of God and prevailed. (Acts 19:19, 20)

Burning occult books in the sight of all men, Steve thought. *Now, that would be like having a bonfire downtown! If we did something like that with records, we'd probably get arrested!* Still, the idea intrigued him, and later he mentioned it to a friend.

"You ought to call a television station and see if they would come out and cover the event for you!" the friend said, his eyes flashing at the prospect.

"I think I'm going to do just that," Steve muttered. After all, if the early Christians were to set such an example for their contemporaries two thousand years ago, it must be just as right today.

On Friday night, as about 100 young people sat soberly trying to swallow the bitter pill that Jim had just fed them—namely, that their favorite rock music might be fraught with evil—Steve began to recount the public burning of occult paraphernalia at Ephesus. Carefully he drew the parallel between that incident and the present circumstances, challenging the audience to take a stand against evil and demonstrate their commitment to Christ. It was a well-received message and Steve followed it with a reminder to return in two weeks for a full presentation.

Those two weeks proved hectic for the Peters as news of the coming seminar spread like fresh gossip. None of the family could remember another event that had created such an overwhelming response, and it made them somewhat nervous. Since curiosity about the burning seemed to be fanning the flames of controversy, they began to wonder if it was such a good idea after all. The Book of Moses, however, provided solid biblical assurance: "The graven images of their gods shall ye burn with fire: thou shalt not desire the silver or gold that is on them, nor take it unto thee, lest thou be snared therein" (Deut. 7:25).

God was saying, "Don't keep them around. Don't give them to your friends. Don't even sell them. Destroy them."

That was good enough for the Peters brothers. Together with Dad Peters, they decided to stage the burning on the day following the seminar. That would allow the kids time to gather their records, receive their parents' permission, and, most importantly, make a private, unemotional, personal decision.

By starting time on the night of the presentation, more than 350 curious kids and apprehensive adults, some from even 40 miles away, filled the small Zion church. As Steve and Jim charged through their two and a half hour rock music exposé, the crowd sat transfixed. It was obvious the Peters had hit a nerve.

Steve then closed with a word from Isa. 59:19: "When the enemy shall come in like a flood, the Spirit of the Lord shall lift up a standard against him." A standard is a banner—a rallying point—under which people will fight. A standard is also a model of excellence against which others can be measured.

"If you're sick of the devil's influence in your life through rock music,"

Record albums being prepared for burning after a seminar. Young people are never coerced into bringing their albums to be destroyed.

Steve and Dan Peters overseeing a record-burning. This practice of burning follows the example of the believers at Ephesus, recorded in Acts 19:19, 20.

Steve challenged the hushed crowd, "we want to give you an opportunity to take a stand for Jesus Christ—to be a standard for others." Then he invited them to the "burning celebration" to be held the next evening on the Zion campgrounds. While the invitation was met with applause and cheers, no one expected the scene Saturday night brought.

By 5:30 Saturday afternoon, Camp Zion was bedlam, as young people hauled in their records. To meet fire codes, it was decided to burn only the album covers, so a crew was hastily assembled to separate the disks from their jackets—a monumental task due to the unexpected volume. Elsewhere, other enlistees were busy starting a fire, pulling yards of tape from cassettes, preparing a statement for the media, and directing the large crowd to the burning site.

With cheers, the young people began to heap their once-prized rock albums onto the fire, nearly choking it with sheer weight—about $15,000 worth of music, up in smoke. Television cameramen combed the camp, reporters cornered the kids. Focusing on the fire, the perplexed media men sought out— quite belligerently—its meaning for the young people there. Consistently, the teens responded with maturity and certainty, not empty emotionalism; they were aligning their lifestyles with their Christian commitments, cleansing out their lives. Radical? Yes, it was radical—but wasn't Jesus radical too? It was an issue they were to face over and over as news of the rock seminar dispersed.

The Fire Spreads

In the following weeks and months, literally hundreds of thousands of words were published and broadcast about the Peters brothers, their seminar and burning. Requests for more seminars followed, and soon, what originally was planned as a "small talk with a few slides thrown in" evolved into a major international ministry. To date, more than 10 million dollars worth of records and tapes have been destroyed, and countless young lives have been redirected toward the one goal that is worth attaining: a life founded on the only Rock mentioned in the Bible, Jesus Christ (1 Cor. 10:4).

As the rock industry continues to mushroom, creating a social force determined to undermine today's youth in ways unimaginable only a few short years ago, the Peters brothers have vowed to take a more militant stand. Not only do they aggressively pursue every new opportunity to share their seminars, but they also confront, face-to-face, an increasing number of secular rock producers and musicians. They hope to defeat this new assault right at its source.

Their first opportunity to do so came on Ted Koppel's *ABC Nightline*. Present for the confrontation was Joseph Smith, board chairman at Electra Asylum Records. When Koppel asked him whether rock musicians had the right to advocate "smutty" material, "the sort of thing you and I would not want our children listening to," Smith defended the industry by saying that

Dan and Steve with Ted Koppel on ABC Nightline.

Dan and Steve at one of their rock seminars.

musicians were merely reflecting society's present values—not promoting new ones.

He said that musicians didn't intentionally produce records designed to corrupt youth. "Our artists have enough trouble rhyming words, let alone producing satanic references in their music," he added. Smith also pointed to motion pictures, theater, and books and magazines as being similar social "reflectors." He referred to the number of questionable songs recorded in the last 20 years as a "miniscule amount," and then objected to Dan's suggestion of a rating system for music, similar to that used by the motion picture industry.

"We've been under attack—rock and roll music—intermittently now, for 25 years. Elvis Presley was blamed for everything, including the common cold. The music will last. It has permanence. It will outlast this flare-up as well. And 10 years from now, somebody else will come along and attack us and attack our music. They're attacking nonsense."

Are rock music artists simply mirroring society? Is the way of life that rock stars preach "normal"? Should musicians be allowed total freedom of expression, as Smith suggests? Are the Peters brothers just picking on innocent guitar pickers? Read the rest of this book, then judge for yourself under which standard you wish to rally.

5

KISS and Tell

PLACE: WCCO-TV, *Five P.M. Report,* Minneapolis, MN
TIME: Friday, February 18, 1979
CAST: Gene Simmons (KISS), Anchorman Don Shelby, Dan Peters

SHELBY: The person you're about to see is a fellow named Gene Simmons. He is one of the most talented and creative of all current rock stars. He plays in a group known as KISS. We also have an individual of interest who is named the Reverend Dan Peters of Zion Christian Life Center in North St. Paul, Minnesota. . . . Reverend Dan Peters believes that the rock music in KISS is the work of the devil, and that it is a corruption of youth. Simmons believes that rock music is fun, it's enjoyable, it's harmless to everyone—except preachers who are a bit frightened by it. Now, you may know that Gene Simmons is in makeup here in the picture we see, and that is the way he is always seen by the public because he doesn't want anyone to see what he really looks like—for his own purposes.* Gene, are you there?

SIMMONS: Yeah, I'm right here.

SHELBY: Okay. Now, the Reverend Dan Peters is downstairs in our newsroom, and we're going to be hooking him up. Here's a picture of him. Gene, I don't know if you have a monitor—

SIMMONS: (gasp) Oh! What ghoulish makeup!

PETERS: (chuckling) I don't have any on, Gene.

SIMMONS: Oh, I'm sorry. I'm sorry.

SHELBY: Now you two have had a running battle here ever since one came to know the other, and we want to carry it on here. First of all, let's let Dan—I understand that's what you prefer to be called?

PETERS: Yes, sir.

NOTE: KISS has since "unmasked" but, by their own admission, the group's members have not changed their lifestyles, lyrics, intentions or concert antics.

SHELBY: Okay. I would like you to state your case briefly so that we can get Gene, here, on the phone, to respond to you. What is your case? Why don't you like KISS?

PETERS: It's not that we dislike Gene Simmons personally. It's just that we do not appreciate some of the things he stands for, some of the things he sings about. We do feel we have a responsibility to one another as part of our society, to encourage one another to live good, godly, moral lives, and it's just that so many of the things that Gene has stood for in the past—including making plaster of Paris molds of men's genitals—we are just not really in favor of children being encouraged to do—

SIMMONS: What have I done? What did you say?

SHELBY: What he said, Gene, you made plaster of Paris molds of, uh, of male genitals.

SIMMONS: I think you better get your story straight. You must be talking about somebody else.

> The plaster's getting harder and my love is perfection
> A token of my love for her collection. . .
> If you wanna see my love, just ask her. . . .
> —from "Plaster Caster"
> on KISS's *Love Gun* album

PETERS: Well, I'm talking about the song, "Plaster Caster," and some of the things we talked about on the phone last week, Gene. I'm just concerned about the general trend of morals in America.

SIMMONS: Let's first straighten out something. What, uh, Dan—who prefers to be called Dan instead of "Reverend"—what Dan asked me in an interview about a week ago was what "Plaster Caster" was all about. I told him then that it was a song about "groupies," actual fans that exist—female variety—who once lived in the Chicago area, and who did make plaster casts of rock stars' (pause) certain parts—parts they preferred. That's their story. My story is writing the song, and—

PETERS: Which you dedicated to them.

SIMMONS: Of course! It's unfortunate that you didn't like it, but listen, millions of people have, and still do, and life goes on.

SHELBY: The point is—to clarify, Gene—Dan here is saying that you do "ungodly" work, unholy—

SIMMONS: Who's God? Who determines what "ungodliness" is? And who is Dan? I represent myself and my own viewpoint, and if they happen to coincide with a certain rock and roll lifestyle, then that's the way it goes. Who does Dan represent? Who is he?

> I was raised by demons, trained to reign as Thor
> God of thunder, and rock and roll . . .
> And I command you to kneel before the god of
> thunder, and rock and roll. . . .
> — from "God of Thunder" in their movie,
> *KISS Meets the Phantom of the Park*

SHELBY: Okay. Let's find out. . . . Dan, now, who is to say that Gene is *not* doing God's work?

PETERS: Our main concern is that the Bible—and of course, Gene coming from a Jewish background could appreciate the story of Cain and Abel—the Peters brothers have expressed concern that we are all responsible for what happens to each other. We have to accept some kind of responsibility to one another in society for what happens to them and that's why we don't appreciate rock musicians who sing about standards that would be immoral and—

SIMMONS: I do agree that there are some standards that are on the "maybe" mark for some people. I do want to point out, though, that your hair is a little long for a preacher, don't you think?

PETERS: Well, I don't think the Bible really teaches much of a standard as far as hair goes—

SIMMONS: Now wait a minute! Ten years ago, when I was growing up and hearing ministers and all shake their fingers at us and telling us to "get a haircut" and be "righteous, God-fearing people" . . . so what are you doing with long hair, there—hippie person?

PETERS: You see, you're trying to draw a parallel between me and the Inquisition—something else that's been done in the name of God. Now, I'm not trying to group all rock musicians together, Gene. But we are concerned about the things that you sing about. In fact, didn't you say in one of your interviews that KISS has probably gone to bed with more teenage girls than any other rock band?

SIMMONS: No, I didn't say KISS—I said I have!

PETERS: Okay—*you* have personally gone to bed with more teenage girls. And when I asked you in the interview [published in the Minneapolis *Tribune*] as far as your own sexual standards, you said you did enjoy group sex. You saw nothing wrong, in fact, with getting involved sexually with . . . teenage girls—maybe 14 or 15 years of age—even if their parents were against it.

SIMMONS: Well, those are your age figures, but I absolutely think that there is absolutely nothing wrong with doing anything between consenting adults.

> Paul Stanley, addressing KISS fans on February 18, 1983, at Met Stadium in Bloomington, MN, immediately after their interview with the Peters brothers:
>
> STANLEY: Do you feel good tonight? (Screams from crowd.)
> STANLEY: Do you care what your parents think about us?
> CROWD: NO!
> STANLEY: Do you care what those *preachers* think about us?
> CROWD: NO!
> STANLEY: We don't give a (expletive deleted)!

SHELBY: Okay, let me step in here. . . . So what we have here is not hysterics, but what I see is a disagreement in lyrics.

SIMMONS: Well, I think there is a basic problem here. The problem is that I make no bones about who I am, who I represent. It's very clear in the songs. . . . What I write is pretty much a belief in a certain lifestyle which is a free soul, a free person, doing basically what he wants to do without hurting anybody else. And I represent myself and a certain viewpoint.

> I guess I always wanted to be God. What that means really is that I want to be It. Mr. Cool. Mr. Top. And there's nothing higher than God.
>
> —Simmons in *Circus,*
> September 13, 1976

Dan Peters face-to-face with KISS

The brief skirmish you have just witnessed is just one episode in the battle being fought over rock music, but hopefully, you are beginning to visualize some of the important "banners" under which each side is fighting.

Although, to be fair, it certainly cannot be said that Gene Simmons speaks for everyone who loves or is involved with rock music (and Gene Simmons may have dropped out of the rock scene altogether before you ever read this book); still, the flag under which Simmons fights is quite universal: namely, that he is a "free soul" speaking and acting only for himself, his own pleasures and purposes. And let the rest of the world be hanged—as if the whole issue were really quite amusing.

The Peters brothers, however, are in earnest. They believe each person's actions affect other people, that each person is his "brother's keeper." If Gene Simmons—or any rock celebrity—is flaunting a destructive lifestyle, promoting unhealthy lyrics, peddling sexually suggestive album covers, or advocating immoral causes, you most probably will be influenced by it, and you have a right to know.

PART TWO

Rock Music's Four Fatal Flaws:
Lyrics, Lifestyles, Goals and Graphics

Introduction to Part Two

Detective Joe Friday, on the old *Dragnet* television series, was fond of interrupting a long-winded eyewitness to remind her, "I want the facts, ma'am, just the facts." Friday was interested in the bare facts because he knew the sooner he had uncovered the truth, the sooner he would be free to solve another crime.

Jesus had the same principle in mind when He told the disciples, "You will know the truth, and the truth will set you free" (John 8:31, GNB). The truth gives us freedom because it allows us to cast off every false concept as we would excess baggage. So far in this book, you have learned the history of rock music—to get a clear idea of rock music's past and its future. Now it is time to explore the rock music of today. Here are the plain facts, the truth about rock, so you can understand *why* rock music appears to be one of Satan's grandest schemes.

This documentation is not given to entertain, and certainly not to titillate, but to convince you that listening to rock music can harm your spiritual, emotional and mental health. Please read with an open mind. The facts stated here are well-documented, and taken from accurate, credible sources—not from sensational, muckraking "rags." If you have questions, or areas of disagreement, hold them until Chapter 14; there we will answer the most common questions, arguments and misconceptions.

We are in a battle for our culture, which has been both subtly and overtly corrupted by the media—television, radio, film and records—which, as we have seen, are influenced and exploited by rock and roll. And the general trend in rock and roll music is away from God, for it promotes values which oppose Judeo-Christian values. As we begin to explore rock music's lyrics, lifestyles, goals and graphics, let's note how that trend affects our cultural values in six specific areas: (1) despondency, suicide or escapism; (2) human-

59

ism and commercialism; (3) rebellion and violence; (4) hedonism (the pursuit of worldly pleasures); (5) occultism or Satanism; and (6) drug and alcohol use and abuse.

6

Lyrics

Rock music isn't the only music that communicates to us—all music does. However, as author Steve Lawhead admits in *Rock Reconsidered*, ". . . add to this phenomenon the rapidly degenerating subject matter dealt with in the lyrics of most rock, and a distinctly ugly and malicious animal emerges. An animal capable of devouring or at least maiming or scarring its keepers."[1] We need to ask ourselves: What ideas do rock lyrics promote? Are they pro-Christian, or do they defy God or question His existence? Do the lyrics encourage or discourage Christian growth—growth as a stable, productive, loving human being? Do the lyrics promote a close relationship with God, or do they hinder it? In short, do the lyrics promote truth or deceit?

Is That All There Is?

In his article entitled "Between Rock and a Hard Place," Jerry Solomon points to one of the most persistent and pernicious themes in rock music today—nihilism (a negative attitude toward life in general), and the despondency which often accompanies it:

> As rock music increasingly moves from the beach blanket and the dance floor to the marketplace of ideas, nihilism's big lie (God is dead, life is absurd) is big business. Large segments of the youth market apparently jump at the chance to spend their money to be told all is not well.[2]

Rock lyrics have strongly espoused the "what's the use?" philosophy since the Beatles engulfed America, saturating songs with themes of despair. For many youth, daily doses of nihilistic themes, combined with a growing awareness of personal and global problems, are simply too much. Add a liberal dose of increased isolationism, a climbing divorce rate, and nightmarish episodes of the *Six O'Clock News,* and soon they're overloaded. Without proper solutions, young people often escape through drugs, abandonment of solid values, and tragically, sometimes suicide.

Black Sabbath's rowdy sound is a good example of the negative philosophy about which many bands are singing. Some of Sabbath's song titles include: "Electric Funeral," "Hand of Doom," "Nativity in Black."

"Don't Fear the Reaper," a morbid tune originally recorded by Blue Oyster

Cult, convincingly beckons the listener to join in a teenage suicide pact, just as the romantic (but fictional) couple, Romeo and Juliet: "Romeo and Juliet, together in eternity (Romeo and Juliet)/Forty thousand men and women every day (like Romeo and Juliet) . . ./More than forty thousand coming every day (and we can be like they are)/Come on, baby, (don't fear the reaper). . . ."

Skimming the lyrics may not initially give you much of a jolt. However, imagine the lyrics set to a memorable melody, and sung and played to a relentless, driving beat by talented musicians. Imagine hearing this romanticized message to join Romeo and Juliet in their "eternal bliss," not once, but repeatedly. The effect can be devastating, as you will learn in Chapter 11.

Punk rockers caught the nihilistic bug early on, and have been screaming their brand of rage at the world since the early seventies. Iggy Pop, at that time with the group Iggy and the Stooges, put out the hard-hitting *Metallic K.O.* album. A top seller, the album was described as possibly "lethal in the wrong ears" by *Super Rock* magazine.[3] In the album's song, "The Idiot," Pop laments, "Though I try to die, you put me back on the line/Oh, damn it all to hell, back on the line . . . hell. . . ."

Pink Floyd, a successful punk group which has sold more than 12.5 million copies of its LP, *The Wall*, offers the theme of suicide and death in many of the album's songs. Titles include: "Goodbye Cruel World" (which was on the charts for 17 weeks in 1980), "Empty Spaces," "The Thin Ice," and "Comfortably Numb." The record's cry of despair was described by *Rolling Stone* as "a foursided scream of alienation so disturbing it made [John] Lennon's primal Plastic Ono Band seem like a Saturday afternoon sing-along."[4]

Since John Lennon's death, however, widow Yoko Ono has continued to milk the former Beatle's name and image, producing several albums which can hardly be labeled "sing-alongs." One album, entitled *Heart Play—unfinished dialogue,* plays on the public's morbid fascination with Lennon. The album consists solely of excerpts from 22 hours of conversation with the late singer and his wife, made in 1980, for a *Playboy* interview.

Another album, *Season of Glass*, which deals with loss, loneliness and despair, has a cover shot of the shattered, blood-spattered glasses Lennon wore at the time of his death. One song begins with four gunshots, followed by a blood-chilling scream. In another, Yoko Ono sings, "You bastards!/Hate us/Hate me." One reviewer noted, ". . . ultimately, one wishes that Yoko's feverish melancholia were equaled by her rather bland popish [sic] rock."[5] The power to persuade, however, is still as intense, despite the lack of musical talent. And through the headphones of an impressionable, young listener, Yoko's screams following Lennon's senseless death are as vivid and real as today's headlines.

In Jackson Browne's "Sleep's Dark and Silent Gate," the singer reviews his life with both confusion and pessimism: "Wishing I could fly away/Don't know where I'm going/Wishing I could hide/Oh, God, this is some shape I'm in. . . ."

The Cars, a new wave group, has a release written by Rick Ocasek entitled "Since You're Gone." The lyric goes: "Since you're gone/I'm throwing it all away/I can't help it/Ev'rything's a mess."

The song's recurring theme, that life is not worth living after a loved one has gone, is particularly dangerous for young ears to hear, since lack of experience makes it difficult to realize that things do get better and pain eventually does go away (despite its intensity at the moment).

"Crystal Ball," a tune sung by Rainbow, has the same desperate cry. However, this tune asks for help from evil powers: "My back's against the wall/And I can't hold on much longer, so I come to you my friend/For my life seems at an end. . . ."

Life can seem "at an end" at times, especially when facing, for the first time, some of life's difficult and hurtful situations. Songs that help a young person see he is not the only one who has ever faced—and triumphed over— a particular problem would provide wonderful support to a troubled teen. "Crystal Ball," however, and the many songs like it, serves only to reinforce feelings of alienation. It offers no positive answers.

Billy Joel, in "Close to the Borderline," contemplates the absurdity of life, madness and suicide. Bruce Springsteen's album, *Nebraska*, does more of the same, as he bemoans problems seemingly without solutions.

Escapism is the solution offered in the haunting tune entitled "Put Me On and Play Me Loud," by Styx. The song invites the listener: "Put me on and play me *loud*/Turn your stereo up *all the way*!/ . . . Now your body's immersed in sound/So let the synthesizer play! [demonic laugh]." The raw-lunged vocals continue to call the listener to obey "the madman screaming in your living room . . . turn your stereo all the way up." Then, following ear-rending riffs and awareness-heightening synthesizer-melodies, the song switches instantly to a dreamy, beckoning call to escape: "And now you're in the mood/ Let the melody just drift your cares away/It's got to do you good/As it mesmerizes you in its own way/So drift away. . . ." Clearly, the message promotes escapism, and the effect can be even more devastating if the listener is using drugs.

The Swiss heavy-metal head bangers, Krokus, have an album entitled *Headhunter*, which includes songs such as "Screaming in the Night" and "Ready to Burn," with violent, nightmarish lyrics such as: "Eat the rich . . ./ Don't you know that/Life is a bitch."[7] Another heavy-duty group, AC/DC, maintains its cult-like following with hypnotic, repetitive tunes such as: "Gimme a Bullet" and "Shoot to Thrill" ("Shoot to thrill—way to kill/I got my gun and I'm ready/ . . . pull the trigger, pull it"). AC/DC's songs have inspired more than one avid fan to follow their former lead singer, Bon Scott, down the suicide road to self-destruction.

There's a Way Which Seems Right

"Imagine there's no heaven. . . . No hell below us, above us only sky. Imagine all the people, living for today . . . nothing to kill or die for and no religion, too."

64

Those are the thoughts of John Lennon, as written and recorded in his very popular song, "Imagine." He goes on to sing, "You may say I'm a dreamer, but I'm not the only one. I hope some day you'll join us, and the world will live as one."

It sounds right, doesn't it? Certainly, we all want peace and we want people to stop killing people. Even Jesus, on the night before He died, prayed "that they may be one, as we are" (John 17:11). If you knew you were about to die, wouldn't you pray for whatever is uppermost on your mind? We can conclude, then, that peace and unity were very important to Jesus. But a few minutes before He prayed over His disciples, Jesus had told them that He was leaving with them the gift of peace, not "as the world does" (John 14:27, GNB). In other words, man's idea of peace is not God's idea of peace. No matter how man tries to imitate God's gifts, he can never equal them. He always falls short.

John Lennon is viewed as a man who strived for peace in the world. How tragic that he never discovered the source of real peace. A relationship with Christ would have given Lennon a peace "which is far beyond human understanding" (Phil. 4:7, GNB). Instead, Lennon chose a philosophy which has come to be termed "humanism." Humanism, which was originally called by its leaders the "Religion of Humanity," is a philosophy that asserts man's worth through his own reason, and rejects supernatural creation. The most tragic result of this thinking is there are no absolutes by which to judge situations or guide actions. The Bible warns against this philosophy when it says, "There is a way which seems right to a man, but its end is the way to death" (Prov. 14:12, RSV).

Dr. Francis Schaeffer pointed out that while humanists (including many composers) often point to some of the real problems of man without Christ, they can't possibly arrive at the right answers. "What they can never do," he said, "is to give us accurate, sufficient, intellectually complete answers on the basis of their knowledge and perspective."[7]

Humanistic answers to today's problems and concerns can be as soft and inviting as Lennon's "Imagine," or as rousing and propaganda-filled as Tom Robinson's "Don't Take No for an Answer," a clenched-fisted cry for gay liberation. Lyrical humanism can cause confusion, as in Prince's single "Controversy," where he sings over an edgy beat, "Am I straight or gay? Do I believe in God?" On the longer album version, and in concert, Prince responds to his own questions by reciting the Lord's Prayer, and then one of his own making: "People call me rude/I wish we all were nude/I wish there was no black and white/I wish there were no rules."[8]

Queen promotes the same "open mindedness" in "Play the Game": "Open up your mind and let me step inside/Rest your weary head and let your heart decide. . . ." Likewise, Christopher Cross questions life and love in the song "I Really Don't Know Anymore," but falls short of any real answers.

This call for no absolutes is sharply condemned by God. Elijah once challenged Israel, when it slipped into the same tepid state, "How long halt ye between two opinions? if the Lord be God, follow him: but if Baal, then follow him" (1 Kings 18:21).

Even more insidious is the trend creeping into some rock lyrics that makes man little more than (or better than) a machine, and suggests the two are interchangeable. Bob Larson, a well-known rock critic, points to Earth, Wind and Fire's record album *Raise*, which "illustrates a melding of the human and non-human by depicting the amalgamation of a spaceship and an Egyptian goddess."[9] Ultravox, a group that's been around since 1977, "when new wave was still called punk," has produced such "numusick ditties as 'I Want To Be a Machine'," and demonstrated an obsession with robotics.[10] While these groups may not take their songs seriously, they do exert a tremendous amount of influence on vulnerable listeners. We have seen the results of some rock-promoted trends in the past. It remains to be seen how pervasive humanism will be in the adult of tomorrow.

Perhaps just as dangerous as rock's humanistic answers to life's serious questions is the lighthearted, schlock-rock approach that commercialism brings to pop music. Glib responses and easy answers presented through the rock music format can be very misleading to impressionable adolescents, for they paint a picture of life that simply doesn't exist. "Commercialism can work in music just as it works with soda pop," says Steve Lawhead, "by distorting the music's importance."[11] Its power to move people to action and to change opinion is enormous.

Rock music-makers, however, have never taken responsibility for the power they hold. At a recent International Music Conference, the spokesman for a major record industry advertising firm stated:

> Record companies and music publishers have earned many millions of dollars from extolling the virtues of drugs. Would one turn out phonograph records extolling the virtues of forceful rape, armed robbery or kidnapping? The answer, I think for many companies, is "yes," as long as there is some money in it, and they don't go to jail.[12]

In pursuit of the almighty dollar, rock music artists often offer pure fluff and soap opera plots as if they were the wisdom of the ages. But there are also several rock songs right now—popular ones—which extol the "virtues" of rape, stealing and lawlessness. Kidnapping? Perhaps it's not on the charts yet, but rockers have long been boasting they are stealing kids away from their parents, so it's just a matter of time before they sing about it.

The Clenched Fist

Violence and rebellion have been shaking their fists at the world through rock music since its inception. Though rebellion, in one form or another, is present in the lives of many of today's youth, constant meditation on anger and alienation, through listening repeatedly to rock music, magnifies and distorts those feelings. Eventually the alienation can grow out of proportion and even out of control. "Rebellion, which is often on the mind of young people," says writer Jerry Solomon in *Shofar* magazine, "finds it's way into many songs. Violence is not far behind. A sensitive chord is strummed when someone hears a song that aligns his feelings of frustration and anger."[13]

Jefferson Airplane/Starship became infamous with one of the most radical albums of the sixties, *Volunteers*. Glorying in revolution, the album advised everyone to become "outlaws in America." Steeped in controversy, the song contained the cry, "Tear down the walls, Motherf* * *!"

Elton John joined in the fight on his *Goodbye Yellow Brick Road* LP. In the song, "Benny and the Jets," he advised teens: "We shall survive, Let us take ourselves along/Where we fight our parents out in the streets/To find out who's right and who's wrong."

The United States wasn't the only country rocked by early themes of violence and lawlessness. In Rod Stewart's million-seller, "Anarchy in the U.K.," he ranted, "I am the anti-Christ. . . . I want to be—anarchy! . . ."

Tom Robinson Band's debut album, *Power in the Darkness*, featured aggressive songs about racism, oppression, women's rights and gay liberation. Songs like "Long Hot Summer," a power-filled ballad about a street battle, urge young listeners to join in the struggle.

The infamous KISS, in songs such as "Flaming Youth," also encourages young people to rise up and use their power to rebel. And AC/DC exhibits a "couldn't-care-less-what-you-think" attitude in nearly all of its music.[14] The Clash, one of England's most notorious punk bands, features the same attitude in the song, "Straight to Hell," on its 1982 hit album, *Combat Rock*.

For lessons in punk grammar and gripes, however, you just can't beat Pink Floyd. On their "Another Brick in the Wall, Part 2," they boast: "We don't need no education, We don't need no thought control. . . ./I ain't did nothing to you. I ain't dumb, I ain't stupid. . . ./Hey, teacher, leave us kids alone. . . ."

The Rolling Stones traditionally has been not only one of the dirtiest bands in rock and roll, but their songs have been some of the most violent and anarchistic. *Undercover*, the group's twenty-third LP (not counting anthologies and outtakes), includes songs with titles like: "Too Tough," "Too Much Blood," and "It Must Be Hell." In a *Rolling Stone* review, Kurt Loder described the album: *"Undercover* exhibits a sense of political scorn that seems fueled by more genuine disgust than the Stones have spewed up in years. Rich in repugnant detail . . . [it] slams the message home with inarguable power."[15]

In these times of troubled nations, inflationary woes, wars and threats of wars, today's youth need to hear a message of optimism tempered by realism. Young people need to know they can put their trust in a source beyond their own limited vision. Instilling trust in a loving Father, however, cannot be done without open and on-going communication between parents and their children. Although it's hard to admit that rock's heroes are today's villains, it is obvious their music is often designed to thwart that communication.

Rock Music's Three-Letter Theme Song: Sex

Sex has been rock music's number-one message since the medium was born. In the early days, as we have seen, references to sex in rock and roll were veiled in double entendre and obscure jargon. Rock has grown up, though, just as quickly as society's standards have gone down. As a result, sex in the lyrics of rock songs is increasingly obvious. And, as an article in *U.S. News and World Report* pointed out, "Unlike X-rated movies and books, this music is broadcast, performed in concerts and available on records to any listener, regardless of age."[16]

As early as 1967, Andrew Oldham, manager of the Rolling Stones, declared, "Rock music is sex and you have to hit them [teenagers] in the face with it."[17]

Aerosmith's manager voiced a similar sentiment: "When you're in a certain frame of mind, particularly sexually-oriented, there's nothing better than rock and roll . . . because that's where most of the performers are at."[18]

In an article for *Circus* magazine, Debbie Harry of the band Blondie agreed. She said, "Rock 'n' roll is all sex. One hundred percent. Sometimes music can make you come. . . . I don't know if people [expletive deleted] to my music. I hope so."[19] (If detailed quotes like Harry's rile you, remember, not only do rock celebrities debase sex repeatedly in their interviews, more importantly, they fill their songs with lyrical pornography.)

A 14-year-old rock fan wrote in a letter to the editor of *Hard Rock* magazine, "Rock and sex mix like rum and coke!"[20] The following sampling of lyrics is a tiny portion of the songs that affirm that assessment. *The Rock Book of Lists* notes Jefferson Starship's number-one song, "Miracles" (on the LP version), included the line, "I got a taste of the real world when I went down on you girl."[21] This sexual reference to oral sex slipped by many radio deejays, and received widespread airplay. Lead singer, Gracie Slick, admitted that double entendre was also included in the group's album *Earth*:

> There's a line where I say, "if you've got one, bring it out. I wanna see it." In other words, "if you've got a [sexual slang], let's see it." . . . There's another song, totally talking about a male apparatus, which is called, "Across the Board." It goes, "Seven inches of pleasure/Seven inches going home/Somebody musta measured the old bone." Now, a bone could be a barhandled .38 or a [sexual slang]. I use the double entendres to get past the record company.[22]

Elton John doesn't bother with double meanings in most of his lyrics, however. His song about lesbianism, "All the Girls Love Alice," is blatant about it's content: "She couldn't get it on with the boys on the scene/But what do you expect from a chick who's just sixteen?/. . . It's like acting in a movie when you've got the wrong part/Getting your kicks in another girl's bed. . . ."

The tune ends with the suicide of Alice, after she has had sexual relations with many married women. John's more recent hit, "I Guess That's Why They Call It the Blues," deals with a heterosexual love affair gone sour. The singer remembers "Living like lovers/Rolling like thunder/Under the covers." His tune "Sweet Painted Lady" touts the virtues of prostitution, and another of his songs, "Jamaica Jerk-Off," can be interpreted as promoting masturbation.

Circus magazine calls Aerosmith's song lyrics "crude but authentic."[23] One might wonder, *authentic what?* when hearing them sing, "Met a cheerleader, was a real young bleeder/You ain't seen nuthin', 'till you been down on a muffin."

"Cut the Cake," sung by Average White Band, is equally as crude, though couched in double meanings: ". . . Give me a little piece/Let me lick up the cream/Cut the cake, do you know what I mean?/Little lovin' on the side/Just to keep me satisfied. . . ."

It's easy to see why teenagers—and adults—often confuse "love" with what the Bible would term "lust," after listening to a steady diet of this type of music. Many of Led Zeppelin's recordings involve this sort of bizarre sexual behavior. In fact, one tune, entitled "Whole Lotta Love," a song filled with sexually explicit lyrics, ends with a simulated orgasm. Jimmy Page expressed Zeppelin's outlook when he told *Circus* that "rock and roll is [expletive deleted] -you music."[24]

Dr. Hook and the Medicine Show, a seven-man rock band of the seventies, viewed rock with similar sentiments, setting blatant pornography to music. In their album, *Sloppy Seconds* (referring to gang rape), the lead song, "Freaker's Ball," describes a pervert convention: "Don't forget to bring your whips/We're going to the Freaker's Ball." Verse two hints that teens should bring drugs; verse three gives a guest list that includes male and female homosexuals, sadists with leather fetishes, sado masochists (those who derive sexual pleasure from pain), and junkies; and verse four urges brothers to have sexual relations with sisters and sons with their mothers. Another heavily promoted Hook sex album, *Makin' Love and Music*, includes the songs "Sexy Energy," "Let the Loose End Drag" (about a 12-year-old boy with a disproportionately-sized sex organ), and "What a Way to Go," a one-man sexual odyssey with seven women.

Face Dances, by The Who, contains a song vividly describing masturbatory impulses while asking, ". . . how can you do it alone?"[25] The Knack sings that "Good Girls Don't, but I Do," the Rolling Stones beg "Let's Spend the Night Together," and Foreigner extols the virtues of quick, self-gratifying sex "in the middle of the night," in their song, "Urgent."[26]

According to Stephan Demorest, of *Hit Parader,* Ted Nugent's lyrics are "vulgar in both senses of the word: (1) coarse and obscene, and (2) common, with lots of explicit sex."[27] Nugent seems to agree. Describing the song "One Thousand Knives," from the album *Cat Scratch Fever*, he said: "[It's about] when you're in school and you wanna get your [expletive deleted] and you gotta do it yourself or use an electric cattle prod" . . . *ad nauseam.* "Just your average love stories," he said of the album, then offered a further description too vulgar to print literally, which catalogues sexual violence, mutual oral copulation, and vomiting.[28]

Some of Nugent's tunes include: "Wang Dang Sweet Poontang," "Spit It Out," "Yank Me, Crank Me, Just Don't Wake Me Up to Thank You," and "Violent Love," which has been banned on some AM stations. "I hope you throw up when you listen to it," Nugent (who calls his fans "the lowest form of human existence")[29] once said of the latter song.[30]

When monster rock stomped onto the stage, it added a new element to the already sexually-glutted lyrics of rock—sado-masochism. KISS debuted in 1977 with *Love Gun*, an obvious sexploitation. The lyrics of the song "Almost Human," from that album, include: "You're so smooth and tender . . ./ I'm listenin' for your scream./I'm almost human. I'm almost a man/. . . Baby, baby, please don't run away."

The crude sadomasochism display on the album cover provides a context for "Almost Human" that carries grisly overtones for a child who is "smooth and tender." KISS loves to recall how the members devised their now-discarded stage personnae—by delving into their own deepest personalities. Gene Simmons provides an excellent case-in-point; he admits the band is concerned with "sex and little else."[31]

Another monster rock ribald is Alice Cooper. In his album, *Million Dollar Babies,* he sings, "I Love the Dead," an anthem of necrophilia (sexual intercourse with a dead person): "I love the dead before they're cold/the bluing flesh for me to hold." Other Cooper hits include "Cold Ethyl" (on the same subject as above), "Only Women Bleed," and "Muscle of Love."

David Bowie introduced homosexual love to monster rock with *The Man Who Sold the World* (an album banned in many parts of the U.S. for its homosexual connotations), *Ziggy Stardust* and *Hunky Dory*. Bowie has presented himself both directly and indirectly as a homosexual, bisexual and/or transvestite on his tours and television appearances. He has been a major influence in the acceptance of androgyny (having male and female characteristics) in the U.S.

On the platform heels of monster rock came the metal mashers with their music for the "masses." *Circus* says one of the cardinal requirements for qualification as a "people's band" is that it speaks the people's language,[32] but AC/DC's obscenities has kept the group off limits on many radio stations until just recently. "AC/DC takes a walk down rock's decidely seamier side," *Circus* commented, "and song titles like 'She's Got Balls,' 'Beating Around the Bush,' and 'Walk All Over You' (and those are the love songs) made it a wonder their LPs didn't come in plain brown wrappers."[33]

Explaining the background of their song, "The Jack" (which is about venereal disease), one of the band members said, "We were living in this household of very friendly ladies and everyone got it [venereal disease], so we wrote this song."[34]

In another sex serenade, "Let Me Put My Love Into You" they sing: "Don't you worry, cuz it's your turn tonight/Let me put my love into you, babe."

Journey, called by some the "faceless" band, and by others the "most beautiful band in the world,"[35] sing: "Lay It Down," about needing to have a double shot of whiskey, wine and women in order to get through the night; "Keep One Runnin'," describing "cruisin' " with a girl and finding some "back seat rhythm and blues . . . down we go . . ."; and "Stone In Love," about sex in the clover, obtaining "burning love."

"Cruisin' " is the name of another tune—this one by the gay-rights group, Village People. The disco tune goes: "I'm in need of someone today, I'm a cruiser. . . ./If the right person should pass my way/I do not wait to make myself a play. . . ." The song states emphatically that they are looking at everyone passing by, not just women. That same theme is also made clear in their song, "San Francisco" ("Freedom is in the air/Searching for what we want—pleasure, pleasure . . ."), and in the disco hit "Y.M.C.A."

When disco was hot in the seventies, Donna Summer was its fire. At the height of the disco craze, she topped the charts with "Love to Love You Baby." A *Circus* article dubbed her "Queen of the Orgasm," since during "Love to Love" she had "managed to slur, wheeze and seductively chant the title phrase over 122 times during the course of the song, with the sterling addition of a marathon 22 orgasms stretched over the 19 minutes of the composition."[36]

Several women rock stars have used sex to sell their music, and the eighties seem to be the decade for the hot female rock vocalist. In Suzanne Fellini's hit single, "Making Love on the Phone," *Us* magazine said she "coos, pants, and belts her way through the tune, too hot to be kept on hold."[37]

Kim Carnes, the former Breck girl, produced a number-one hit and Grammy winner in 1981, with her raspy, sensuous "Bette Davis Eyes" (". . . she'll take a tumble on you/Roll you like you were dice/Until you come up blue . . .").

Millie Jackson, whose songs had received little airplay because of their offensive lyrics, changed all that when she walked away with her Grammy for "If Loving You Is Wrong, I Don't Want to Be Right." *Us* said, "Her notorious X-rated raps on love and lust have turned five of her eight albums to raunch 'n' roll gold." Jackson added, "It's amazing! My first gold album was my first dirty one, and it was the first one I produced myself. Now, when it's time to do a new one, they want to know: 'What's the dirt this time, Millie?' "[38]

Punk rock's Patti Smith knows how to dish out the dirt too. Of her album, *Horses,* an article in *Circus* observes, she "talks of lust, love, death, dreams, and demons. . . . Pattie talk-chants the beginning of her poem 'Oath': 'Jesus died for somebody's sins—but not *mine*. My sins are my own, they belong to *me*.' Patti is in the guise of a cocky seducer here: ('She looked so sweet/I took the plunge'), . . . choosing sweet lust and life instead of rules and regulations."[39] Another song on the same album, entitled "Land," is probably the only recording in existence where a boy is raped by another boy in a high school hallway, and within 80 seconds of the beginning of the song! In reference to the tune, a *Circus* journalist remarked, "Patti Smith could write a song about the Great Wall of China and it would be sexy."[40]

Other popular female stars selling sleaze for a living are: Pat Benatar, described by *Us* as a "rock tigress in heat and beat"[41]; Chrissie Hynde, female lead of the Pretenders, who sings of a quasi-rape scene in "Tatooed Love Boys"; Annabella Lwin, whose lyrics are described by one fan magazine as having "come from *Playboy* magazine"[42]; and Debby Harry, whose lyrics are loaded with sexual innuendo—"I'll give you some head—and shoulders to cry on"— and yet, her songs get radio airplay.[43]

Prince is another rock star clever at sneaking loaded lyrics on the air. In his 1979 hit, "I Wanna Be Your Lover," he croons, "I wanna be the one you come for. . . ." In his early 20's, Prince singlehandedly wrote, produced and played all the instruments for each of his LPs: *For You; Prince;* and *Dirty Mind. Rolling Stone* said of the third:

> Nothing could have prepared us for the liberating lewdness of *Dirty Mind.* . . .
> The cover photograph depicts our hero, smartly attired in a trench coat and
> black bikini briefs, staring soberly into the camera. The major tunes are paeans
> to bisexuality, incest and cunnilingual technique. . . . At its best *Dirty Mind* is
> positively filthy. Sex, with its lasting urges and temporary satisfaction, holds
> a fascination that drives the singer to extremes of ribald fantasy.[44]

In "Head," a tune from the album, Prince sings of seducing a bride in her wedding dress on her way to be married; in "When You Were Mine," he cries, "I never cared . . ./When he was there/Sleepin' in between the two of us"; and in "Sister," he sings with relish, "Incest is everything it's said to be."[45]

Rick James, the self-styled king of punk funk, exhibits a similar style with his hot single, "Give It to Me, Baby," claiming he'll "make you holler 'til you've had enough."[46] Another punker, Elvis Costello, in his song, "The Year's Model," sings the praises of the trendy Farrah Fawcett-Majors types: "You see yourself rollin' on the carpet with this year's girl. . . ." Punk lust is the subject, too, of the Dead Boys' morally degrading "I Need Lunch": "I don't really wanna dance, girl/I just wanna get in your pants. . . ." Iggy Pop makes even more clear what is on his mind when he sings, "Pull up your shirt— Lemme take satisfaction. . . ." The Cars sing of "Lust For Kicks." And Wild Cherry, in the song, "I Feel Sanctified," describe—among other sex acts—a woman caressing a man's genitals.

When sexual precocity is packaged and promoted by rock music, when it is held up to be the norm, it is no wonder that an age group (which child development experts label as fiercely conformist) falls prey to the pressure. At no other stage in life are one's peers so strong an influence, and authorities agree that peer pressure is one of the most important causes of premarital sex in teens aged 15 to 19.

With a steady bombardment of sex through all media, especially rock music, today's teens face tremendous opposition if they decide to remain virgin. Psychologists agree sex before the age of 16 or 17 is counterproductive.[47] However, Wilson Key, author of *Media Sexploitations* and *The Clam Plate Orgy*, concludes, "Media, as a circulation-advertising gimmick, has for several decades pushed the notion of mate-swapping, orgies, casual sex, and perversion of a dozen varieties." He maintains that the incredible confusion, uncertainty and guilt today's young people experience in regard to sex is a direct result of their trying to "adjust" the conservative, biblical teachings they receive from the adults in their lives to the "anything goes" hedonism preached through their electronic "peers," the media.[48] While it might be easy to scoff at the effect of rock music on the cultural value system of our young people, to do so abandons them to a situation that is dangerous not only to their sanity, but their souls.

Up Jumped the Devil

Rock and roll has long been labeled "devil's music" by concerned preachers and parents, often to the great amusement of both rock's stars and fans. The term sounds somewhat archaic in our modern, computerized world. Any military strategist would tell you, however, that it is dangerous to underestimate the enemy—and foolhardy to pretend he doesn't exist. Satan loves for us to misjudge his powers, and better yet, scorn his existence. That is why he is a master of disguise. He and his servants can disguise themselves as "angels of light" and sometimes fool even the wisest of men (2 Cor. 11:13).

There is no need for you to be fooled, however. Satan is alive and well, and he prowls about this tired, old planet like a hungry lion, seeking to devour souls. And at a time in history when the world seems to be on a collision course, when we can't help but wonder if there will be no "future" for mankind, and when mankind is searching for answers, it is easy to be deceived. The recent revival of Satanism, witchcraft, occultism, spiritualism and mysticism is evidence of that search.

As Hal Lindsay wrote in *The Late Great Planet Earth,* "It is a mystic time. Famous movie stars and wealthy socialites [and one could add, rock stars] are traveling to the countries of the Far East to consult with 'holy men.' The influence of spiritualism in our popular songs, jewelry, and even clothing, is obvious. . . . In churches and on college campuses mediums are receiving speaking invitations. . . . More than forty colleges now conduct psychic research under the title of parapsychology. The interest in these subjects is growing in proportion to the increase in astrology and prophecy."[49]

Sadly, many of these promoters of old and new religious cults have found their way into the rock music industry, and many young people, while sincere, follow these false pipers.

As pointed out in Chapter 2, the Beatles were probably the first to color their music with the misguided message of mysticism. George Harrison's album, *Somewhere in England,* is a good example. It is a strange, entrancing blend of religion-oriented pop hymns that come across like plain, old-fashioned love songs. Although the music has AM radio appeal, it doesn't fail to drive home its point.[50]

Lyrics of one song on the album go, "They call you Christ, Vishnu, Buddha, Jehovah, Our Lord. . . ." Obviously, in Harrison's mind, all religions are alike, and Jesus and the Father (Jehovah) are on equal footing with all the others mentioned. Jesus, however, said, "I am the way, the truth, and the life: no man cometh unto the Father, but by me" (John 14:6).

Tom Scott, who played with Harrison on several of his LP's, says, "George is a tremendous student of Hindu religion. He can tell you an awful lot about it, about who the various deities are and what they stand for. . . . The messages that come through in the lyrics are very clear. That's how he feels philosophically. . . ."[51]

Soon after the Beatles lent credence to the godless Eastern religions through their Maharishi meetings, a flood of misdirected religious fervor washed over the rock music community, and found expression in rock music.

One of the biggest commercial successes for The Strawbs was their album *Grave New World*, released in 1972. In it, the lead singer includes a quote from Buddah and a prayer of praise dedicated to the Egyptian sun-god, Ra. (Ra was the supreme deity of the ancient Egyptians and is represented as a man with the head of a hawk, crowned with a solar disc.[52] Symbols and references to him can be found on numerous other rock recordings.)

In the same year, the Jefferson Airplane/Starship released their album entitled *Long John Silver*. In it, Jesus Christ is described as a bastard who had an affair with Mary Magdalene. Soon after, they recorded a Paul Kanter song, "Your Mind Has Left Your Body," a song about astral projection, or out-of-the-body experiences, an occult phenomenon. Another Airplane album contained the song "Light the Sky on Fire," dedicated to "the great god Kokoa Kan."[53]

Steve Tyler is the androgynous-looking lead singer of another highly-successful seventies group, Aerosmith. In their song, "Seasons of Whither," he wails, ". . . Loose-hearted lady, sleepy was she/Love for the devil brought her to me. . . ."

Bad Company, one of the seventies groups that flirted with the occult, recorded its 1977 album, *Burning Sky*, in a French studio supposedly haunted by the ghost of Frederic Chopin, a 19th-century composer. The album closes with "Master of Ceremonies," a song described by *Circus* as a "standout bizarre jam under the mind-altering influence of Chopin's ghost."[54]

The band's guitarist, Mick Ralphs, explained, "The control room is where all the weird things go on. The machines go off and on, for no reason. And we used to hear voices coming through the speakers."[55] Ralphs also mentioned that Elton John cut "Honky Chateau" in the same ghostly setting. John's long-time lyricist, Bernie Taupin, would have been right at home in the studio; he has told *People* magazine that he decorates his walls with "Satanic art," and admitted "the occult fascinates me."[56]

A group with a name like Bad Company might be expected to be a poor example to youth, but what of groups with supposedly squeaky-clean images? Groups such as the Beach Boys or the BeeGees?

The BeeGees' Maurice Gibb once had a bout with heavy drinking, and brother Robin "wallowed" in speed and downers, but both claim they have come clean.[57] However, it is this band's references to the occult that most tarnish its image. One of the most popular groups since the chart-busting Beatles, the Brothers Gibb own title to the second biggest-selling album of all time—*Saturday Night Fever*. Their careers, however, were floundering until the album *Main Course* was cut. That LP included the song "Shenandorah," based on the name of an evil spirit.

In the late seventies, following a string of hits, they released the *Spirits Having Flown* LP. Barry Gibb insists the album is fraught with references to reincarnation, and according to a *Rolling Stone* interview, both Maurice and Robin lay claim to the psychic power of ESP.[58]

The Beach Boys, an on-again-off-again group since the sixties, seem to exude the All-American Boy image as well. They, too, have made references to the occult in their music. While their early tunes were usually odes to the wonders of a surf board or a 409 engine, Beach Boy Mike Love's decade-long affair with Transcendental Meditation began to surface when they dedicated an album—*M.I.U.*—to the Maharishi International University, in Fairfield, Iowa. The school was founded by followers of the Beatles' guru, Maharishi Mahesh Yogi.[59]

Recorded on *M.I.U.* is the quiet little ditty, "Transcendental Meditation," which says: "Anyway you do it, well, it's bound to work I know . . ./Transcendental meditation should be part of your time." Though the lyrics are somewhat tongue-in-cheek, and the tune has the unmistakable Beach Boys bounce, the message is nonetheless persuasive, especially to an impressionable teen searching for answers.

Blue Oyster Cult, like its British cousin, Black Sabbath, took mysticism and the occult one step further, by playing what some call "Satan Rock." One of its sinister songs, "Divine Wind," begins with stereotyped ingredients of a witch's brew, then declares, "If he really thinks we're the devil/Then let's send him to hell. . . ."

Ronnie James Dio, formerly a member of Rainbow (as well as Black Sabbath, before forming his own band, Dio), has noted that the Rainbow song "Stargazer," from the *Rainbow Rising* LP, is written from the viewpoint of an Egyptian slave. "He is serving the Wizard, who observes the skies and stars and becomes obsessed with the idea of flying. The slaves are building a tower of stone so the Wizard can jump off the top and take to the air. Finally this Wizard falls to his death."[60]

Ritchie Blackmore, also of Rainbow, is described by *Circus* as a songwriter who laces his lyrics with occult references, and believes in séances. When asked if he believes in the songs he writes, such as "Tarot Woman"—a song dealing out fortune-telling cards and fornication—Blackmore answered, "It scares me to death. But it's really true."[61]

Brian Johnson, AC/DC's replacement for the late lead singer Bon Scott, recently admitted he was occasionally "scared to death" as well by the energy in the group's music.[62] The heavy metal group's songs include: "We're Back in Black," "Evil Walks," "Inject the Venom," "Highway to Hell"—a song that claims hell is the "promised land"—and "Hell's Bells": ". . . I'm gonna take you to hell . . ./I'm gonna get 'cha—Satan got 'cha. . . ./If God's on the left, I'm on the right./If you're into evil, you're a friend of mine. . . ."

When Ronnie Dio migrated to Black Sabbath, he must have felt right at home, for the band seems to go out of its way to promote demonic notions in its songs (e.g. "Wizard," "Voodoo," "Stonehenge"). Bill Ward of the group admits "Satan could be God"[63]; bassist Geezer Butler has claimed he is Lucifer, and that he has seen the devil;[64] and main composer, Tony Iommi, insists black magic and sorcery are his legitimate interests, not gimmicks. Their albums include: *Sabbath, Bloody Sabbath*; *Heaven and Hell*; and *Born Again*.

Led Zeppelin, one of the original metal mashers after which Black Sabbath was patterned, has recorded albums such as *House of the Holy*, depicting on the cover a child sacrifice to demons. The group often puts subliminal satanic messages into their recordings as we shall document in Chapter 12. Robert Plant and Jimmy Page, former members of the now disbanded group, both profess an interest in the occult, and their album *Presence* displays an oddly-shaped object that Page claims symbolizes the force that enables the group to profoundly affect audiences—a power simply called a "presence."[65]

Uriah Heep, a group launched in 1970 as a heavy metal band similar to Led Zeppelin, received almost unanimous press hostility. One critic moaned, "If this group makes it, I'll have to commit suicide." Their albums include *Abominog* and *Demons and Wizards*, with many pro-occult songs, including "Traveler In Time," which deals with astral projection.[66]

On his phenomenally successful first album, *Bat Out of Hell*, Meat Loaf (Marvin Lee Aday) sings about a mutant biker who comes out of hell. Composer Jim Steinman said, "I've always been fascinated by the supernatural and always felt rock was the perfect idiom for it."[67] However, after recording the album, Aday lost his voice for two years and his career nose-dived.[68]

Medical attention was also necessary for singer Bruce Dickinson of the torturous group, Iron Maiden; while on tour he slipped a disc when mimicking a demonic seizure.[69] Iron Maiden has come under fire for making more satanic music than any other band except Ozzy Osbourne. Many of its songs refer to the Antichrist; most of the lyrics are obsessed with hellish imagery ("Purgatory") and ghoulish themes ("Transylvania"); and seven out of the eight songs on one album alone pertain to themes of death and assorted evils.[70]

Todd Rundgren dedicated his album, *Ra*, to the Egyptian sun-god. The album includes song lyrics dealing with Japanese and Egyptian mysticism.[71] He also professes a belief in astral projection and reincarnation.[72] The devil is welcomed back in a bizarre, sinister song entitled "Hell Hotel," by the group Blackhorse, and Styx sings of having a one-way ticket on a hell-bound train in "Witch Wolf."[73] The Moody Blues' album, *In Search of a Lost Chord*, refers to the mystical reincarnation concept that says if one hears the right super-natural chord struck, he obtains instant nirvana—enlightenment through a transcendent state of mind.[74]

In the very popular song, "Hotel California," the Eagles sing of demonic possession and power: "You can check out any time you like/But you can never leave."

Alice Cooper sings of similar nightmares in his albums, *Alice Cooper Goes to Hell* and *Welcome to My Nightmare*. His ominous lyrics and music are designed specifically to create a frightening atmosphere. That same devilish climate was created by Rick Derringer in one of his group's songs, "Sweet Evil": "Show me where to sell my soul/A promise sealed in blood."[75]

Earth, Wind and Fire sings the haunting song "Jupiter" (a time-traveling god who comes to "make them free"), and Jackson Browne shares his belief in reincarnation in the mythological "Rock Me on the Water."

BowWowWow howls its punk rock release, "Prince of Darkness": "Who's going to hell? What's his name? . . ./Open the door and let me in/I am the Prince of Darkness." At this point in the song, it's as if the devil actually takes over, speaking through the group, saying he wants to possess the listener.

As a listener, you need to stop and consider just what this music is telling you. Hopefully, reading some of the lyrics, without their catchy, lilting melodies, has helped you recognize the evil and potential danger within rock's entanglement with the occult.

The late Jimi Hendrix once told *Life* magazine, "Atmospheres are going to come through music, because music is a spiritual thing of its own. You can hypnotize people with music, and when you get people at the weakest point, you can preach to them into the subconscious what we want to say."[76]

Ask yourself this: If the Holy Spirit can bless spiritual hymns and songs, and allow them to lift the soul of the listener, can the devil—the deceitful one, the counterfeiter, as he is called in Scripture—create the opposite effect? The answer is yes. And whether you consciously listen to the lyrics or not, your subconscious mind—which is the seat of the soul—is influenced. Are you allowing avowed occultists to "preach" into your subconscious, as Hendrix boasted?

Common Ground

What is it that students, sports heroes, suburban housewives, jail inmates, top executives, ghetto kids and rock stars all have in common? Drugs. Twenty-two million Americans smoke marijuana regularly, and another 54 million have at least tried it. Surveys show that one of every ten high school seniors gets high *every day* (smoking a joint up to twenty times more potent than those used a decade ago).[77]

Cocaine, it seems, has crossed the ghetto barriers and is now the drug of the very "chic," with 15 million having tried it and another 4.5 million using it regularly.[78] Likewise, heroin, with its high risk of overdose, is making inroads into affluent suburbia. There are now more than 400,000 heroin addicts in this country.[79]

After a low in the seventies, both PCP (angel dust) and LSD are making a comeback among young people in many areas, and the use of stimulants and sedatives is increasing. Alcohol, however, remains the prime recreational drug. Now 3 out of 10 high school students are "problem drinkers," and by 10th grade, 7 out of 10 are using alcohol at least occasionally.[80]

Responding to a Gallup youth survey conducted in 1977, adolescents listed "drug use and abuse" as the foremost problems facing their generation.[81] The heart-rending, overwhelming nature of this nation's current drug problem leaves parents, clergy and authorities asking "why?"

According to the book, *Parents, Peers and Pot,* published by the U.S. Department of Health and Human Services for the National Institute on Drug Abuse:

> The main difference between growing up in the 1950's and growing up [now] is the pervasive influence today of the commercialized and glossily packaged, popular youth culture. Like other facets of American consumer society, the commercialized pop culture depends on a constantly expanding consumer market. It uses all the sophisticated techniques of modern marketing to create new desires and "needs" in its customers.
>
> *One element in this pop culture is rock music* [authors' italics]. . . . The rock scene is permeated by the values and practices of the drug culture. Many rock stars have become cult heroes, and many of them take drugs. . . . Since the [mid-sixties] many rock lyrics have had drug overtones. The explosion of psychedelic imagery in the music of the 1960's—based on the visions stimulated by LSD, mescaline, and high-potency marijuana—was exotic and poetic enough to disguise much of its drug orientation. Few adolescents or their parents identified popular songs like "Lucy in the Sky with Diamonds" with LSD.
>
> As the protests of the 1960's faded away, however, merchandisers of the rock culture expanded their sales pitch to appeal to a broader youth market—one that increasingly included younger children. At the same time, changing marijuana laws and increasing tolerance of its use led to more overt drug language in the lyrics of rock music.
>
> Few parents, their ears conditioned to a different decibel level, could even hear the words that blasted through their homes, much less understand the slang drug references.[82]

Many music promoters have accused concerned parents and citizens of finding a convenient scapegoat in rock music for the rising problems of drug and alcohol abuse, but, as just cited, even health officials of the United States government accuse its artists and merchandisers of greatly contributing to drug-culture values. However, as the authors note, parents often don't hear the drug references on records because they can't make out any of the words. As an aid, we will cite just a few top-selling, drug-pushing rock hits.[83]

"Sergeant Pepper's Lonely Hearts Club Band" and "Lucy in the Sky With Diamonds"—both Beatles hits—were mentioned earlier as having had a profound impact on the acceptance of psychedelics worldwide. Another Beatles' ditty, "Dr. Roberts," jests about a true-to-life New York doctor who would prescribe pills to anyone just for the asking. "Tomorrow Never Know," originally (and more accurately) called "The Void," is a Beatles' song inspired by the sixties drug guru Timothy Leary's book, *The Psychedelic Experience.*

The Jefferson Airplane/Starship's "White Rabbit" is a through-the-looking-glass trip: ". . . One pill makes you larger [uppers], and the other makes you small [downers]."

"Sister Morphine" is a Rolling Stones classic tribute to both morphine and cocaine, as is the Mamas and the Papas' "Trip, Stumble and Fall."

"I'm Mandy—Fly Me" is a 10cc tune, inspired by an airline campaign slogan, but it tells of the use of downers in a dream sequence.

Recorded by the Byrds, the song "5–D" promotes the supposed "insight" that comes with drug use.

"Along Comes Mary" (the Associations) and "Proud Mary" (Creedence Clearwater Revival) were both songs sung in praise of marijuana, otherwise known as "Mary Jane."

ZZ Top, a seventies band now enjoying a revival thanks to MTV, sings "Arrested for Driving While Blind": "We broke open a case of 'proof 102' . . ./ You could say we was out of our minds/But let me tell ya, we was flyin' while blind."[84]

AC/DC invite their listeners to "Have A Drink on Me" ("Come on, have a good time/And get blinded out of your mind . . .").

Ambrosia's "Apothecary," tells the tale of a severe drug addiction; Donovan's "Sunshine Superman" and "Mellow Yellow" both praise the numbing effects of drugs; and Bob Dylan's top hit in the sixties, "Mr. Tambourine Man," was sung about a drug pusher.

The punkish Lou Reed moans the lyrics: ". . . it's my wife and my life/ Because a mainer to my veins leads to a center in my head/And then, I'm better off dead. . . ." In another tune he instructs a junkie in the art of disposing of an overdosed, dead girl friend.

"Fantasy," by Aldo Nova, offers a fantasy life that's "outasite" if you're willing to "powder pleasure [cocaine] in your nose tonight. . . ."

Pink Floyd extols the sensation of being "Comfortably Numb" in its LP,

The Wall: "I can ease your pain, And get you on your feet again."[85]

Even without drugs, the childhood-to-adulthood transition is a hard one. It's also one of the most crucial times for development of values. How much of an influence do the lyrics of rock music have on a young person just beginning to make challenging choices, just beginning to face adolescence's unique problems? No one can say for certain, but music, as even the ancient Greeks understood, does have a direct affect on the mind.

At the beginning of a concert in Detroit, David Roth, lead singer of the group Van Halen, called out: "We are gathered together in celebration of sex, drugs and rock and roll."[86] Young person, don't join in that deadly celebration.

7

Lifestyles

Heroes are an important part of our lives—they give us someone to admire and emulate. Psychologist Kenneth E. Clark says hero admiration can be a healthy part of growing up: "Most young people are looking for lives to copy. It's very hard to decide how to set up your own life by reading a book or by analyzing it. You have to see somebody that you admire and that you want to copy."[1]

The danger in hero worship, however, comes when we abandon our own beliefs in order to pattern our lives after someone else. Clark says there is a great, unsatisfied need for more modern heroes—people who inspire and motivate others because of their unselfish virtues and values.

Perhaps that is why many young people seem drawn toward charismatic characters such as today's rock celebrities, whether or not the stars exhibit truly admirable qualities. The Bible, however, says, "Do not be fooled: bad companions ruin good character" (1 Cor. 15:33, GNB). In other words, don't be fooled by immoral people—if you listen to them long enough, you will become just like them. Take a look at the lifestyles of most of rock's heroes, past and present. Do they live in ways after which God would want us to pattern our lives? Do their lifestyles promote laudable goals? Do they demonstrate personal sacrifice and high morals? Would we want to follow their lifestyle? Do they have true joy? For isn't that the outcome of a good life? You can "spot check" a rock star's lifestyle in the same six areas which pointed to defects in rock music's lyrics: despondency, suicide or escapism; humanism and commercialism; rebellion and violence; hedonism; occultism; and chemical abuse.

It's Hard to Be Happy

John Cougar Mellencamp, a rock and roller who seems to be having trouble lately with his rough, bad-boy image, claims he's a pessimist who "goes forward with an optimist's attitude." In other words, he hasn't completely given up on life, but sees little in which to hope.

He admits, too, that his violent, anti-everything songs contain humor primarily so he won't "get depressed hearing them over and over again."[2]

"When you get older . . . it's hard to be happy," he says. "I have never had a full good day since I was 21."[3] If Mellencamp, and other rock stars like him, knew Jesus Christ, that would not be the case. Jesus said He came to give each person a joy that nothing can take away (John 15:11), and He keeps His word. A life lived for Jesus produces good fruit—and one of those fruits is joy. It's the age-old principle of "you reap what you sow"—or as Jesus put it, "You shall know them by their fruits" (Matt. 7:16). The results in people's lives show if they are on the right path, and the most obvious results will be—in addition to joy—love, peace, patience, kindness, goodness, faithfulness, gentleness and self-control.

If Mellencamp—and so many others like him—finds it hard to be happy when he is successful, wealthy and comfortable, shouldn't that be a sign to would-be followers that he is on the wrong path? It's not hard to see why Mellencamp, and other rock stars as well, writes music with such despairing suicidal themes: they have "won the whole world" but have no life (Matt. 16:26).

At a time when it has never been quite so difficult growing up, the teenager of the eighties, already faced with the pressures of adolescence, needs to see positive values taught by positive role models. The National Center for Health Statistics now claims suicide is the second leading cause of death among teenagers.[4] Furthermore, there may be up to five times more teen suicides than are reported, and perhaps as many as fifty serious suicide attempts for every one that succeeds![5] Let's look at the lives of a few more rock stars and see if they have something positive or constructive to teach us—if their lives exhibit "good fruit."

Jim Morrison, song writer and notorious lead singer for the now-disbanded Doors, once said, "I'm interested in anything that is about revolt, disorder, chaos, especially activity that has no meaning."[6] Rock's number-one sex idol was destined, however, to self-destruct, and he seemed to know it. He said of his fondness for drink, that it was "the difference between suicide and slow capitulation."[7] Morrison's words became his epitaph, when his body, ravaged by alcohol and drugs, simply gave out at the age of 27. Such was the "fruit" of Jim Morrison's life.

Another major musical force in the sixties was the Grateful Dead. Robert Hunter, lyricist for the group, expressed his view of the "fruit" of rock and roll in a cynical parody, "The Ten Commandments of Rock 'n' Roll," published in *The Book of Rock Lists*. One of those "commandments" was: "Destroy yourself physically and mentally and insist that all true believers do likewise as an expression of unity."[8] While obviously tongue-in-cheek, the observation rings true. The "fruit" of Hunter's life, by his own admission, seems to be self-destruction, not joy.

Freddie Mercury, of Queen, says he is very emotional, and "may go mad in several years' time."[9] Where is self-control?

Roger McGuinn of the Byrds once said of Beatle George Harrison, "George didn't believe in anything when I met him. He said, 'We don't believe in God.' It was like he didn't have a personal mind or ego of his own."[10] Where is faith?

"I am something of a madman," Ozzy Osbourne once proclaimed to the press, "I can do nothing in moderation. If it's booze, I drink the place dry. If it's drugs, I take everything and then scrape the carpet for little crumbs. I took LSD every day for years—I was spending about $1,000 a week on drugs . . . I OD'd about a dozen times."[11] Where is self-control?

The Exorcist's hit theme song, "Tubular Bells," was written by Mike Oldfield, who remained a virtual hermit for a long time afterward. He credits his emotional instability to the creation of that music: "To write something like that," he admitted, "you have to be a bit unbalanced. It was written by someone terribly insecure."[12] Where is peace?

Johnny Rotten/Lydon, formerly the Sex Pistols' head-gunslinger, received his position in the band, neither because of musical ability (which many peers have said was nil), nor personality, but because, according to *Rolling Stone*, "(1) his face had the pallor of death; (2) he went around spitting on people he passed on the street; and, (3) he was the first to understand the democratic implications of punk."[13] The group has since fizzled out, due partially to its brazen use of commercialism, but mostly, because of the death of the group's bassist, Sid Vicious (John Simon Ritchie). He committed suicide by overdosing on heroin after murdering his 20-year-old girl friend. Rotten's pseudonym alone demonstrates the lack of love in his life; and Sid Vicious also lived up to his stage name—there was no gentleness in his sad, short life.

When Adam Ant (real name: Stuart Goddard) entered rock and roll, following several years as a graphics design student, he noted the musical scene looked "very decadent—very drug-oriented and wasted." He added, "A line in one of my songs goes, 'Everybody I've met says they're going to die' . . . That sums up a lot of rock and roll mythology that isn't particularly pleasant. It's strange that there are very few great rock artists who can become legends without dying."[14]

Such pessimism prevails in rock and is reflected in both the lives and the lyrics of the artists. Pete Townshend, of the on-again-off-again band, the Who, agreed with Ant when he said, "Rock is going to kill me somehow. Mentally or physically or something, it's going to get me in the end."[15] It was Lou Reed, however, who probably put it most sadly and succinctly: "All the people I've known who were fabulous have either died, flipped or gone to India!"[16]

Even more sad, however, is that many ardent rock fans have followed rock's misguided minstrels down the same road.

Brother, Can You Spare a Dime?

During the radical sixties, when flower power blossomed, many of California's musical generation began to espouse a lifestyle that sounded very good on the surface—peace, love, and brotherhood. Unfortunately, most of their attempts at communal living failed miserably.

The Monkees' guitarist and singer, Peter Tork, opened his Hollywood Hills mansion to any number of hangers-on and leeches. Eventually, they depleted his fortune, and he was left sleeping in a rented room in the basement. Jefferson Airplane and the Grateful Dead ran open crash pads that were plagued with drug raids, and Dennis Wilson, of the Beach Boys, virtually gave over his estate to the grisly Manson commune. Lou Gottlieb, of the Limelighters folk group, formed a commune called "Morning Star Ranch," a place with no organization, no rules, open to anyone. While all these attempts were well-intentioned, they sadly failed.

The key to their failure lies in the philosophy of humanism. Each of these attempts—and all others based on the inherent goodness of man apart from the creative power of God—were built on shifting sand instead of immobile rock. Many paid dearly trying to live out their naively humanistic ideas, yet recall that period of rock's history with nostalgia. They have forgotten the runaway "flower children" panhandling for food and begging dimes to buy drugs. They choose not to remember that "talkin' about freedom and bein' free are two different things," as Jack Nicholson said in *Easy Rider*. Talking about love and really loving are two different things as well.

Though many would like to follow the bright and beautiful people of the rock generation to their simplistic utopias, and teach the world to sing in perfect harmony, it is all a pipe dream without the reality of Jesus. He taught that love was laying down our life for a friend. Unless we're willing to pick up the cross, the humanistic jibberish of "try to love one another right now" espoused by so many rock stars is simply a sham.

Perhaps even more sad than the lifestyles led by many rock stars who unwittingly drag others down with them are the lifestyles specifically planned and promoted to produce media hype for the stars.

Punk rock entrepeneur, Malcolm McClaren, is probably the most flagrant promoter of sensationalism in the rock business. His proteges include Adam Ant, the Sex Pistols, and BowWowWow. Not only has McClaren, described by Boy George as "a modern-day Robin Hood,"[17] managed and commercialized the private lives of these rockers, he has also used the talents of fashion designer Vivienne Westwood, long-time collaborator and former lover, to create the punk look. It was she who hyped the torn T-shirts, pins in the skin, studded brassieres, bondage trousers, and the generally angry, sullen punk style. It was an improvisation on the themes of death, sadomasochism, rape and bondage, and more than once, the entire stock of her Chelsea boutique was confiscated by police.[18]

McClaren, however, added his own touches—promoting Adam (then with the Ants) through a pornographic video about a sex club for kids; using 14-year-old Annabelle (then with BowWowWow) as a nude feature in a preteen

84

sex magazine; and, of course, engineering the media blitz fiasco of the Sex Pistols.

Drummer Steve Smith of Journey summed up the whole commercial aspect of a rock star's lifestyle this way:

> The strange thing for me is that jazz and classical musicians are respected for their technical prowess, but rock stars are known for how many women they can take home or how much drugs they can consume. All rock stars are afraid of not seeming bigger than life, and that's why they lie and that's why they are exploited and that's why they get screwed up."[19]

Although it seems some rock stars will say or do just about anything to get attention—especially media attention—and seem to live by the adage that the more bizarre the better, it's sad that in their efforts to attract the public notice they so desire, they are leading astray many teens, and preteens, who view them as heroes. The consequences for such actions are on their shoulders, for Jesus said, "If anyone should cause one of these little ones to lose his faith in me, it would be better for that person to have a large millstone tied around his neck and be drowned in the deep sea. How terrible for the world that there are things that make people lose their faith! Such things will always happen—but how terrible for the one who causes them!" (Matt. 18:6, 7, GNB).

On the Road Again

Another theme many rock stars' lives promote is rebellion, which often breaks into violence. Rock's resident crazy, Ozzy Osbourne, has been a prime example. He recalls that in 1978, " 'I did insane things. One time I took an axe and chopped down every door in my house. I wanted to build a black cathedral behind my house. I dragged my wife around our house by her hair.' . . . These days most of the mania gets discharged [on stage]."[20]

Osbourne's on-stage antics include the slaughter of live animals, but sometimes he leaves that to his fans, after he's whipped them into a frenzy and splattered them with buckets of offal. The San Antonio, Texas, City Council banned Osbourne's performances in their city facilities for different reasons, however. It seems Osbourne had the gall to urinate on their Alamo. You can subject a Texan to almost any outrage, but don't deface his shrines![21] "I'm just as evil and crazy as ever," Osbourne boasted of his performances to a *Hit Parader* reporter,[22] and yet, he was elected *Billboard's* Singer of the Year in 1983.[23]

Molly Hatchet's tours are anything but peaceful. What fuels the flames of their rowdy times? "Ah, mother's milk, life's blood," guitarist Steve Holland said with a grin as he hoisted a quart-sized bottle of Jack Daniels into the air. "This is the stuff that keeps you going. . . . Every January we load as many bottles as we can into our equipment truck and then we just keep touring until we run out. It's the only way to live."[24]

The members of Van Halen, another successful metal band, have also found that fame enables them to indulge in excesses. When asked in an interview, with Scott Cohen of *Circus*, how Van Halen compares to Attila the Hun, Roth replied, ". . . very closely. It's a group of barbarians who are sweeping around the world non-stop and have a few basic goals in mind and when it's done have a good old barbarian party—after each city is conquered. . . . And after it's over, we sack the village. We go looking for women and children."[25]

REO Speedwagon, like many other groups, is able to rearrange hotel rooms within minutes. Gary Richrath of the group explained it all with a shrug of the shoulder. "We can get crazy drunk, or do 'sports' instead."[26] But when the band's publicist, Joan Tarshis, was asked if she doesn't occasionally fear for her life when she's on tour with the band, her instantaneous reply was, "At *all* times."[27]

One of rock's hottest bands, the Pretenders, boasts a female singer/songwriter who likes to mix it up with the boys. She's Chrissie Hynde, who is fast earning a reputation as rock's "bad girl," according to *Us* magazine.[28] *Rolling Stone* says she has "established quite a reputation as a boozing, brawling broad."[29]

Freddie Mercury, of Queen, blames quirky personalities and tender psyches for the mayhem the group causes. "Yes, we're all very high strung. Once Roger squirted Brian in the face with hair spray in a tiny, steaming dressing room. They nearly came to blows. We've all got massive egos, my dear."[30]

But Alice Cooper probably nailed down the root cause of all the destruction when he gloated, "If I were a kid, Alice would be my hero. He's a rebellion symbol. He doesn't have to answer to anybody."[31]

Though many rock stars have become famous for the destruction of their hotel or dressing rooms, either as a way to break tension, overcome boredom, or sadly, as a warped sort of status symbol, it is this attitude of sheer rebellion that is most devisive. Such a lifestyle generates the attitude that authority figures are ignorant, that adults can't be trusted, and that a problem can best be handled by spitting at it—or someone. Unfortunately, though the violence and rebellion may reap press notices, they solve nothing. Their end result is more often bitterness and depression—a far cry from the promises the Lord makes: "Happy are those who have reverence for the Lord, who live by his commands. Your work will provide for your needs; you will be happy and prosperous" (Ps. 128:1, GNB). In other words, happiness and good fortune are the fruit of respect for God and His laws.

Hedonism—A Media Masquerade

"The media—TV, movies, records, magazines—all play up the hedonistic lifestyle. Whether it's cars, stereos, clothes, sex, or drugs, what we want is a good time."[32] So says *Cornerstone* magazine, and with good reason. Our society is told that pleasure is the primary goal—the main focus—of our existence. It's even guaranteed in the U.S. Constitution: the pursuit of happiness. Of course, there's nothing wrong with being happy. Contrary to the Stoic philosophers of ancient Greece, who taught an indifference to pleasure (an attitude which in some cases slopped over into Christian thinking), Jesus taught, "Fear not, little flock, for it is your Father's good pleasure to give you the kingdom" (Luke 12:21, RSV). But while God wants to give us the desires of our hearts, Jesus also warned against constant pleasure-seeking in His parable of the man who, upon becoming tremendously successful, developed an attitude of taking it easy, eating and drinking, and having a good time, to the exclusion of God from his life. That attitude destroyed him; without warning God said to him, "You fool! This very night you will have to give up your life; then who will get all these things you have kept for yourself?" (Luke 12:20, GNB). Jesus said this is how it will be for people who have piled up riches and pleasures on earth, but aren't rich in God's sight, because they don't know Him personally.

As *Cornerstone* pointed out, it takes little investigation to discover what is foremost on the minds of most entertainers today—their lifestyles show they are consumed with pleasure-seeking and self-gratification. Though their actions speak louder than their words, many rock stars blatantly use both.

Creem, a hard-rock fan magazine, published a devastating article that captures the rotted essence of the pleasure-seeking sex-rock scene: "There's gonorrhea, syphilis, crabs, NSU, venereal warts and herpes to consider. . . . I mean you'd be simply amazed at the number of times one has to schlepp to the V.D. clinic; it's almost a regular stop for some groups on the way to or from a gig. . . . The intrigue, the search, the wallowing through the muck and mire of *sleaze* is all part of it. It's all part of the rock and roll lifestyle, isn't it?"[33]

Even though the "sleaze" is granted to be part of the rock and roll reality, some stars veil their hedonistic tendencies because they want to maintain a clean image.

The Beatles kept a low profile until they were well-established and could afford to be less discreet. Hunter Davis, in his official biography, *The Beatles*, sheds light on the personal background of each of them. John Lennon's first wife, Cynthia, alleges he beat her—he was known as the cruelest Beatle. Even in their pre-Beatle days the men of the foursome were no angels.[34] But after success came, Lennon described their tours as orgies, and said their rooms were always full of dope.[35] McCartney was recently cleared in a paternity suit by a West German woman who contends he fathered her 17-year-old daughter during the Beatles' early Hamburg days.[36]

With a shrug of the shoulders, the lead singer of The Who, Roger Daltry, informed his wife of the promiscuous lifestyle he leads on the road: "When you're in a hotel, a pretty young lady makes life bearable."[37]

Perhaps Daltry's wife is willing to overlook such adultery, but Rod Stewart's wife, Alana, was not. She told the British press their rocky marriage was washed up:

If he wants to go around with mindless moronic young models rather than be with me and our two children, then good luck to him. I don't think I'm losing anything. He's lost a warm and loving family. We've lost a mixed-up kid. I don't want him back unless he changes completely and grows up.[38]

One of Stewart's "young models" was the Swedish-American beauty, Britt Ekland. In excerpts from her autobiography, she states, "[From the moment we said we loved each other] we were inseparable, kissing and cuddling in our new-found passion. We were oblivious to the stares and embarrassment we caused. . . . Very soon we were making love three or four times a day. . . . There had been past affairs in Rod's life. He admitted that he had an illegitimate child . . . who was later put up for adoption. 'She was a pretty little thing, but just like any other baby,' said Rod. . . ." Soon Ekland experienced the bitterness of her paramour's reckless ways, however. She says, "My love and respect for Rod crumbled. There was nothing left, except for a burnt-out shell. . . . She then married Stray Cat's Jim McDonnell."[39]

Mistresses are rampant in rock circles. According to *People* magazine, January 16, 1984, Anita Pallenberg was Rolling Stones' Keith Richards' mistress for years, and had two children by him. Brian Jones was romantically linked with her as well. While Mick Jagger was known for affairs with Marianne Faithful, Bianca, Jerry Hall and others, the late Brian Jones had a reputation "he had acquired for near satyriasis [uncontrolled sexual conduct]," as Gary Herman put it in *Rock 'n' Roll Babylon*. "Sixty women a month was the figure bandied about."[40]

The late Jim Morrison, of the Doors, was also well-known for his sexual escapades, especially on stage. However, a young woman who lived with him for some time told *Esquire* magazine about his sad state:

He wanted dirty talk from me. It excited him. I had to do things to him. He was mostly impotent . . . sometimes when it didn't work he would turn violent, choke me and beat me. . . . Twice, I think, I was very close to getting killed.[41]

A companion of the late Jimi Hendrix noted, "He had an incredible sexual appetite and would often sleep with three or four girls on the same night."[42]

Gene Simmons of KISS blames high tech for his hedonistic ways. When asked what his hobbies were, he said, "I'll put it this way. I *love* my fans. Well, I love push-button technology. It's sexy—you push the right button—it turns on. Just like a girl. . . ."[43] The groups' rhythm guitarist, Paul Stanley, seems to agree. He offered, "You know what we've been getting a lot of lately? Letters from 16- and 17-year-old girls with little Polaroid pictures of them naked. That's amazing. That's great. There's nothing like knowing you're helping the youth of America—" "Undress," filled in Simmons.—"We really appreciate that," Stanley quipped.[44]

The video rock stars of Duran Duran have disclosed they receive the same kind of fan mail. Says *Rolling Stone*: "Tons of letters from little girls (not to mention the X-rated photos they receive, mainly from America)."[45]

Easy sex and fast cash lure many to ambitiously seek rock stardom. Angus

Young of AC/DC explains, "I'm generally lazy and I figured that this is the easiest way to make money. This is what I do best. I saw all the women," he continues, "and I figured that looked good; I was horny. I got a guitar off my brother and I started playing anything."[46] Jim Lockhart, of the band Horslips, is even more crass in his response to *Circus* magazine's question, What appeals to you in a woman? He says, "One that's short enough to turn upside down, and look at and send on her way." Barry Devlin, spokesman and bassist for the same group, replied to a similar question, "I tend to like any woman who will come across inside the next 15 minutes."[47]

Elton John admitted his homosexual tendencies early on. He adds, "It's a subject that seems to be brought up quite frequently . . . but I never realized that by me saying, 'Big deal, I'm bisexual,' I would get all those letters from people—especially in England—who live in a completely different, frightening environment."[48] Then in 1984, as if to set straight the record, he married on Valentine's Day. Both he and his bride wore white.

David Bowie's sexuality has always been in question. Back in the seventies, he boasted, "It's true—I am bisexual, but I can't deny I've used the fact very well. I suppose it's the best thing that ever happened to me. Fun, too!"[49] Later Bowie told a journalist that he was "pretty much over my affection for men."[50] Nonetheless, fans keep reminding him of his Ziggy Stardust persona.

Presently, however, Bowie seems to be showing some regret. In 1972 he lamented to a *Rolling Stone* interviewer, "The biggest mistake I ever made, was telling that . . . writer that I was bisexual. Christ, I was so young then. I was experimenting. . . ."[51]

Daryl Hall, of Hall and Oates, concedes to similar experimenting: "The idea of sex with a man doesn't turn me off. I had lots of strange experiences with older boys between when I was four and fourteen."[52] He appeared in drag on one of their album covers.

Appearances to the contrary, Prince, the young man with a penchant for posing in his skivvies, says he's not gay, and has a standard refusal for forward male fans: "I'm not about that; we can be friends, but that's as far as it goes. My sexual preferences," he explains, "aren't really their business."[53] Known for his lewd lyrics, outlandish costumes and sexually explicit stage antics, he claims sex in general is more than just a business—it's his mission.

Two other bands closely resemble Prince in their mission of salvation through sex—Vanity Six, and Time. Vanity Six is a trio Prince formed as a backup. Now they're on their own, singing Prince-type tunes with plenty of references to teenage sex. *Rolling Stone* says the group strives to be as sexually direct as its founder and that the members even perform in their undies. The Time, *Rolling Stone* claims, is basically an "outlet store" for Prince's damaged goods, and the group shadows both his recording style and format.[54]

In the same vein is Ted Nugent, the performer *Circus* magazine claims has the "foulest mouth this side of the concert stage." Nugent allegedly has an egomaniacal belief in his own greatness and endeavors to prove it over and over again. "I do not live like a normal white man," Nugent remarked in an interview with the magazine. "I do not go to sleep, not because I'm high. I would stay awake for three, maybe four nights. I'd be playing in the basement, hooked up to my amps . . . just hammering my brains out. Not because anyone was holding a gun to my head, but because I loved it." When asked what tips he would offer a girl who wanted him to like her, he responded, "Drop trou' [trousers] for starts." During the entire interview, the writer says Nugent was bounding off the sofa, screaming at the top of his lungs, re-enacting scenes with flailing arms, bugged-out eyes and "a smile that borders on a menacing sneer."[55]

A singer-bassist told interviewers his main interests weren't with his young fans' attentions, but with his mother. In fact, he was quoted as saying he desires sex with his mother: "Always have done. Not so much now, because she's getting older. She's losing her grip on her looks. She's a cute little French girl."[56]

Ann Wilson, of Heart, suggests a "cannabilistic thing . . . happens with rock stars' groupies" [the young whores who follow rock stars on tour], in which the guys and girls meet solely for sexual purposes, and "eat each other alive for awhile." Her sister, Nancy, adds that she has seen "rock and roll guys so delirious they don't know who they take home."[57]

Sex is so easy in the rock business, it is even more of a power game than on the street, and reputations help build that image the rock stars want to promote. The defunct Thin Lizzy's Phil Lynott said, ". . . there's a lot of women for you if you're a star, and I love it all, every one of them when I get the chance."[58]

A lead singer betrayed a similar attitude when he told an interviewer he "always checks the birth control method of 15-year-olds before seducing them."[59]

The Tubes, a group brought together in 1972, is known for its crazed events, such as the "Streaker's Ball," which admitted all naked people free of charge. The group appeared in the skin flick, *The Resurrection of Eve*; and one of its most popular songs is entitled "White Punks on Dope."[60]

Nudity was also the subject of an interview with Queen's Roger Taylor. He says the band members were entertained by nude female mud wrestlers and topless waitresses during tours. "This is what rock and roll is all about," he went on. "Like our music—designed for quick and temporary gratification."[61] The drummer admitted in another interview that he likes "strippers and wild parties with naked women. I'd love to own a whorehouse. What a wonderful way to make a living."[62]

One female singer doesn't seem to need quite so many around for her sexual escapades; in fact, she says masturbation is an important key to illumination. *Circus* says she didn't realize a woman could masturbate until she was 25, and she regrets having lost out on a lot of "illumination." The singer has also related that she dreamed, as a child, of having sex with the Holy

Ghost, and that she enjoys "brainiacamours"—her term for sexual excitement through reading sexually explicit material.[63]

Another female vocalist, Pat Benatar, was not afraid to state her lifestyle preferences. In an article in *Us*, she mentioned her high school years, saying, "I was a cheerleader. You know how cheerleaders are; they're bad—not real bad, just promiscuous." Benatar keeps that image going with what *Us* calls "sexploitation, set off by the suggestive LP covers and advertisements."[64] The combination seems to work for her, as she was voted Favorite Pop Female Vocalist by the 1984 American Music Awards.

Judas Priest, heavy metal's answer to motorcycle gangs, portrays a good deal of sadomasochism in its stage performances. When asked by *Rolling Stone* if the image reflects the members' off-hours life, lead singer Rob Halford replied, ". . . to a certain extent. Sexually I have always been to the fullest extent of the experience that S-M has to offer. It's quite nice to experiment."[65]

Not only does the Plasmatics' Wendy O. Williams enliven her stage performances with sexually explicit antics, she takes her stage style right into personal appearances. In a Los Angeles record store, she recently coaxed the pants off a male fan. As the fan sheepishly accommodated her, Williams exposed herself as well. The singer was at the store to autograph copies of the group's LP, "New Hope for the Wretched."[66]

The whole episode, however, as well as all the other facts and quotes stated here, doesn't give the rock fan hope. Instead, it yields death. For the sad error most rock stars make in embracing and promoting hedonism is warned against in the Bible: "Although they claimed to be wise, they became fools. . . . Therefore God gave them over in the sinful desires of their hearts to sexual impurity for the degrading of their bodies with one another. They exchanged the truth of God for a lie. . . . Even their women exchanged natural relations for unnatural ones. In the same way the men also abandoned natural relations with women and were inflamed with lust for one another. . . . Although they know God's righteous decrees that those who do such things deserve death, they not only continue to do these very things but also approve of those who practice them" (Rom. 1:22–25, NIV).

Reverend Jesse Jackson, the nationally known civil rights leader, has charged, "Our children's minds are being adversely affected and there is a definite correlation between the rising rate of illegitimacy and increasing numbers of abortions and songs about sex."[67]

One out of every ten teenage girls gets pregnant—with the sharpest increase among those under fourteen. Venereal disease is rampant among adolescents, accounting for 25% of the one million reported gonorrhea cases every year.

And yet, with all the heartbreak and death that overemphasis on pleasure-seeking can cause, not to mention the alienation from God, rock stars continue to run headlong after "the good life," leading their young fans along the same ruinous path.

Cults and the Occult

Although an interesting phenomenon, the rise of deviant "religions" is one of the most alarming developments of our time. As promoters of old and new religious cults become more active and evangelistic than ever, millions of searching individuals, even naive young Christians, are sucked into unorthodox beliefs that are nothing but false, satanic cults. Dr. Dave Breese, a noted Christian minister, writer and broadcaster, describes a cult as "a religious belief and practice calling for devotion to a segmented religious view centered in false doctrine. It is an organized heresy.[68] Breese believes cults are now thriving in the Western nations because they feed on the pathetic spiritual naivety of people who have become interested in Christianity, or who have been converted to Christ, but are still "vulnerable to the childhood diseases that stalk the convert in the nursery years of his Christian life."[69] Many rock stars who have succumbed to cults are pulling undiscerning young fans with them into their false beliefs. Sometimes well-meaning, other times as diabolical as Satan himself, these rock stars can greatly influence the lives of impressionable teens, still young and untested in their faith. A look at the lifestyles of many rock VIP's will quickly divulge to whom they mistakenly pledge their allegiance.

The Kingston Trio was once one of folk/rock's hottest groups, whose 1959 version of a 90-year-old ballad, "Tom Dooley," ignited the folk boom of the early sixties. Dave Guard, a member of the group who has remained on the music scene since the group's demise, says that in 1976 he became a student of the guru, Swami Muktananda. "I'm into a lot of good health, yoga, meditation," Guard says. He studies Sanskrit (the old Indic literary language), Indian philosophy and Indian music.[70]

Also involved with Eastern religions were, of course, the Beatles. Perhaps even more destructive, though, was their anti-Christian stance. Their former press secretary, Derek Taylor, once said, "They're completely anti-Christ. I mean, I am anti-Christ, as well, but they're so anti-Christ they shock me, which isn't an easy thing [to do]."[71] George Harrison put his money where his mouth was when he invested in two films which poke fun at Christianity to the point of sacrilege: *The Life of Brian* and *The Long Good Friday*.[72] Not to be outdone, Lennon wrote a book, *A Spaniard in the Works*, in which Christ is unsubtly portrayed as Jesus El Pifico—a "garlic eating, stinking little yellow, greasy fascist bastard Catholic Spaniard."[73]

Bob Marley was one time considered the King of Reggae (a form of rock music made popular in the Caribbean, and now receiving wide acceptance). He wrote hits such as "I Shot the Sheriff," "Stir It Up" and "Guava Jelly." Marley, a proud but reverent man, swayed many into Rastafarianism, a belief that the late emperor of Ethiopia, Haile Selassie (whose given name was Ras Tafari), was the spirit of the creator sent to earth in human form. Marcus Garvey, a Jamaican revolutionary in the thirties, first prophesied the coming of this spirit named Jah. Rastafarians believe in the Bible, but distort its message. They are also nature-lovers, and use marijuana as a sacred herb in their religious rites. Marley once said, "Me don't have a religion, just a natural t'ing you supposed to have."[74]

Ike and Tina Turner, who broke down many television standards during the seventies with their erotic, sizzling performances, are best known for their rendition of "Proud Mary." "I'm a Buddhist," Tina once admitted, "and chanting gives me strength. I use chanting to become at one with myself."[75] An article in *Rolling Stone* says, until she started chanting she fought her exotic, animal image. "Now I've come to accept the sweat and the wildness that's Tina Turner. Chanting helps me to get rid of all the crap in my life."[76]

Stevie Nicks, who sings successfully solo, as well as with Fleetwood Mac, flirts openly with the occult. According to *Rolling Stone*, she would like to build her own pyramid and live in a little "witch house" on a cliff overlooking the ocean. "I love the symbolism of the three roses," Nicks said, "which is very pyramid, very Maya." Occult terms which she frequently uses include the word Maya (also known as Devi, the Shakti goddess), and Rhiannon, which became the name of a smash hit for the band. Rhiannon, it seems, is the name of a Welsh witch, and Nicks often dedicates songs at Mac's concerts to "the witches of the world."[77]

Several rock stars attribute their meteoric rise to stardom to the powers of darkness. Suzanne Fellini told *Us* magazine that when she had her astrological chart compiled, "and the horoscope quoted things that actually went down—like I would be signed by a record label with a big C (Casablanca). It also said that in 1980 I'd do a European tour, where my first record would release from Spain."[78] When the predictions came true, Fellini became a believer and puts her faith in the stars. But God says the astrologers Fellini believes in now will some day desert her, and will be of no help at the time for God's judgment—"none will be left to save you," He warns (Isa. 47:15, GNB).

Utopia's Todd Rundgren has expressed, through his music, his interest in Eastern religions, psychic energy and Egyptology. An article in *Circus* says of his house, "A cursory glance around the premises also reveals a number of small pyramids on bookshelves and tables, reflecting Todd's interest in their psychic energy and Egyptology in general as displayed on Utopia albums like *Ra* and *Oops! Wrong Planet*."[79]

Earth, Wind and Fire, long-standing jazz-rock group with hits such as "September" and "Got to Get You Into My Life," are led by Maurice White, a former student of Buddhism, now into mysticism. While banning cigarettes, alcohol and drugs, the group tunes into "higher powers."[80] Says White, "The key to what's happening is . . . self-understanding—the powers that you have in yourself—and allowing them to flow through you. Doing so, you allow the magic to be viewed. I put that magic out and let people view it, dig, and not being afraid of allowing them to view it is the magic." White says he believes in reincarnation, as well. The members of the group "carry on" before each performance. "We stand in a circle and hold hands and we basically kind of communicate to each other. We all say a prayer, each in his own way and then we join the forces of harmony and we do what we do. . . . You feel the energy flowing from one body to the next."[81] The problem with White's kind of "power" is that it doesn't come from God who says, "Your wisdom and knowledge mislead you when you say to yourself, 'I am, and there is none besides me!' " (Isa. 47:10, NIV). Though White may be leading a "cleaner" lifestyle than many in the rock community, he is still being deceived.

The black arts have attracted the interest of Ritchie Blackmore. An article in *Circus* says he has long been interested in psychic phenomena, ghosts and séances. "When we formed Deep Purple," says Blackmore, "we had a bassist called Nic Simper. He used to do all these séances. I was totally opposed to all that, till I saw what was going on. I got intrigued with it all out of curiosity. I believe in religion because I see what goes down in an evil sense. I don't practice evil stuff, but I see how effective it is."[82]

When asked what he considered ideal conditions for a séance, and if it were crucial that séance participants believed in what was taking place, Blackmore responded, "You can't be very tired. And you can't have weak personalities present; otherwise, you'll get possession. . . . You can go crazy if you're not careful. A lot of people go too far, too soon. Mental hospitals are full of people who are actually possessed by trouble-making spirits."[83]

Unfortunately, Blackmore doesn't realize that people should not attempt séances at all, for God has warned often of the results of such practices: "But people will tell you to ask for messages from fortunetellers and mediums. . . . They will say, 'After all, people should ask for messages from the spirits and consult the dead on behalf of the living.' You are to answer them, 'Listen to what the Lord is teaching you! Don't listen to mediums—what they tell you will do you no good' " (Isa. 8:19, 20, GNB).

Brian Johnson's religious views are unclear according to an interview with *Cornerstone* magazine. The AC/DC lead singer stated that if he has any religious beliefs, he keeps them to himself. "If I go to church, I'll go when the priests aren't in or the people aren't in. I don't like going with anybody else." Commenting on TV preachers, Johnson claimed that he put his foot through a television set on two occasions when he didn't like what he'd heard. "It's one big hype," Johnson concluded. "Religion in the States is one big hype."[84]

"I believe in God, but not in religion," echoed drummer Kevin Godley when *Circus* interviewed 10cc. Guitarist/vocalist for the band, Eric Stewart, added dryly, "Religion's become a commercial industry. We *do* mention it in songs like 'The Second Sitting for the Last Supper,' that makes cracks about religion." Godley added, "We don't push religion. It's the sacred cows we like to have a go at now and then."[85]

Singer/bassist/screen sex symbol Sting, from the popular Police, enjoys villainous movie parts. His credits include *Dune* (a sci-fi fantasy); and *Brimstone and Treacle* (he plays a satanic drifter), and he's auditioned to be Pilate

in *The Last Temptation of Christ.* When asked by *Seventeen* magazine, why
the penchant for bad guys, Sting offered, "I don't want people to think, 'Oh,
he's a good guy.' As soon as a label's tacked on you, you're trapped. People
never allow you to be free. I want people to think, 'Well, what on earth is this
guy about?' " Then as if to make it clear what he was "about," Sting added,
"Bad guys—we're the life and blood and salt of the earth."[86]

Does Sting seriously prefer to be evil? Whether he was speaking sincerely
or not, the fact remains he spoke as one of rock's most popular and persuasive
stars, glorying in the benefits of evil, to a magazine readership of 1.5 million
teens.

Isaiah might have been speaking directly to Sting, as well as others in
the rock industry, when he warned: "Woe to those who call evil good, and
good evil; who substitute darkness for light and light for darkness; who substitute bitter for sweet and sweet for bitter! Woe to those who are wise in
their own eyes, and clever in their own sight!" (Isa. 5:20, 21, NASB).

While in his original group, Black Sabbath, which was formed in 1969,
Ozzy Osbourne joined in black masses before concerts, complete with nude,
blood-sprinkled female sacrifices on an altar. The band featured a witch on
the cover of its first album. Though he has since claimed the occult trappings
were merely an attention-getting gimmick, many of his albums are covered
with a collage of satanic things—from naked girl sacrifices to vampires and
werewolves.

Daryl Hall of Hall and Oates, voted 1984's Favorite Pop Group by the
American Music Awards, is a dedicated follower of Aleister Crowley. Crowley
was a notorious mystic, infamous throughout the world as one of the most
wicked men who ever lived. Noted for heroin addiction, murders, and sexual
perversion, Crowley literally renamed himself, "The Beast 666."[87] Hall's song
"Winged Bull" is dedicated, he says, to the ancient Celtic religion (witchcraft).[88]

Jimmy Page, the London-born organizer of the heavy metal vanguard,
Led Zeppelin, is a collector of Aleister Crowley books and artifacts, and owns
Crowley's Boleskine Manor in Scotland.[89] Page's fascination with the occult
and black magic has grown over the years from a between-tour hobby to a
full-time obsession. He now owns an occultist bookstore in London, so he can
more easily obtain the occult books he wants.[90]

Page, Zeppelin's lead guitarist, was asked to compose the music for a film
to be called *Lucifer's Rising.* The film is the life's work of Kenneth Anger,
long-time friend and occult arts tutor of Anita Pallenberg, the Rolling Stones'
paramour. The part of Lucifer was originally to be played by Bobby Beausoleil, a guitarist in a band called Love, and member of the Charles Manson
cult. Mysteriously, after months of filming, Beausoleil bowed out.[91] Mick Jagger, it has been said, was asked to step in to play Lucifer in the film, with his
side-kick, Keith Richards, as Beelzebub. While Jagger refused, Beausoleil
eventually encouraged him to replace Page as the film's musical score com-

poser.[92] The film finally emerged under the title, *Invocation to My Demon Brother*.[93]

A string of tragedies within the band seem to haunt Page, who is also a Zen master. The sad events include the death of the group's original drummer, John Bonham; the death of lead singer Robert Plant's son, Karac; the mysterious death of a Zepp "roadie"; and an auto accident in which Plant and his wife were seriously injured. The chain of events has led even hardened rock writers to speculate that Page's involvement with the occult might be the band's "jinx."[94]

The Beatles' John Lennon once said, "Christianity will go. It will go. It will vanish and shrink. I needn't argue about it. I'm right, right and will be proved right. We are more popular than Jesus now. I don't know which will go first, rock 'n' roll or Christianity."[95]

What was Lennon saying and why is it important to us today, when the Beatles are a thing of the past, and Lennon is dead?

Lennon seemed to be saying not only that the Beatles were a phenomenon unlike anything that had ever occurred before or since—which was probably true—but that they were equal in importance to Jesus and to the salvation He brought through His death on the cross. Unfortunately, Lennon, for all his clever quips and peace-loving quotes, did not have the power to save even himself, let alone anyone else. Prov. 11:7 reminds us that the expectations of the godless come, in the end, to absolutely nothing.

Lennon used drugs heavily from a young age, allegedly beat his first wife and lived with Yoko Ono before his divorce was final. He and Yoko released numbers of sexually explicit pictures and films. Lennon carried on an affair for years with his secretary while married to Yoko. He was both anti-religion and anti-Christ. And while he promoted peace, he often drank to excess, then annihilated hotel rooms and friends' entire houses. Perhaps his worst offense, though, was preaching his views to teens who thought he could do no wrong.

It is important to expose the life and views of Lennon because his works live on though he has died. Recordings made before his death repeatedly climb the charts; taped interviews are rehashed; and, with 1984 being the 20th anniversary of the Beatles' appearance on *The Ed Sullivan Show*, the media is hyping "Beatlemania," misted over with a nostalgic longing for "the way things were."

We need ammunition to resist the kind of thinking that comes from media-promoted, latter-day false prophets such as John Lennon. That ammunition can come only from careful study of the Truth, as presented through Scripture. Likewise, we need to rid ourselves of as much of rock's destructive effects as possible. Otherwise we may be swept away by the undertow of cult doctrine prevalent in the rock music industry today.

One Toke Over the Line

When asked what difference he had noted in today's drug scene, versus that of a few years ago, Dr. Charles Schuster, director of the Drug Abuse

Research Center at the University of Chicago, said, "The aspect . . . that worries me more than it did a few years ago is the fact that there are younger people involved. It has gotten down now into the grammar school, junior high school age."[96] Likewise, psychologist Gary Forrest, author of *How to Cope with a Teenage Drinker*, says the average teenager begins to drink between the ages of 13 and 14. In fact, 3% to 5% of teens in grades 7 through 12 are already daily drinkers.[97]

Though laws prohibit the use of alcohol and illicit drugs by minors, the laws won't stop chemical abuse. Children model their drug and alcohol habits after their parents' and their peers' habits. And since young people spend an average of barely 15 minutes a day in conversation with their parents (with all but two minutes tied up in "What's for dinner?" and "Who's taking the car?"), it is their peers that assert the most pressure to imbibe.[98] A study conducted for *Parade* shows that in 1960, teens felt their value systems were most highly influenced by (in order) parents, teachers, friends, and clergy, then counselors and popular heroes. The same study taken in 1980 showed a tremendous shift. Teenagers now list friends as their prime source of influence, followed by parents, then the media—television, radio/records, and movies. Since rock music proliferates in the media and since rock stars are "sold" as the teenager's friends and peers—in opposition to adults—it becomes clear why the loose drug standards, so prevalent in the rock industry today, have a profound affect on young people.

Says rock chronicler Gary Herman:

> Once upon a time drugs were seen as a route to a new form of musical expression. Today, with all the emphasis on "recreational drugs" as new consumer commodities, drug-taking in quantity is all too often seen as the reward and proof of rock stardom. And between taking drugs to make music and making music to take drugs, the performers, the music and the fans have lost more than the law could ever take.[99]

Do you still doubt that rock music and its stars can highly influence young people's value systems? David Crosby doesn't. Crosby is one-fourth of the highly successful group, Crosby, Stills, Nash and Young, which *Top Pop Artists and Singles* calls, "One of the great assemblies of contemporary music talent." He has been on the rock scene for over 15 years. Crosby was convicted of carrying a concealed weapon (a .45 caliber pistol), as well as drug possession (he was "in the process of getting the cocaine ready").[100] The sentence is being appealed.

Crosby says of the influence of rock music, "I figured that the only thing to do was steal their kids. I still think it's the only thing to do. By saying that, I'm not talking about kidnapping. I'm just talking about changing young people's value systems which removes them from their parents' world very effectively."[101]

Beach Boy Dennis Wilson, another veteran in rock circles, and writer of the soulful song, "Slip on Through," slipped away forever from his fans in late

December, 1983. *Rolling Stone* described Wilson's lifestyle as "weirdness." It included marriage and divorce—twice to the same woman; arrest for contributing to the delinquency of a minor; and fathering a child by his cousin's (Mike Love) daughter—whom he later married. "And while other band members dabbled in TM or health food," the article says, "Dennis Wilson went straight to the top: Charles Manson, under whose spell he fell for a period in 1968."[102] That "spell," according to one of the band, was an attraction to the sex-and-drugs lifestyle Manson represented. It seems Manson sponged about $100,000 off Wilson and also wrecked his uninsured $21,000 Mercedes before moving on to murder. But Wilson found other ways to squander his money to the tune of $600,000 a year. Steve Love, the Beach Boys' manager during most of the seventies, said, "It's hard to imagine that anyone could blow so much money, but Dennis did. He was totally unrestrained and undisciplined; he was foolishly, self-destructively generous."[103] In the end, the Beach Boy who was the epitome of a surfin' summer had no home, and spent each night either at a friend's place, or crashing—drunk and alone—in some cheap hotel.

While Dennis Wilson was battling a drinking problem, his brother Brian fell victim to the effects of mind-altering drugs. He is known to have spent years in virtual solitary confinement, incapable of writing the music he loved— or doing much of anything else. Under constant supervision and psychiatric care, rumored to cost $50,000 a month, the Beach Boy who, until the mid-seventies, was considered to be the guiding genius behind the group, proved that LSD, cocaine and booze were not synonymous with summertime fun.[104]

Pink Floyd lost its founder, Syd Barrett, due to drug-related problems.[105] Eric Clapton found out the hard way, too. He told *Rolling Stone* magazine, "I had my first taste and thought, 'Oh, you know, one snort can't do me any harm.' But . . . dead wrong!"[106]

Linda McCartney, Paul's wife, was nailed for marijuana possession twice in three days, in January 1984, but her husband was unrepentant about the drug bust (in both instances they were fined). He told reporters: "This substance is a whole lot less harmful than rum punch, whiskey, nicotine, and glue—all of which are perfectly legal." Asked if he would now give up smoking marijuana, as he had pledged after a previous conviction, the singer-song-writer winked and said, "Never again."[107]

The Rolling Stones have a long record of run-ins with the law over drugs. *Time* says, ". . . by one account, in order to pass a blood test to enter the U.S. for concert tours, [Keith Richards] had a physician drain his own heroin-tainted blood from his body and replace it with transfusions from more sedate citizens."[108] Richards has been quoted as saying, "I only get ill when I give up drugs, [and] I only gave up drugs when the doctor told me I had only six months left to live."[109]

Another member of the Stones, Ronnie Wood, told the *London Sun* about his drug addiction treatment over the 1983 Christmas holiday: "We all talked in group therapy about how we were going crazy. They reduced you to tears and things." Although Wood claimed he'd been spending more than $2,500 a week on cocaine, he proclaimed himself cured after only a few weeks in the five-week treatment program. However, *Rolling Stone* magazine reports he'd promised himself he would keep on drinking. "I didn't want to end up like some religious fanatic who couldn't even enjoy a drink," he said in defense.[110]

Was (Not Was) mastermind, David Weiss, explained in an interview his need for drugs: "I take drugs to get in an unpleasant frame of mind and then I try to find a catharsis for it. It's a self-sacrifice."[111] In a later interview, Weiss admitted he had stopped experimenting with certain drugs, and had "gone recreational with the leaf." Weiss said he used drugs to get himself into a "Negative Rocky state"—a self-willed, isolated depression—so that he could write the off-beat concoction of psychedelic funk, jazzy-heavy-metal, and rock-and-roll Was (Not Was) is known for.[112]

The now-disbanded Eagles' drummer Don Henley claimed in 1970 he had slowed down, but in November 1980, he was fined $2,500, given a two-year probation, and required to take part in a two-year drug diversion program, due to a prosecution on possession of cocaine, quaaludes and marijuana, as well as contributing to the delinquency of a minor. (A naked 16-year-old girl, suffering from a cocaine overdose, had been found in Henley's house. Henley was 33 at the time.)[113]

Alice Cooper has experienced much of the bondage excessive alcohol can bring. "I was drinking two quarts of whiskey a day after my three-month treatment [in a sanitorium] just to keep going," Cooper once admitted.[114]

One well-known guitarist declared, "I used to sniff glue. It expanded my consciousness better than acid."[115]

David Bowie lamented in 1978, to *Rolling Stone*, "Actually I was junked out of my mind most of the time. You can do good things with drugs," he said, "but then comes the long decline.[116]

A former guitarist and singer experienced blackouts from his heavy involvement with drugs, especially amphetamines. "I was so into speed," he said, "I mean I don't even recall making the first album."[117]

The majority of the top rock performers in the late sixties and early seventies were using drugs heavily, and thus earned reputations as "heads." But Ron McKernan, Grateful Dead's keyboardist, only earned a death certificate. He died of drug and alcohol abuse in 1973.[118]

Janis Joplin, another victim of drug abuse, described the ambitions she pursued: "I wanted to smoke dope, take dope, lick dope, anything I could get my hands on I wanted to do. All my life I just wanted to be a Beatnik, meeting all the heavies, get stoned, get laid, have a good time." Little more than a year later she was dead.[119]

Grace Slick, of the seventies success, Jefferson Airplane/Starship, confessed soon after Joplin's death, "The only difference between Janis Joplin and me is I'm still here."[120] However, Slick asserts motherhood has changed her ways. "It's hard to keep an eye on the kid," she admits, "while you're hallucinating."[121]

Heroin was the poison-of-choice for another of rock's female stars, Debbie Harry of Blondie. Before Blondie's meteoric rise to success, Harry earned spending money as a Playboy bunny and drifted into heroin addiction along with her drummer-boyfriend. When he died of an overdose, she went home to clean up her act.[122] "I got smart," Debbie reflects. "I was a victim. Addiction," she now warns, "is never the right thing to do."[123]

Drugs almost killed Sly Stone also, the founder and lead vocalist of Sly and the Family Stone, a successful, psychedelic soul band, known for innovative music, as well as extraordinary clothes. The group's hit "Everyday People" earned a gold record and was the number-one single in the U.S. in 1969. The group rocked on for another five years, but Stone's penchant for drugs caused many delayed and no-show concert dates, and public scandal.[124] Experiments with PCP ("Angel Dust") have stymied Stone's talent and threatened his health, but he still claims to use cocaine.[125]

Barry Gibb, of the BeeGees, was correct in his assessment of the drug scene in rock music today. He said: "I think cocaine is the threat of the music industry right now. People in the streets and in the offices are taking it. But it destroys creativity, health, and causes antagonism. I've seen it destroy too many people."[126]

Reggie Vinson, who has performed with Alice Cooper, KISS, John Lennon, and Elvis Presley, recalled that before he was converted to Christ, he "was taking close to $100 a day of hard drugs. Though I was living the glamorous life of a rock star I was seeing the unhappiness of many entertainers. I saw some become homosexuals and some commit suicide."[127]

Bonnie Bramlett, too, has played with some of the biggest names in rock music, and yet she admits she planned to commit suicide. "I was beyond contemplating suicide," the former alcoholic admitted. "I had decided I was going to do it." Fortunately, God intervened; Bramlett put down her gun and sought help.[128] She is now a popular Christian singer.

Rock, drugs, and death—somehow they seem forever entwined. Rock critic Bob Larson explained it this way: "The stewardship of our leisure time is always an inviting target for the Enemy. Spare moments not fully committed to the lordship of Christ can become the devil's playground."[129] In other words, the devil is most free to toy with our minds when we are most relaxed unless that time has been thoughtfully planned to coincide with what Jesus wants for us. Eph. 5:15, 16 instructs us, "Be very careful, then, how you live—not as unwise but as wise, making the most of every opportunity, because the days are evil" (NIV).

We need to watch the way we spend our time, especially the sparetime pleasures we pursue. They are open territory for the devil and his motley crew. Steady doses of rock music, through radio, television, movies, etc., can erode our lives. And the powerful persuasion of the hyped rock star lifestyle only adds to the problem.

8

Goals

Spencer Dryden of the recently-revived Jefferson Starship once said, "Get them when they're young and bend their minds."[1] What did he mean by that? Is he an isolated case, or do most rock stars have definite intentions for their music? Although some musicians are simply out for a fast buck, or a chance to jam with the good ol' boys, many rock stars go beyond that—they have a message to preach and a gospel to sing. You as a listener need to know precisely what that message is. Furthermore, you must ask yourself: Does money I spend on rock music actually promote the singers' immoral lifestyles and values? And if so, is that wrong?

Frank Zappa has been a major figure of the rock scene since his Mothers of Invention absurdist albums lampooned anything and everything held dear in the mid-sixties. Zappa explained his theory of the effects of rock music this way: "I realized that this music got through to the youngsters because the big beat matched the great rhythms of the human body. And I further knew that they would carry this with them the rest of their lives."[2]

While Zappa's theory on the beat of rock and roll is perhaps questionable, his opinion regarding rock's staying power has proven prophetic. His goal was merely to ride rock's vortex to stardom, and insure his own staying power in the process; the commercial content of his music made that goal a reality. Zappa has produced over 30 LP's in his 15-year history, culminating in an ode to "Valspeak," with his daughter Moon Unit—a spoof on California "valley girls" which fostered a fad that swept the nation in the early eighties.

As a goal, crass commercialism is probably the least destructive of the many intentions rock stars have had for their music. One of the most shocking situations we have uncovered, in our investigations, is the specific and often dangerous designs many of rock's promoters have had for their tunes—designs that go well beyond simple money-making.

Those intentions fall into the same six categories which characterize the dangers present in rock music's lyrics and rock stars' lifestyles, namely: (1) nihilism and escapism, (2) humanism and commercialism, (3) rebellion and violence, (4) hedonism, (5) occultism, and (6) chemical abuse. A quick examination of rock's notable quotables clearly reveals the intentions they have for their music.

100

The Terminal Generation

One goal rock stars often promote, either as a reflection of their own sad view of life, or as a gimmick to bolster record sales, is the life-is-a-drag-so-let's-end-it-all (suicidal–nihilistic) theme, or the let's-run-away-to-where-life-is-beautiful-all-the-time (escapism) theme.

One promoter of the first of these two themes is Melle Mel, lyricist of Grandmaster Flash and the Furious Five, whose members fancy themselves apocalyptic rappers with a heavier-than-heavy metal sound. Writer Merle Ginsberg, of *New Sound* magazine, described the group, saying, "They refuse to look away from ugliness, and they don't expect, or even desire, that the ugliness will go away."[3] For example: their single, "New York, New York," recounts a teenager's dumping of her newborn child into the trash.

Melle says, "I wanted to create my own image. It's a way of being anti-Christian. . . . The lyrics are so serious because that's the way we feel, and because if you're going to make a record with a groove, it's very easy to get a subconscious message across. . . ."[4]

Furious Mel is correct—his attitude *is* anti-Christian. When Paul the apostle was in prison, and there was Christian opposition against his work, as well as pagan persecution of the Church, he wrote to his Philippian friends, "Fill your minds with those things that are good and that deserve praise: things that are true, noble, right, pure, lovely and honorable" (Phil. 4:8, GNB); and twice he encouraged them to rejoice in *all* circumstances. That should be the attitude we have today. We should willingly recognize the problems around us—the world does not need Christian "Pollyannas" anymore than it needs anti-Christian "Oscar the Grouches"—but we also should put our trust in God to provide the solutions.

Another group which intentionally designed its music and image to create chaos, havoc and despondency was the Sex Pistols. In late 1975, Malcolm McLaren, who until then owned a London clothing shop called Sex, matched up four grungy-looking characters with no musical experience whatsoever, and christened them the Sex Pistols. McLaren declared at the time, "I'm going to change the face of the music scene. . . . The Sex Pistols are from the street. They can't play very well, but that's not important; it's their attitude."[5]

Their attitude was pure nihilism. As *New Sounds* magazine says;

> From the start, the Sex Pistols made a point of letting everyone know that they stood for nothing, that in fact they were against everything. . . . "There's always something to fight," said Johnny Rotten to a British reporter in '76, "mostly apathy. We're in a band because we're bored with all that old crap, like every decent human being should be."[6]

The Sex Pistols weren't the first band to offend the public, but they were the first to flaunt their offensiveness.

The same depressing mood still predominates the harsh punk rock scene. When *Cornerstone* asked guitarist Matthew Ashman and bass player Leroy

Gorman about BowWowWow's songs which extol adolescence and living it up, Ashman commented, "If there's a message in the music, it's 'have a good time while you can before the bomb goes off,' and all that sort of boring stuff."[7]

German singer/songwriter Peter Schilling echoes that theme in most of his work. One of his songs, a reworking of the standard Christmas hymn, "Silent Night," exposes Schilling's hopeless view of a world filled with starvation, wars and terrorism. "I hate that Christmas song," states Schilling. "I'm glad that my version got a negative reaction from some Christians because I want to tell them that it's not a silent night and a holy night, that everything is not well."[8]

Unfortunately, Schilling and other rock nihilists, don't understand that a Christian is happy not because he has blinders on, but in spite of his and the world's circumstances. That is not to say the Christian should not be concerned and compassionate, for Jesus reminded us to clothe and feed the needy, welcome strangers, and visit the sick and imprisoned. It is simply that Jesus' spirit of joy is in each person who is living for Him, and that joy is full and unexplainable—and available for the asking.

Just as far from the truth as nihilism is the flight-to-fantasyland rock star who uses his music to promote escapism. Perhaps most successful is the Peter Pan of Pop, Michael Jackson. Having performed on stage for 20 of his 25 years, it's understandable that Jackson has a distaste for reality. "Jackson has a rich fantasy life," says *New Sound* of the young record maker-and-breaker, "and to enhance it he has made his California estate an extension of it." There, the magazine says, Jackson keeps a boa constrictor, a llama, a macaw, fawns, and other exotic animals. Some rooms in his home are filled with mannequins and Disneyesque robots.[9] Both Peter Pan and E.T. (The Extraterrestrial) play a big part in his life, as do horror movies and things scary. He visits Florida's Walt Disney World so often, *USA Today* reports, that he now has a hotel suite named for him.

"I love to create magic," says the young superstar, "to put together something so unusual, so unexpected, that it blows people's heads off."[10] Creating magic, as Jackson puts it, can be rewarding, exhilarating. But that sort of "magic" is just short of madness—and therein lies the danger. Elvis Presley lived to weave magic for others, and was soon caught under his own spell—trapped in his own alter-image—until life became unreal.

Of his penchant and talent for dancing—as much a part of his act as his haunting, popping, clicking, moaning-to-the-beat vocals—Jackson says, "Dancing will never disappear, it's instinct, it's God, it's escapism, getting away from everything and having a good time just moving your body and letting all the tension and pain out."[11]

When Jackson received the Award of Merit at the American Music Awards, along with awards for Favorite Pop Single, Favorite Soul and Favorite Pop Album, Favorite Soul and Favorite Pop Video, Favorite Pop Male and Favorite Soul Male Singer, he confided to the audience, "I put all my heart and my soul in my work. . . ." With such intensity devoted to providing escapism for his fans, it is easy, perhaps even unavoidable, to be caught up in the myth. And while Jackson espouses a rather straight life, compared to most in rock circles—no smoking, no drugs—his connection with the cult of Jehovah's Witnesses leaves him vulnerable to satanic influence.

The escapism Michael Jackson offers his adoring fans through his magical, musical make-believe is as spiritually unhealthy as any drug or cigarette would be physically, because it disconnects those fans from the real world and their real purpose for being here. A person can still have fun, but he needs to remain alert. Paul once instructed the Corinthians to discard "imaginations"—anything that would take God's place in their lives—and "bring into captivity" every thought (2 Cor. 10:5). They weren't to let their imaginations run free, but bring them under control so that everything they did would be done for and with Christ. In the same fashion, He should be *our* motivation always.

In contrast, Jackson's main motivation seems to be what he describes as "the force within"—something he draws from and expresses in his music. "The thing that touches me is very special," he says. "It's a message I have to tell. I start crying and the pain is wonderful. It's amazing. It's like God.[12]

Newsweek describes this solid gold, show business phenomenon as "a black giant who sacrificed his childhood to become a pop idol . . . a lonely prophet of salvation through the miracle of his . . . music."[13] Yet the magazine questions Jackson's powerfully popular hits such as "Billie Jean," "Beat It," "Wanna Be Startin' Somethin'," and "Thriller." "Each one," the article says, "is quirky, strange, deeply personal, with offbeat lyrics that hint at Michael's own secret world of dreams and demons."[14]

Pretty Packages

Many of rock's wayward messages are tied up in pretty packages so their corrupt, evil nature is not detectable. Such is the case either when rock's stars intend to promote themselves purely for commercial reasons, or when they intend to promote their particular brand of secular humanism through their music.

Adam Ant, the rocker who invented himself, is one of the former. It appears that Ant is the sort of fellow who will wear anything—or nothing—if it will sell more records. For nearly a decade, he's changed costumes and personas continuously. This clothes chameleon, whose one constant is a gold skull-and-crossbones earring in one ear, has sold over a million copies, collectively, of his first three albums. His fourth, *Strip*, carries lyrics *People* magazine refers to as "soft-core smut."[15] On the inner-sleeve photo of the LP, Ant wears little more than the earring and a tatoo. "I'm concerned with escapist entertainment," Ant remarked. "I'll dance or sing or stand on my head to tickle an audience's imagination."[16]

Rock magazine questioned such blatant commercialism when its writer spoke to Malcolm McLaren, the mastermind behind Ant's, as well as BowWowWow's images: "When you got her [BowWowWow's former lead singer Annabelle Lwin] to pose semi-nude for their *Last of the Mohican's* LP, you were accused of terrible exploitation, and her mother went to court to try to stop the U.S. tour." McLaren replied, "Yeah! That was great! Of course I exploited them—and I'm quite proud of it!"[17]

Debbie Harry of Blondie is quite pragmatic about rock's commercial emphasis: "The major goal of any entertainer is to become easily identifiable. You have to find your own personal twist and play it up. Once you've done that, you start to click, regardless of your product. It's a psychological approach to sales."[18]

Chic's bassist, Bernard Edwards, explains rock's continual character mutations this way: "We make the group for the public. If tastes change, we will too."[19] And John Lennon put it even more bluntly when he remarked, "You have to be a bastard to make it, and that's a fact. And the Beatles were the biggest bastards."[20]

Despite their success, the Beatles employed any method to ensure the commercial value of their recordings. In 1968, when concerts and tours became too dangerous, due to fan violence, the Beatles hit on another gimmick for record promotion. According to *Rolling Stone,* they included on the *Abbey Road* album and its cover approximately 25 subtle suggestions that Paul McCartney was dead. Experts, it appears, had demonstrated hidden persuaders, such as fear, sex, the occult and death, were powerful sales tools. The Beatles set out to prove the theory, and sold thousands of records in the process.

Dregs member, Steve Morse, candidly placed the issue of commercialism in perspective: "If you spit in people's faces, you get publicity. If you break things and piss on the audience, you get in *Rolling Stone.*"[21] Morse added, sarcastically, that a musician is better off if he can't play well (and in many cases, he's right). In our free, capitalistic Western society, we seem to have the notion we can take any product, no matter how bizarre, base, or immoral— even if it has the power to destroy people—and package it attractively, and sell it on the open market, as if the selling of that product validated its message.

Crass commercialism of this sort is fairly easy to detect. Not so simple to discover is the intent to diffuse humanism into society, for often it is done by well-meaning, but misled, people. The Bible offers the answer, however; it says we should examine ourselves, as to whether we are "in the faith." We should be continually proving ourselves and our thinking—and the ideas we pick up from the world—to make certain it goes along with what God teaches us.

Boy George of Culture Club is a case in point. He has stated he wants people to celebrate with him—that is the goal of his music. "That's what I want. I want people to celebrate. Dress up for the evening." On the surface that sounds harmless enough. However, Boy George doesn't stop there: "I don't want people committed to an ideal," he added, " 'coz ideals go out the window after a while. Things aren't black and white to me. I could say something to you now and tomorrow something could happen that would make me change my mind. . . ."[22] That is relativism, which essentially says, "My will be done." It is the humanistic standard of situation ethics, and it is anti-God.

Some rock stars aren't afraid to state their thoughts more overtly. Guitarist Craig Chaquico observed, "Rock concerts are the churches of today. Music puts them on a spiritual plane. All music is God."[23] Leon Russell offered similar sentiments when he said, "I'd like to say that organized Christianity has done more harm than any other single force I can think of in the world." And as an alternative, he offered "the religion of rock and roll."[24]

Sting, the Police's keystone cop, promotes a view of life which is a sad combination of his own past—bits and pieces of the faith in which he was raised, polluted with humanism and mysticism. "Looking outside yourself is a waste of time," he says. "I'm looking inside for awareness." He then adds with pride that his six-year-old son already has a "concept of God he invented himself."[25] Sting's goal, from the time he was eleven, and first heard the Beatles sing, has been to "become a musician. My religion would be music," he says, "and I had just received my first sacrament."[26]

This sort of delusion is forecast in Scripture as a sign of the end time. Paul spoke of those days when he said, "For the time will come when men will not put up with sound doctrine. Instead, to suit their own desires, they will gather around them a great number of teachers to say what their itching ears want to hear. They will turn their ears away from the truth and turn aside to myths" (2 Tim. 4:3, 4, NIV).

Widening the Gap

"Our music is intended to broaden the generation gap [and] to alienate children from their parents," one member of the Jefferson Airplane/Starship proclaimed with hostility—and he's not alone in that intention.[27] The *St. Paul Dispatch* once described Billy Joel as having a perpetual chip on his shoulder. "He has exhorted his fans from the stage," the article claimed, "to follow what appears to be his personal philosophy: 'Don't take any [expletive deleted] from anybody!' "[28]

Other musicians with the same mentality and mission include Alice Cooper and Freddie Mercury.

Alice Cooper says, "Rebellion is the basis for our group. Some of the kids who listen to us are really deranged; but they look up to us as heroes because their parents hate us too much."[29] Queen's Freddie Mercury agrees: "We want to shock and be outrageous."[30]

That same spirit is present—perhaps even more so—in heavy metal rock. *Newsweek* magazine says most adults will claim heavy metal is noise. "It's not just the earsplitting sound and the relentless beat," contends *Newsweek*.

"Kids at a heavy metal concert don't sit in their seats; they stand on them and move—it's the spirit of rebellion."[31]

Allen Lanier, of Blue Oyster Cult, admitted that violence and rebellion are key ingredients of most heavy metal. "Rock and roll has a real violent catharsis to it. It brings out violent emotions. There's a lot of violence, a lot of aggression in the music."[32] Lanier is misguided, however, when he says violent music is cathartic, a means to alleviate restless inner emotions. Violence and rebellion, contrary to what many child-rearing "experts" have said, are not simply outgrown. It is not healthy to allow them to be expressed at will. For rebellion is compared in Scripture to the evils of witchcraft and idolatry. The only cure is repentance and obedience (1 Sam. 15: 22, 23).

While teens should be allowed to develop personal viewpoints and self-reliance, the unbridled rage and alienation of heavy metal rock is evil in God's eyes. First Samuel 15 goes on to say that rebellion against the Lord's commands puts one in danger of being rejected by God.

Rock stars embrace that danger when they spell out their intentions as did Brian Setzer of the Stray Cats:

> Rockabilly . . . it's definitely teenage rebellion. . . . The lyrics to our songs are the things I know about: cars, bikes, getting kicked out of school, all the good things in life. Dumb stuff. Nobody wants to listen to Mom and Dad, me included. So you want a song to go with that, something you can play really loud on your stereo so Mom and Dad can hear it! It's not just the music. Half of it is being an individual. A rebel. This is what I choose to be . . . a rockabilly rebel![33]

Another key figure in the punk/New Wave music of the seventies is Elvis Costello (real name Declan MacManus). Although he sports a rocker-as-nerd, horned-rimmed-glasses image, he has from the beginning projected himself as an angry young man. "The only two things that motivate me and that matter to me," he says, "are revenge and guilt. They are the only emotions I know about. Love? I don't know what it means. It doesn't exist in my songs."[34]

The saddest truth about the whole rock-and-roll rebel mystique is that although so many of rock's most popular bands promote it, many don't believe in it for themselves. In a moment of honesty, David Lee Roth admitted to a *USA Today* reporter, "The best thing about being a singer in a band like Van Halen, is that I can be exactly what everyone expects of a rock singer and people love it. We like the fact that the masses see us as rock 'n' roll rebels," he said, reclining in the band's plush Hollywood office. But the image stops when Roth comes offstage. He employs bodyguards full time, even when he's not touring, so he can be protected from fans who expect a certain type of behavior from him. And though the performers "act nuts" on stage, their multi-million dollar business is run with cagey business savvy, and though they preach rebellion, they are firmly (and hypocritically) entrenched in the establishment.[35]

Rock Music: Pornography Set to a Beat

Rock music's deluge of pornography is not by accident. Many of rock's most popular groups purpose to promote, and even perform, sexual debasement through their music. It takes but a brief overview of rock stars to discover their songs are written to sell sex; and sex, in turn, sells their songs.

Jan Berry, of the sixties sensation, Jan and Dean: "The throbbing beat of rock-and-roll provides a vital sexual release for its adolescent audience. . . . I believe that the next trend in rock-and-roll will be to relieve the sexual tensions of the preadolescent set."[36]

Jim Morrison, of the Doors: "I feel spiritual up there performing. Think of us as erotic politicians."[37]

Punk rock manager, Malcolm McLaren: "Rock 'n' roll *is* pagan and primitive, and very jungle, and that's how it should be! The moment it stops being those things, it's dead. . . . That's what rock 'n' roll is meant to be about isn't it? . . . the true meaning of rock . . . is sex, subversion and style."[38]

Rick Derringer: "They [fans] think we're all sexy and they want to go to bed with us." *Circus* magazine notes, "For Rick Derringer, this is what rock 'n' roll is all about."[39]

Circus magazine on Patti Smith: "Patti says that pornography is one of the few frontiers that hasn't been explored to the 'nth' degree. . . . Patti Smith wants to write rock 'n' roll pornography that will be totally illuminating. Patti says to die before total illumination is a sin."[40]

Composer/producer/artist Johnny Bristol: "Sex is where it's at in music . . . and I like it."[41]

Teddy Pendergrass, the gruff, sexy-voiced singer whose concerts—before he was sidelined to a wheelchair by an auto accident—used to be billed "For Women Only," as reviewed by *Us* magazine: "Almost every song he sings has to do with love, spelled s-e-x. Turn off the lights and everything will be all right—that's the message that exudes from an evening with Pendergrass."[42]

Blondie guitarist Chris Stein: "Everyone takes it for granted—rock 'n' roll is synonomous with sex."[43]

Shaun Cassidy, as described by *Circus* magazine, in concert at Madison Square Garden for an audience comprised mainly of girls (average age: 12): " 'This is what rock and roll is about,' he shouts, caressing his bottom with his back turned to the audience. . . . His swagger is Mick Jagger's, his exaggerated hip undulations and slyly suggestive microphone play [at one point he dangles it seductively between his legs] are straight from Elvis Presley."[44]

Keyboardist of Blue Oyster Cult, Allen Lanier: "Rock and roll is just mindless fun."[45]

Doug Feiger of the Knack: "We've been accused of writing about women as sex objects, and I don't think that's so bad. Everyone wants to be a desirable sex object. Everyone. It's a human thing."[46]

Author Tony Scaduto in his bestseller, *Mick Jagger: Everybody's Lucifer*: "Jagger is unfortunately sucked into his own image. . . . Sometime during that 1969 tour he began to get into the whole evil-dirty-rapist-drag queen image."[47]

Village People's manager Jacques Morali: "I am sincerely trying to produce songs to make gay people more acceptable. [It is a] protest against Anita Bryant."[48]

Freddie Mercury of the group Queen, whose songs' lyrics range from the unprintable sexual solicitation of "Get Down, Make Love," to the widely-accepted anthem of gay liberation, "We Are the Champions": "We want to shock and be outrageous."[49] He also proudly reveals that the band's name and androgynous performances are designed to connote its gay connections.[50]

Holly Near, who hired a PR firm to help promote her albums which are love-hymns to lesbianism (The result was sales of 30,000 copies of her LP, *Fire in the Rain,* during its first month's release, as well as appearances on *The Today Show* and *Sesame Street!*): "I want to do songs about lesbians in such a way that both gay and straight teenagers will ask their parents to come to concerts."[51]

John Oates (of Hall and Oates, voted by American Music Awards, 1984's Favorite Pop Group): "Rock and roll is 99 percent sex."[52] Oates said of Daryl Hall: "You should see Daryl when he sings 'Sarah Smile.' He walks to the edge of the stage and blatantly rubs his crotch. There's not much more you can do to communicate other than [sexual term] the whole front row."[53]

Can the pornographic music of some rock and roll, intentionally meant to promote promiscuity and perversion, really persuade the public? Experts think it has that power. As D. H. Lawrence wrote in *Sex, Literature and Censorship:* "Pornography is the attempt to insult sex, to do dirt on it. . . . Ugly and cheap they make the human nudity, ugly and degraded they make the sexual act, trivial and cheap and nasty."

Speaking of the latest craze among rock stars, the androgynous look (of singers such as Boy George, Michael Jackson, Annie Lennox, and the actress in the rock-cult movie *Liquid Sky,* Anne Carlisle, who played both male and female parts), a crisis counselor told *USA Today:* "For some kids, it has created a confusion in themselves." Dr. John Money, a psychologist at Johns Hopkins University, says, "More than anybody knows, we're dependent on clothes to give us our first impression of whether you're a man or a woman."[54]

Rock artists tend to agree. Reggae rocker Peter Tosh said, "I am a musical messenger . . . and I want to educate people through music."[55] Singer Huey Lewis concurs: "It [rock and roll] can help you with life; it can teach you how to live."[56] However, David Lee Roth claims his sexual antics onstage and off, as well as his musical lyrics, have no message. Even though his fans tend to describe him in terms of sexuality, not musicianship, he once declared to *ABC Nightline,* "I have no message. I dare not preach to somebody. . . . I'm having a good time, and you're invited."[57]

Yet, the pornography he and other rock stars portray through their music educates. Without question, it teaches that human beings are merely animals, that people can be exploited and then discarded as just so much garbage. It says there is nothing precious and private and permanent.

When rock stars portray perverted sex, they are not telling the truth about sex; they are selling a lie, but you don't have to buy it. You can stay clear of rock's perverting influence, having no fellowship with such "unfruitful" works. Proverbs suggests instead, "Buy truth, and do not sell it; buy wisdom, instruction, and understanding" (Prov. 23:23, RSV).

Stairway to Heaven?

"I am the Lord your God who brought you out of Egypt, where you were slaves. Worship no god but me" (Ex. 20:2, GNB). This is the first of the Commandments God gave to Moses. Perhaps one of the most difficult conditions the Jewish people suffered through during their Egyptian slavery was their lack of freedom to worship God and practice their faith as they wished. In fact, at the time of Moses' birth, to simply be born a Hebrew male was a capital offense.

There was great celebration when the Jews left Egypt, knowing they now would be able to worship as they pleased. Egypt was, after all, a nation inundated with false gods and occult religious practices.

However, in the desert, the Hebrews began to question the wisdom of their exodus, and they grumbled: "Why did we ever leave? Things weren't so bad. At least we had food to eat. Now we're going to starve." Life's cares bogged them down and veered them off the track. However, God took care of their physical needs, and each time He did, He reminded them He was the Lord, their God.

Times don't change much. Even though we in the Western nations are free, as no other people on the face of the earth have ever been, to worship our God, we too, get bogged down in the problems of everyday life. And often, we, too, place other gods before us, or search for wrong answers to our problems. A number of rock stars, while honestly seeking answers to the problems they see (within their lives and without) mistakenly look to false gods and false religions for their answers. Some have even, as we have already seen, used the powers of Satan to fulfill their needs.

Since religion is a deeply personal thing, an expression of a yearning for God which is at the very center of one's nature, a person cannot help but live out his beliefs. And to make matters worse, many rock stars seem to flaunt theirs—whether they believe in spiritualism, in satanism and witchcraft, the Eastern mystics, or one of the so-called New Age heresies. The most urgent problem, when rock stars begin to proselytize, is that their listeners are young and vulnerable. Young people generally step back a pace or two from their parents' beliefs in order to examine them and, hopefully, embrace them. If those beliefs are on shaky ground, however, and if those young people are presented with a "logical" alternative by a trusted source, they may be duped into following false religions.

Elvis Presley was one of the first of rock's heroes to fall into, and subsequently promote, a false religion. Raised on a diet of superstitious, quasi-Christian practices, and suffering from a mind destroyed by drugs and a spiritual life corrupted by pleasure-seeking, Presley developed a fascination for all sorts of spiritualistic pseudo-religions; he even maintained a library of occultic reading material, from *The Urantia Book* to *The Rosicrucian Cosmo-Conception*. One of his favorites, according to biographer Albert Goldman, was *The Impersonal Life*, a book supposedly dictated by the voice of God directly to Joseph S. Benner. Goldman says:

> . . .from this time forth you could never come into the presence of Elvis Presley, whether at one of his homes or in a motel room or an airplane cabin, without finding a copy of his book [*The Impersonal Life*] either in his hand or near his person. Over the course of the next thirteen years he must have given away hundreds of copies of this book.[58]

Another false prophet, whose writings intrigued Presley, was the spiritualist, Madame Blavatsky. Presley so favored *The Voice of Silence*, her purported translation of the most ancient runes of Tibet, that he "sometimes read from it onstage and was inspired by it to name his own gospel group, Voice."[59]

John Denver, whose very name seems to signify everything that is wholesome in America, has admitted his dedication to the pseudo-religious practices of est—the Erhard Seminar Training method. Although many may not consider this mind-control technique a false religion, research by such experts as Dr. Walter Martin shows est is, in truth, a cult; in other words, it is people's attempt at finding God apart from the Lord Jesus Christ. Those who indulge in est are taught they are "perfect . . . gods who have created their own world."

On one of his album covers, Denver wrote: "My purpose in performing is to communicate the joy I experience in living. It is the aliveness within you that my music is intended to reach. Participating in est has created an amazing amount of space for joy and aliveness in my life. It pleases me to share est with you." Denver sings in one of his tunes that he was "born again" in the summer of his twenty-seventh year, when he went back to a place he'd "never been before." When Denver was later asked about the lyrics, he said he did have a religious experience—through the occult science, through yoga, through self-centered est; however, but not through Christ. "Some day I'll be so complete," he once boasted, "I won't even be human. I'll be God." Now he proposes to present the counterfeit experience to others through his music.[60]

Maurice White believes in another New Age, para-religion falsehood: reincarnation. Believers in reincarnation deny Jesus' death is sufficient atonement for our sins. They contend Jesus was simply a man who reached the perfect state of "Karma" through good works in His past lives. Remember, though, that Heb. 9:27 tells us that "everyone must die once, and after that be judged by God" (GNB). White believes his former life "had something to do with the 900 years before Christ," he says, "and the Egyptians and the

Great Teachings and Africa and America.... Maybe this was not the first time I came this way."[61]

Ozzy Osbourne professes a belief in reincarnation as well. In fact, he believes one of his previous lives "was lived as a servant of the devil."[62]

A Ouija board influenced the life of rock-star-cum-horror, Alice Cooper. Many people mistake a Ouija board for a harmless toy, but a book written by a former queen of witches labels the board an occult device. It is used to tell fortunes, and, according to Alice Cooper, it was consulted when a name for the group was chosen. The board spelled out Alice Cooper, which the rocker later discovered was the name of a 17th-century witch. Cooper contends that he is the reincarnation of that witch.[63]

Demonic overtones accompany many of rock's most popular groups. The members of KISS, which have won the hearts of many preteens, have used devilish makeup and demon-like fire-breathing to mesmerize their fans. Peter Criss once boldly announced to *Rolling Stone,* "I find myself evil. I believe in the devil as much as God. You can use either one to get things done."[64] Hoping to appeal to the next hoard of pre-adolescents, the men of KISS have washed away their makeup, but they can't wipe clean the perversions they have dumped on the minds of thousands of teen fans.

Seals and Crofts, the guitar and mandolin duo who blend country sounds with rock and roll, also blend in the Baha'i faith on their recordings. A final song on their *Takin' It Easy* album is a tribute to Abdu'l-Baha, and is actually a translation of a Persian poem. Prefacing the song is a solo on the Persian *santour,* probably the first time that instrument has been played in America.[65] Baha'i is based on the writings of a 19th-century Persian prophet, Baha'u'llah, who claimed lineage with both Christ and Buddha. The Baha'i faith denies the deity of Jesus, His atonement for our sins, His bodily resurrection, and His literal return.

Though instruments such as the *santour* are perhaps not harmful in themselves, there certainly can be an aura—a spirit—which comes through the music they produce. It enhances the proper frame of mind in which one is susceptible to the philosophies the music is designed to promote. Another instrument which has been utilized in much the same way is the *sitar,* first incorporated into rock music by ex-Beatle George Harrison.

"It was the spiritual side of Indian music that first attracted me," Harrison once said. "The only reason for being is to have full understanding of life's spiritual aspects.... The idea is to become one with God through meditation and yoga."[66] Harrison's music is filled with references to and praises of Hinduism and the Lord Krishna, the supposed Hindu god-man, whose "inspired" book, *Bhagavad-Gita As It Is,* is sold by Krishna's followers in airports and on street corners. The book contains a foreword written by Harrison, and a significant portion of his record royalties goes to support the Krishna cult.[67]

Another Eastern religion now captivates singer/songwriter Cat Stevens, well known for his mellow seventies hits. In 1981, he announced he had become a Muslim and changed his name to Yosef Islam. Professing he was through with music, he auctioned off his entire assortment of instruments and equipment, and donated the proceeds to the Companions of the Mosque, a London-based organization that oversees Muslims throughout the United Kingdom.[68]

Names have significance, and often in the world of rock, a band will choose its name to spell out its intentions. Hence, names such as Styx—one of the rivers of Hades, the nether-world kingdom of souls of the dead; Ambrosia—the food of the Greek gods, which gave them wisdom and immortality; Iron Maiden—connoting torture, it was a nickname given to a hideous, medieval torture device; Mahavishnu Orchestra—obviously dedicated to the Hindu god Vishnu (The founder of the now-disbanded group, John McLaughlin, introduced each of his songs with an explanation of the metaphysical implications of the lyrics).[69]

Perhaps most shocking are the groups whose name are chosen for, or whose intentions are linked with, the demonic. Whether as a gimmick, in jest, or in deadly earnest, these misled unfortunates are flirting with real danger when they dabble in the occult and black magic. Some rock stars, such as Iron Maiden's Bruce Dickinson, say they are "not into the occult that much"; however, that is self-delusion. Playing around with the devil is like playing Russian roulette. Perhaps the first time a person pulls the trigger, the gun won't fire, but if he keeps playing long enough, he's liable to blow his head off.

"We just enjoy doing songs about fantasy subjects," says Dickinson. "It's more of a horror movie mentality than anything else. . . . Eddie [the rotting corpse that serves as the band's mascot] comes on stage to do battle with the devil, and I can tell you that Eddie really kicks his [expletive deleted]. It's Maiden's way of showing that rock and roll can overcome anything."[70]

Don't be too sure. The devil has just one purpose in mind—to see as many souls as possible damned to hell with him. Does that sound like fooling around? The Bible says, "It is like sport to a fool to do wrong" (Prov. 10:23, RSV).

The Rolling Stones, who have melded their name to the devil's on a number of projects, such as *Their Satanic Majesties Request*, say, "We receive our songs by inspiration, like at a séance."[71] Even *Newsweek* magazine called Mick Jagger "the Lucifer of Rock, the unholy roller," and spoke of his "demonic power to affect people."[72]

Joni Mitchell credits her creative powers to a "male muse" she identifies as Art. He has taken so much control of not only her music, but her life, that she feels married to him, and often roams naked with him on her 40-acre estate. His hold over her is so strong that she will excuse herself from parties and forsake lovers whenever he "calls."[73]

Many groups have alluded to feelings of being manipulated while performing—as just so many pieces in a giant demonic chess game, or of having out-of-body experiences. Ginger Baker, drummer for Eric Clapton's band, Cream, a major musical force in the late sixties, explained the sensation:

> It happens to us quite often—it feels as though I'm not playing my instrument, something else is playing it and that same thing is playing all three of our instruments. That's what I mean when I say it's frightening sometimes. Maybe we'll all play the same phrase out of nowhere. It happens very often with us.[74]

Stevie Nicks talks about similar experiences: "It's amazing, 'cause sometimes when we're on stage, I feel like somebody's just moving the pieces. . . . I'm just going, 'God, we don't have any control over this.' And that's magic."[75]

Rock critic Andy Secher wrote in *Hit Parader* magazine, "It happens that Jimmy Page does have a fascination with the macabre and black magic, but that doesn't exactly make him the devil incarnate. Rather than hindering his musical abilities . . . this interest helped bring an extra element into Zeppelin's music."[76]

Page says the occult is a fascination for him, not an obsession, but there is little difference. Led Zeppelin's record-breaking song "Stairway to Heaven" was the most requested song of the seventies, and, until Michael Jackson came along, one of the top tunes of all time. Yet both Page and Robert Plant have admitted to not being sure who wrote the number. They claim the whole song was written in just 10 minutes.

What's the harm? you might ask. You may even be tempted to reason: What difference does it make what the artist's intentions were—a song is a song is a song. But music, as has been said before, is a tremendous motivator, and many have used its power to persuade people to investigate and enter pseudo-religions.

For example, The Way International, a heretical cult making inroads into middle-class America with its "gospel," now has a rock band: Takit. According to the *Chicago Sun-Times*, the group has gained entrance to many high schools by posing as simply a rock group with no affiliations. During concerts the group intentionally avoids mention of its ties with the cult. The performers tell their audience to keep "off drugs and liquor, stay in school, make something of yourself." There is no mention of God. Afterward, however, contacts are made and new members are recruited.[77]

Such tactics, along with the general proliferation of occultic material available in easy-reading paperbacks, and the promotion of the occult through the music industry, have stealthily invaded the minds of young people, influencing directly and indirectly every phase of their lives, whether or not it's believed or desired.

The occult is rampant in the U.S. (At least 5,000 witches are said to practice in New York and 10,000 in Los Angeles. And there are nearly half as many witches in the U.S. as there are doctors or clergymen.[78]) And many parents are simply not aware of the proliferation of materials or of the consequences of dabbling with any of the occultic practices mentioned here. It is important, however, that parents and teens alike recognize the dangers present and heed Jesus' words: "But watch at all times, praying that you may have strength to escape all these things that will take place, and to stand before the Son of man" (Luke 21:36, RSV).

California's Bumper Crop

The list of casualties in rock circles due to drug and alcohol abuse is seemingly endless, as the next chapter reveals. However, despite the hell-on-earth which chemical abuse has caused in so many lives, we almost never hear a rock star speak against drugs—and songs extolling the virtues of staying clean are virtually nonexistent.

A prominent rock manager explained why to *Circus* magazine: "No matter what anyone tells you, drugs will always be a part of the rock scene."[79] A major publicist concurs: "Most of the artists I talked to refused to be anti-cocaine because they use it."[80] As documented earlier, many rock stars claim there were whole periods of time—sometimes years—when they were so drugged they now remember nothing about them. The glorification of drugs has caused an inestimable amount of pain and suffering among rock's stars and fans alike.

Albert Goldman poignantly described two of rock's greats, and a great many of rock's fans, this way:

Jimi Hendrix:
His death was an inevitable product of his life . . . rock's flamboyant superstar, snuffed out at twenty-seven . . . [cocaine] swept him along heedless of dangers that made his mere existence a daily miracle. . . ."

Janis Joplin:
Rock's greatest soul belter, also twenty-seven, found dead . . . fresh needle marks on her left arm . . . possessed by a very different demon . . . she gloried in self-destruction, tearing out her throat with every song, brandishing a bottle of Southern Comfort on stage. . . . Dope was as essential to her myth as blues, booze, and the frantic beat. . . .

The rock culture that has become the drug culture:
Convinced that everything is fraud, feasting on films that feed their paranoia, . . . thousands of ordinary kids are a set-up for the pusher—and the "magic" drugs that promise ecstasy. . . . Yet what they are addicted to ultimately is not the drugs but dreams—the myths and fantasies which they have imbibed from the mass media. . . .

"It is within the context of this New Depression," Goldman soberly points out, "that the deaths of the rock stars must be pondered."[81]

The Bible tells us we should always seek to grow in both true knowledge and in good judgment so that we can choose what is best for our lives (Phil. 1:9, 10). It promises we will then have the quality of life we seek to enjoy—a quality only Jesus can produce in us. The Christian doesn't need drugs to chase myths—he has the way to true happiness, rather than death.

9

Dead and Gone: Rock and Roll Obituaries

Let's now "ponder," as Goldman says, the death of some of rock music's greats, not for any sadistic or morbid purpose, but for the purpose of seeking "true knowledge" and "good judgment." Tragic as many of these lives and deaths may be, perhaps we can at least profit from their mistakes.

Johnny Ace (1929–1954)

Died of a gunshot wound backstage at a Christmas Eve performance in the Houston City Auditorium, Houston, Texas. Ace was playing the deadly game, Russian Roulette, in which a bullet is placed in one chamber of a revolver, and players take turns pointing the gun to their temples and pulling the trigger.

Duane Allman (1946–1971)

Known as the world's best on the bottleneck guitar, Allman, one of the original members of the Allman Brothers Band, died at the age of 24, in a motorcycle accident.

Florence Ballard

One of the original members of the Supremes, Ballard met the others at a church gospel meeting in their hometown of Detroit, Michigan. However, she either had been forced out of the group or had quit by the time of their first big hit, "Every Beat of My Heart." She died, virtually penniless, at the age of 27, of cardiac arrest which was medication-alcohol related.

John Belushi (1950–1982)

Belushi, although well-known as a talented comedian and early cast member of *Saturday Night Live*, headed the Blues Brothers Band with fellow comic, Dan Aykroyd. Originally just a stunt, the band developed a following, and soon had produced hit records. *Rolling Stone* magazine said of his death: "Belushi was cranked up on cocaine nearly all the time.... 'He would try anything he could find,' said [girlfriend Cathy] Smith." There were enough drugs in his body to kill even a healthy man, according to the examining

115

116

pathologist, and the autopsy report listed 11 abnormalities, including "pulmonary congestion with distended lung," a swollen brain and heart, "aorta atherosclerosis," and enlarged liver, and obesity (May 13, 1982, pp. 76-7).

Jesse Belvin (1933–1960)

A singer, composer, pianist and member of many fifties groups, including the Cliques (best known for the tune, "Earth Angel"). He died in a car crash.

Bill Black (1926–1965)

An early sixties bass player on many of Elvis Presley's recordings, Bill Black and His Combo recorded a 1960 hit, "White Silver Sands." He died a short five years later. The cause of his death was not made public.

Bobby Bloom

Originally a member of the Imaginations, Bloom came to public attention in 1970 with a light, summery song, "Montego Bay." He died in 1974, the victim of an accidental shooting.

Marc Bolan (1947–1977)

The main force behind the band T-Rex, he was its lead guitarist and songwriter until his death in an auto accident, at which time he was estranged from his wife and family. *Rolling Stone's* March 16, 1972, issue says of Bolan: "He admits to having spent two years . . . living with a black magician in Paris, and claims to have learned how to cast spells, to which he attributes the credit for some of their successful rock records."

Tommy Bolin (1950–1975)

He took Ritchie Blackmore's place in the extremely successful Deep Purple, and also toured with both Sailor and the James Gang. In December 1975, after an all-night party, Bolin's body, dead from an overdose, was discovered by his girlfriend.

John "Bonzo" Bonham (1948–1980)

Former Swan Song Records Vice President, Danny Goldberg, said of the Led Zeppelin drummer, "He was the ultimate rock and roll bad guy." Bonham was known to not only drink heavily but to take "speed balls"—a mixture of heroin and cocaine—and sleeping pills mixed with booze. A suspected heart attack caused his collapse in June 1980, but he continued to abuse his body until September 26, when he was found dead in guitarist Jimmy Page's home. At the time of death he had the equivalent of 40 measures of vodka in his system, and had choked on his own vomit.

Tim Buckley (1947–1975)

A singer/guitarist with hits in the early seventies, Buckley died from a drug overdose at age 28.

Johnny Burnette (1934–1964)

This singer/guitarist was one of the early rockers. He and his brother, Dorsey, and singer Paul Burlison, formed the Johnny Burnette Trio, best known for the 1960 tune, "You're Sixteen." Johnny Burnette died in 1964, in a boating accident. His brother, Dorsey, who had written many rock and country hits, died in 1979 at 47.

Karen Carpenter (1950–1983)

She was the pop rock vocalist of the Carpenters, a group with a string of successful seventies hits. She died, at age 32, of complications stemming from anorexia nervosa, a disease characterized by compulsive dieting and uncontrolled weight loss.

Bill Chase

Chase's group, the Chase, had several songs among the top 100 in the early seventies, but the trumpet player and three other members of the band perished in a plane crash on August 9, 1974.

Eddie Cochran (1938–1960)

Born in Albert Lea, Minnesota, this pompadoured rockabilly star gained major attention in England. His big hits were "Summertime Blues" and "C'mon Everybody." He died at the age of 21, when his car blew a tire in Chippenham, Wiltshire. He was returning to London from a week-long show at the Hippodrome in Bristol.

Brian Cole

Bassist and vocalist for the late sixties group, the Association, Cole died from drug-related causes in 1972.

Sam Cooke (1935–1964)

A black soul singer best known for "Only Sixteen" and "Twisting the Night Away," Cooke was shot and killed after he allegedly raped a 22-year-old woman in a Los Angeles motel.

Jim Croce (1943–1973)

Born in South Philadelphia, Croce was a former truck driver, best known for his narrative ballads. His tune "Bad, Bad Leroy Brown" was a number-one hit in 1973. He was killed in a plane crash just as his career was taking off. His poignant dream song, "If I Could Put Time in a Bottle," sailed up the charts after his death. But as he sang, dreams can't "make wishes come true."

Ian Curtis (1959–1980)

A member of the short-lived British group, Joy Division, Curtis committed suicide when he was just 20 years old.

King Curtis (1934–1971)

Born Curtis Ousley and renowned for his saxophone soul stylings, Curtis was stabbed to death in Harlem at age 36.

Darby Crash (1958–1980)

A punk rocker with the group Germs, he played the lead role in the film *The Decline of Western Civilization*. In the film which LA critic Robert Hilburn describes as "a nihilistic cesspool," Crash often appears stoned and incoherent. He died at 22 from a drug overdose.

Bobby Darin (1936–1973)

In *A Generation in Motion*, author David Pichaske labels Darin the "shlockmeister of the fifties," referring to the sappy, commercialized music of the period. Darin went on from teeny-bopperism to do Las-Vegas-style crooning ("Mack the Knife") and movies. He landed his own TV show in 1973, but died of a heart attack on December 20 of that year, at 37.

James Dean (1931–1955)

The legend—the myth really—on which the post-war generation hung its cause, Dean was the epitome of antagonism toward authority, aimlessness and rebellion. He starred in the movies *Rebel Without a Cause* and *East of Eden*. His life was quickly ended in 1955 by an oncoming car.

Sandy Denny (1947–1978)

This singer and composer, born in Wimbledon, England, was briefly with the Strawbs, then joined one of England's first folk/rock groups, the Fairport Convention. She died as a result of a fall down a flight of stairs in her home.

Nick Drake (1948–1974)

A drug overdose took this promising young English rock singer/pianist of the late sixties.

"Mama" Cass Elliott (1943–1974)

Elliott was the rotund, dreamy-voiced member of one of the psychedelic sixties most popular groups, The Mamas and The Papas. Once boasting that they would become an institution, the group split up after barely three years. Mama Cass choked to death on a sandwich, in the same London flat where Keith Moon of The Who was to die four years later. She was 31 at the time.

Brian Epstein (1934–1967)

Epstein, who ran a record shop until he discovered the Beatles (who claim they discovered him), was the group's first manager. He was a homosexual, reportedly in love with John Lennon, although evidence that the feeling was mutual is sketchy. The man was found dead in his bed, apparently from a drug overdose.

Mel Evans

Mel Evans, a former Beatles road manager, was fatally shot in 1976 by local police officials, following an argument involving a shotgun.

Pete Farndon (1953–1983)

One of the two original members of the Pretenders to die recently. He was found dead in the bathtub, a heroin hypo still in his arm.

Richard Farina (1937-1966)

Until his life ended in a motorcycle accident, at the age of 29, he was one of the prominent members of the folk music scene, and a folk/rock writer.

Alan Freed (1922–1965)

The disc jockey who first named and promoted rock and roll died destitute, after payola scandals ruined his brief career.

Bobby Fuller (1943–1966)

The founding member of the Bobby Fuller Four, an early rock quartet from El Paso, Texas. The group's rough-hewn vocal harmonies gave them two hits in 1966, "I Fought the Law" and "Love's Made a Fool of You." But success was short-lived. Within months, Fuller was dead by asphyxiation from automobile fumes, and the group broke up.

Cassie Gaines

One of three musicians and four members in the entourage of Lynyrd Skynyrd who were killed in the 1977 crash of their private plane.

Steve Gaines (1949–1977)

Another member of Lynyrd Skynyrd to die in the plane crash. (Also dead were the pilot, co-pilot and two roadies.) The group was said to have partied its way through tours.

Tommy Gaither

An original vocalist of The Orioles, a rhythm-and-blues group from the early fifties who pioneered the doo-wop sound of early crossover hits, including, "Crying in the Chapel" and "Tell Me So." Gaither was killed in a car crash in 1950.

Marvin Gaye (1939–1984)

Born in Washington, D.C., Gaye received his musical roots singing in the choir and playing organ at the Washington church where his father was a minister. In 1962, he began a run of nearly 30 top 50 hits with the song, "Stubborn Kind of Fellow," and was well-known also for his duets with the late Tammi Terrell. Forty-four-year-old Gaye died of gunshot wounds, allegedly following a disagreement with his father, with whom his relationship was strained.

Lowell George (1945–1979)

Although this guitarist/singer had found success with the band called Little Feat, he was attempting a solo career when he was found dead of a heart attack caused by a heroin overdose.

John Glascock (1952–1979)

Glascock was Jethro Tull's bass player until dismissed due to ill health. He died in a London hospital at age 27.

Earl Grant (1931–1970)

Known for his hit tune, "The End," Grant met his end during an auto accident.

Pete Ham (1947–1975)

In the early seventies, as the Beatles' reign declined, Pete Ham formed Badfinger as a mop-top reincarnation. The group enjoyed several hits on the top 20, including "Day After Day" and "Come and Get It." By 1975 the group had fallen out of favor. After quitting the group, Ham committed suicide.

Roy Hamilton (1929–1969)

Born in Leesburg, Georgia, Hamilton moved to Jersey City, where he sang in church with the Searchlight Gospel Singers. His first secular hit came in 1954 with, "You'll Never Walk Alone," and his fame was instantaneous. He died of a heart attack in 1969.

Tim Hardin (1940–1980)

This talented singer and songwriter of the late sixties and early seventies died from a drug overdose. He was best known for writing "If I Were a Carpenter."

Alex Harvey (1935–1976)

Born on February 5, 1935, in the slums of Glasgow, this veteran rock entrepeneur attempted 36 occupations before becoming a musician. The Alex Harvey Band recorded a tremendous number of albums as Harvey pushed himself to the limit, despite collapsing while on a European tour in 1976. He died at 41, after suffering a heart attack in Belgium.

Les Harvey

Founding member and lead vocalist of the group, Stone the Crows, which produced its first album in 1970. Harvey was electrocuted by an improperly grounded microphone while on stage at the Top Rank Ballroom, in Swansea, Wales, during 1972. The accident took place before an audience of 12,000 students.

Donny Hathaway (1945–1979)

Hathaway fell or jumped to his death from a hotel window. He had enjoyed a successful career as lead vocalist of his own group, but was better known for a number of duets recorded with rock/blues artist Roberta Flack. Their biggest hit was "The Closer I Get to You," in 1978.

Jimi Hendrix (1942–1970)

Jimi Hendrix, who could play the guitar in what he called "a big flash of weaving and bobbing and groping and maiming and attacking," told writer Albert Goldman that he bought his first guitar from a drunken friend of his father's for only $5.00. However, rock's flamboyant superstar lost his life in but a flash at age 27 when he was declared dead on arrival at a London hospital. Hendrix once said, "If I seem free, it's because I'm always running," but he couldn't run fast enough to hold on to happiness. Drugs became his answer. Eric Burden, of the Animals, said of his friend Hendrix that he "used drugs to phase himself out of this life to go someplace else." On September 17, 1970, Hendrix drank some wine, smoked some pot, and then retired with the aid of a handful of Vesperin—sleeping pills. He subsequently choked on his own vomit.

Gregory Herbert (1950–1978)

A former member of Blood, Sweat and Tears, Herbert's death is attributed to a drug overdose.

Bob "The Bear" Hite (1945–1981)

The founder of the white blues band, Canned Heat, he broke into prominence at the Monterey Festival. Born in Torrance, California, he died a short 36 years later when his heart failed due to drug abuse.

Buddy Holly (1936–1959)

The white root of rock and roll, Holly was the voice behind the early Beatles. He died in an infamous airplane crash, February 3, 1959. Holly, and his comrades, the Big Bopper and Ritchie Valens, had decided to forego the bus which the rest of their entourage rode from Clear Lake, Iowa. They had wanted more time at their destination, Fargo, North Dakota, to do laundry and pick up their mail before their next gig.

James Honeyman-Scott

One of the originals of the four-man group, the Pretenders, he played guitar and keyboard, as well as doing vocals. The Pretenders were lauded as one of "pop's hottest new bands" in 1980; but Honeyman-Scott saw little of the fame and less of the glory when his life was snuffed out on June 16, 1982. He was in his mid-twenties. The cause of death was heart failure due to cocaine. The rocker acknowledged an addiction to speed as well, and was suffering from acute cirrhosis of the liver. Drummer Jim Chambers of the group said of Honeyman-Scott's death:

> So there you are. Silly, huh? The kid was in his mid-twenties, very talented. And it killed him. . . . It's synonomous with rock 'n' roll, this drug business. Everybody has their moments, but it really is a dead-end street. And people think, "It's okay, it's just coke." But it killed Jim.

Johnny Horton (1927–1960)

Johnny Horton died instantly in a car crash while returning from a performance in Texas. His song "Battle of New Orleans" was number one on the charts for six weeks in 1959, followed by another hit, "Sink the Bismark," in 1960. It wasn't until after his death, however, that his biggest hit, "North to Alaska," was released as the title song of a popular John Wayne movie. The tune was a million-seller.

Al Jackson (1945–1974)

A drummer with the band, Booker T and the MGs (Memphis Group), Jackson was shot to death by an intruder in his home.

Brian Jones (1943–1969)

Once the drive and musical inspiration of the Rolling Stones, Jones curtailed his musical career through the heavy use of LSD, and thus contributed little to the Stones' recordings after 1966. He became only a mop-headed mascot. *Rolling Stone* magazine eulogized Jones by saying: "What the Stones Sang, He Was." He died in his Sussex, England, mansion (once the home of A. A. Milne and Christopher Robin), the victim of drowning. However, it was the direct result of an overdose, and many of his vital organs suffered from fatty degeneration that soon would have killed him anyway. When The Who's Pete Townshend was asked to comment on Jones' death, he said, "Oh, it's a normal day for Brian, like he died every day, you know." Keith Richards, the Stones' guitarist, said of Jones, "Brian burnt out all his fuses a long time ago. He'd lived 26 years too fast. A whole lifetime in 26 years!"

Little Willie John (1937–1966)

Soul man Little Willie John had 14 bestsellers as a teenaged singer in the fifties. He died of pneumonia in prison, at 29.

Janis Joplin (1943–1970)

When Janis Joplin heard the sad news that Jimi Hendrix had died, due to drugs, she proclaimed, "Godammit! He beat me to it." A short two weeks later, Joplin was found, her troubled head split open from a fall, after overdosing on heroin. Country Joe McDonald had called the powerful young blues singer from Port Arthur, Texas, "a flashing light," but Joplin saw herself from the inside. She once said, "God, how did it happen? How did I turn into this person, man? . . . Sometimes I look at my face and I think it looks pretty rundown, but considering all I have been through, I don't look so bad." Joplin said all she wanted to do was to party and get stoned. She did accomplish that. At her death, her body was riddled with syphilis.

Terry Kath (1946–1978)

A guitarist/vocalist for the band Chicago, which was highly successful all through the seventies, he died in the Los Angeles home of a friend. In full view of his wife and a member of the sound crew, he accidentally shot himself in the head while playing with a gun.

Johnny Kidd (1939–1966)

The founder of Johnny Kidd (real name, Frederick Heath) and the Pirates, a successful British group in the late fifties. Though not a chart-topper, his group gained a reputation of legendary proportions for classic tunes such as "Shakin' All Over" and "Restless." The eye-patched singer had been reduced to a low-priced support role by the time of his death in a Lancashire, England, car crash.

Patsy Kline (1932–1963)

A crossover country and pop artist with two top hits to her name, "Crazy" and "I Fall to Pieces," Kline died in a plane crash, March 5, 1963.

Paul "Koss" Kossoff (1950–1976)

Originally with the British group Free, he played with a number of bands as a guitarist, then formed Back Street Crawler. Kossoff was the son of a well-known actor in Great Britain. It's thought the stress from that relationship may have pressured Kossoff into drugs. He tried unsuccessfully to kick his heroin habit. By the spring of 1976, at the age of 25, he had suffered two massive heart attacks, the second one killing him.

Kit Lambert (1936–1981)

The discoverer and original manager of The Who, as well as Jimi Hendrix, Lambert was once quoted as saying, "I hope I die before I get old." That quote is to be the title of a movie about the man who, before entering the music profession, was first known as the sole survivor of an Amazon jungle expedition massacred by headhunters. The son of a noted composer and conductor, he died of symptoms purported to have been sustained after a fall down a flight of stairs.

Martin Lamble

The drummer of the Fairport Connection, Lamble died in a wreck of the group's van.

John Lennon (1940–1980)

Singer/guitarist of the Beatles, Lennon went on to form his own band with wife, Yoko Ono. The Beatles used drugs to bolster their energy during hectic days and nights in Hamburg, Germany, where they sometimes played eight hours straight. By the time the Beatles split up, Lennon had a heavy heroin problem, took other drugs as well, and drank excessively—turning into a madman when he did. May Pang, Lennon's lover while he was married to Ono, describes the couple as nervous, paranoid and insecure. "Only when John was alone in bed with Yoko did he think he might be safe," she says, and adds they often stayed in their bedroom for days. Reggie Vinson, a songwriter who once played bass for the Beatles, says he never got to know Lennon well because of John's drinking problems. Commenting on the death of the superstar, Reggie says:

> If John had really known Jesus, I don't believe the fiery darts would have come. He lived in his own world, like Elvis. At the time he died, he was worth at least $235 million, but that didn't do him any good. . . . Lennon's untimely death shows you've got to be ready, you've got to accept Jesus. Otherwise, Satan can come at any time to kill, steal, and destroy.

On December 8, 1980, as Lennon and Yoko Ono arrived at New York's Dakota apartment house where they lived, a lone gunman stepped up to them and fired five shots into Lennon, killing him instantly. The assailant, Mark David Chapman, was immediately apprehended.

Frankie Lymon (1942–1968)

By the time this young black man was 14, he and his group, The Teenagers, had a string of top 10 single hits. Lymon was the darling of the rock and roll raconteurs, who dreamed up the myth that Lymon's hit tune "Why Do Fools Fall in Love?" was the result of the broken love affair of the 13-year-old. He was in the streets, so the story goes, singing the ditty with his buddies, and they decided to cut a demo. Boom! They had a hit! Wealth and fame did come Lymon's way almost in storybook fashion, and he had the status of Elvis Presley or Chuck Berry. When Lymon attempted a solo career, however, the book slammed shut, his career flopped, and Lymon became hooked on heroin. He died from an overdose, penniless and forgotten, a has-been at age 26.

Van McCoy (1941–1979)

This black pianist began his promising career in the early sixties as a writer, producer and arranger for some of the great performers of the time.

Then, during the disco craze, he began singing and performing on his own. His *Disco Baby* album included a song he wrote about a dance he'd never seen, "The Hustle," which the *New York Times* lauded as the "biggest dance record of the seventies." The Grammy winner pushed himself at a grueling pace and died of heart disease at the age of 38.

Jimmy McCullough

From the age of 16, McCullough was deeply immersed in the music scene, and was a veteran of at least five different bands when he joined Paul Mc-Cartney's Wings. (On the Wings' single, "Junior's Farm," "Junior" refers to McCullough.) McCullough drank heavily and also indulged in drugs. He was found dead, in September 1979, from an overdose of morphine mixed with both booze and pot.

Robbie McIntosh (1944–1974)

The drummer of the Scottish band, Average White Band, which he helped form, he was also a talented guitarist and vocalist. The band was just beginning to taste success, when the members attended a party in their honor; while there, McIntosh bought some heroin laced with strychnine. (Some say he thought it was cocaine.) McIntosh was found dead in his motel room the following day. Within five months of his death, the band had its first in a string of hits, "Pick Up the Pieces."

Ron "Pigpen" McKernan (1945–1973)

The drummer who inspired the acid rock band, Grateful Dead, with a passion for rhythm-and-blues, McKernan slowly poisoned himself with alcohol. By the time the Dead were confounding the music industry with their noncommercial marathon tracks, their free concerts, and their on-stage antics, McKernon had been forced out of the band. In 1971, at age 26, he'd ruined his liver, and his body was wasting away. When he died two years later, his internal organs were worn out, he weighed only 100 pounds, and he looked twice his age.

Clyde McPhatter (1933–1972)

Born in North Carolina, in 1933, McPhatter was a member of the Dominoes, the first group in rock and roll history to hit the pop charts (their song was "Sixty Minute Man"). In 1953, he helped form the original Drifters, who had a number of hit recordings. As success slipped from his fingers, however, he began to drink excessively. He died of a heart attack, but his liver and kidneys had also been destroyed by alcohol.

Bob Marley (1945–1981)

Bob Marley (and the Wailers) brought the Jamaican rhythms of reggae to rock music. *Rock and Roll Babylon* says of Marley:

Through reggae and its association with Rastafarianism—a belief that holds the late Emperor Haile Selassie of Ethiopia to be a god, uses marijuana (*ganja*) as a sacrament and preaches the eventual return of all blacks to Africa— Marley represented the unity of the Third World countries against the rest (p. 94).

His impact has been felt in many hits of the late seventies and early eighties. Marley died of cancer at the age of 36.

Sal Mineo (1939–1976)

Mineo, born in the Bronx, co-starred with James Dean in the tremendously successful, "Rebel Without a Cause," as well as several other motion pictures. He also experienced moderate success as a singer, and appeared on the top 10 charts with "Start Movin' " in 1957. He was found murdered, February 12, 1976, in Los Angeles, California.

Keith "Moon the Loon" Moon (1946–1978)

Moon was the drummer of the revolutionary, The Who. Their 1967 hit, "I Can See for Miles," launched them on the road to success. Moon's nickname was well-earned, and his stunts included smearing his own living room walls with human excrement, and several episodes of public indecent exposure. He died following a party thrown by Paul McCartney. The cause of death was listed as an overdose of Herminevrin, a drug sometimes used to help alcoholic patients. He had taken 32 tablets—twice the lethal dose—after consuming a steak in bed. When asked to comment on Moon's death, fellow band member Roger Daltrey said, "In a way, it was a sacrifice. We can do anything we want to now. I have very odd feelings . . . incredibly strong and at the same time, incredibly fragile" (*The Book of Rock Quotes*, p. 49). One can't help but wonder if Moon is feeling as free and strong.

Jim Morrison (1943–1971)

Morrison, the lead of the sensationally successful Doors, was a showman who tried in vain to shock and humiliate his teenybopper audiences, and in the process became rock's number-one sex idol. In *Freakshow*, Albert Goldman describes Morrison as "a hero of classic proportions" for the "messianic generation." He continues:

Abundantly gifted as a singer and songwriter, Morrison is, above all, a powerfully seductive public personality, at his most entrancing onstage. . . . Morrison—in any of his aspects—is energized by a ferocious eroticism. Totally uninhibited he appears to be always in a state of smoldering and eruptive sexual excitement.

Morrison, unfortunately, was destined to self-destruct. Goldman seemed to recognize that when he wrote in 1968:

Like all hero cults this latest one is deeply overshadowed with morbidity. Every week it fosters false reports from all over the country: reports that picture

Morrison blind from drug abuse, maimed from the waist down, locked up in an insane asylum or simply—as the UPI flashed across its wire service recently—"Jim Morrison dead. More later." The worshipers are growing impatient. They want to get on with the rites of mourning (pp. 344–5).

They hadn't long to wait. Morrison, his body wrecked by alcohol, resigned from the Doors and moved to Paris. In July 1971, his heart gave out and he died in his bath. His common-law wife, Pamela Courson, died of a heroin overdose three years later.

Billy Murcia

He was the original drummer of the New York Dolls, a major influence on the East Coast in the seventies. The New York Dolls performed as transvestites and had little or no musical training. Murcia died in 1972 when his girlfriend poured hot coffee down his throat in an effort to revive him during a drug-and-booze party.

Klaus Nomi

A seminal new-wave artist, Nomi died on August 6, 1983, the victim of AIDS. His music lives on, however, and his video, "Falling in Love Again," which *Rock Videos* magazine describes as having "evil sexual images" and women "brimming over with sexuality," has received airplay (April 1984, p. 50).

Phil Ochs (1940–1976)

Ochs was a well-known folk-protest singer and songwriter in the seventies, and a good friend of Bob Dylan. He wrote a number of songs recorded by other artists, but his most well-known was "Draft Dodger Rag." By 1968, Ochs was so paranoid that he suspected the Mafia and the CIA of having a contract out on him; he therefore carried, everywhere, a lead pipe, a hammer and a pitchfork. Insisting there were snipers on the roof, he also required the bartenders in his fashionable SoHo bar to carry meat hooks. In 1976, he performed the ultimate act of paranoia—he committed suicide.

Berry Oakley (1948–1972)

Berry was the bass player in the Allman Brothers Band, best known for its 1973 hit, "Ramblin' Man." That song could have been used to describe Oakley, who had a penchant for the fast life and motorcycles. In the autumn of 1972, before the song had even enjoyed success, Oakley crashed his bike in Macon, Georgia. He refused hospital treatment, and died of a brain hemorrhage. The group Duane Allman had once described as "six enlightened rogues" broke up amid chaos in 1976—despite a success that included five gold albums.

Felix Pappalardi (1942–1983)

Former drummer of Mountain, and noted record producer, he was shot to death.

Gram Parsons (1946–1973)

At 26, Parsons—a guitarist and vocalist with both the Byrds and the Flying Burrito Brothers, as well as a performer on two albums with Emmylou Harris—died from multiple drug use. Found in his body after his death were morphine, amphetamines and cocaine.

William Powell

One of the original members of the O'Jays, which were one of soul music's long-lived groups. Their number-one hit, "Love Train," topped the charts in 1973. Powell was dead by May 1977.

Elvis Presley (1935–1977)

Presley was born in East Tupelo, Mississippi. He was a twin, but his brother, Jessie Garon, was stillborn. Elvis' given name was Elvis Aaron. From the age of four or five, Presley was said to have heard his brother's voice many times, supposedly telling him to be good. Presley biographer Albert Goldman contends this presence soon affected Presley's personality to the point that eventually he split into two distinct characters—the Christian do-gooder who joined President Nixon in his 1970 war on drugs as a "special agent," and the orgiastic merrymaker who sometimes partied with whole chorus lines in his suites. In the book *Elvis: What Happened?* the man is portrayed as having had an obsession with death and an irrational hatred for any singing star he perceived as being a threat to his career. In a post-mortem conference, Dave Hebler, Presley's former friend and bodyguard, said in defense, "How do you protect a man from himself? . . . I think in many ways Elvis was a tormented man. I think he was a victim of himself, the image and the legend." That myth hit a pinnacle in 1973, when Elvis gave what will probably be remembered as his most spectacular performance. It was also an incredible feat of marketing for his manager, Colonel Parker. Elvis' *Aloha Satellite Show*, beamed via satellite from Honolulu to an estimated worldwide audience of over 1.5 billion, was the most expensive special ever taped, but it netted Elvis a cool million—plus sales of a double LP version of the show. A short four years later, at age 42, the legend died.

Dickie Pride

One of the early "stable" boys of British promoter, Larry Parnes, Pride's trademark was always a porkpie hat and a battered leather jacket. He was one of the earliest English rockers to become hooked on heroin, and when his antics began to cause problems, Parnes quickly dropped him. He died in obscurity, from a drug overdose.

Carl Radle

Fired from Eric Clapton's band in 1979, after years of working together, Radle's life quickly deteriorated. The bass player died a heroin addict, in June 1980, suffering from a related kidney infection.

Danny Rapp (1941–1983)

The lead singer of Danny and the Juniors, which scored an international million-seller in 1957, "At the Hop." The group followed up with another hit, "Rock 'n' Roll Is Here to Stay," but then came a string of boring dance-tune failures. Finally, in 1963, the group disbanded. Rapp tried to stage a comeback some years later. However, when his first concert proved unsuccessful, he committed suicide on April 4, 1983.

Otis Redding (1941–1967)

A successful soul/rock singer, Redding, and five teenage members of his backup party, died when his private plane crashed just four miles short of their destination, Madison, Wisconsin. The plane sank to the bottom of Lake Monona. Approximately 4,500 people attended the star's funeral. Ironically, his biggest hit, "[Sittin' on] The Dock of the Bay," became a number-one smash hit after his death, selling four million copies.

Phil Reed

Singer in the duo, Flo and Eddie, died from a fall from his hotel window at age 25.

Jim Reeves (1924–1964)

His velvet-toned vocals made Reeves one of the most successful country/rock crossover artists, and his 1960 hit, "He'll Have to Go," held the number-two spot on the charts for weeks. He was killed while piloting his own aircraft. The plane went down during a heavy rain, crashing in heavy brush.

Keith Relf (1943–1976)

This former lead singer of the important British band, Yardbirds, also founded the group Renaissance. Relf was electrocuted in his bathtub by a shock from his electric guitar.

Randy Rhoads (1958–1983)

A songwriter and guitarist, from a religious English family, Rhoads was part of the original Quiet Riot, then joined Ozzy Osbourne's band. Rhodes, who had been named Best New Talent in *Guitar Player* magazine's 1981 readers' poll, died in a Florida plane crash shortly after agreeing to sing on a Quiet Riot reunion LP. He was 25.

J. P. "The Big Bopper" Richardson (1935–1959)

The Big Bopper's best-known hit was "Chantilly Lace." Undoubtedly, he would have gone on to a successful career had his life not ended at age 23, in the same plane crash that killed Buddy Holly.

Minnie Riperton (1948–1979)

A number-one song, "Lovin' You," put Riperton's band, Rotary Connection, on the charts in 1975. However, this lead singer died of cancer at the age of 31.

Bon Scott (1947–1980)

Scott was the lead singer for AC/DC, Australia's heavy metal group, and his vocals and macho image provided the band with much of its appeal. He was found dead in his car on the outskirts of London, the victim of too much alcohol on a bitterly cold winter night. According to *Rolling Stone*, however, his band hardly missed a beat. Said guitarist Malcolm Young, "I thought, 'Well, . . . I'm not gonna sit around mopin' all . . . year.' So I rang up Angus Young [also of AC/DC], and said, 'Do you wanna come back and rehearse?' This was two days afterward. And I'm sure if it had been one of us, Bon would have done the same thing" (December 25, 1980).

James "Shep" Sheppard

The vocalist on "A Thousand Miles From Home," a 1957 hit by The Heartbeats, and the 1961 hit (reproduced later by the Jackson Five), "Daddy's Home." That second tune which was recorded by the group he founded, Shep and the Limelights, was a 1961 American smash hit. Following some lesser successes, the group split in 1963. Sheppard was found beaten to death in a car parked at the side of the Long Island Expressway on January 24, 1970.

Billy Stewart (1938–1970)

Stewart and his band had enjoyed a string of hits in the late sixties—11 U.S. solo chart entries—including the song, "Summertime." He and three of his band were killed on January 17, 1970, when their car went over a parapet of a bridge. He was 32.

Rory Storm (1940–1974)

This one-time Merseybeat bandleader founded Rory Storm and the Hurricanes, the group Ringo Starr played in before joining the Beatles. Storm was found dead in his home with his head in the oven, the result of a suicide pact with his mother, whose body was discovered nearby.

Stu Sutcliffe

Sutcliffe played guitar with the Beatles in the group's earliest days. He was with the group when it recorded its first three singles in Hamburg, Germany, in May 1961. A year later, he was dead of a brain tumor.

Vinnie Taylor

Vinnie Taylor was a guitarist and vocalist with the very successful group, ShaNaNa, who had their own fifties-oriented TV show in the seventies. Taylor died of an drug overdose in 1974.

Tammi Terrell (1946–1970)

Terrell enjoyed a number of successes in the late sixties, including several duets with Marvin Gaye. Some of her classics include, "Your Precious Love" and "If I Could Build My Whole World Around You." She died after incurring brain damage from a fall down a flight of stairs.

Gary Thain

Thain was the bassist for the Miller Anderson band, and Captain Jack Dupree, before joining Uriah Heep in 1972. He died from a drug overdose in 1983.

Ritchie Valens (1941–1959)

Valens' career was just beginning to soar when he was killed in the Buddy Holly plane crash.

Ronnie Van Zant (1949–1977)

A place crash on October 20, 1977, killed this lead singer and founder of Lynyrd Skynyrd, along with several other members of the group and its road crew.

John Simon "Sid Vicious" Ritchie (1958–1979)

A punk rocker, absorbed in self-mutilation and homosexuality, Sid Vicious was bassist for the Sex Pistols. According to *Top Ten*, "Vicious allegedly knifed his girlfriend to death, and then took his own life through a drug overdose. The whole fiasco was over in a few months" (p. 267). Vicious was 21 when he died; his girlfriend, Nancy Spungen, was 20.

Gene Vincent (1934–1971)

Vincent was an early American rocker who made it big in England and became one of the most influential leather-and-grease rockers of the fifties. His biggest single was the 1956 release, "Be Bob a LuLu." He and his band were known to drink heavily, cause riots, and destroy motel rooms. An Army injury, reinjured in the same accident that killed Eddie Cochran, became ulcerated, causing Vincent severe pain. Pain, and the alcohol he drank to relieve it, left his career and life in a shambles. He died, fat and debilitated, of a seizure resulting from a perforated ulcer.

Thomas Wayne

Wayne sang with a fifties group known as The DeLons. Their tune "Tragedy" hit the top 10 in 1959. Wayne's death was listed as due to accidental causes.

Dinah Washington (1924–1963)

One of jazz and blues music's most influential singers, Washington also sang a number of hits with Brooke Benton and with Lionel Hampton. She recorded several top 10 hits before her untimely death by an overdose of sleeping pills.

Clarence White (1944–1973)

From 1968, White was a guitarist and vocalist for the Byrds, who brought the social commentary of folk music to the popular medium of rock and roll, thus creating "folk rock." White died of a stomach hemorrhage when hit by a car before his 30th birthday.

Danny Whitten (1945–1972)

This guitarist/vocalist of the seventies band, Crazy Horse, died from drug-related causes.

Billy Williams

A popular hit singer of the late fifties, when "pop" was becoming rock and roll, Williams sang, among other hits, "I'm Gonna Sit Right Down and Write a Letter" and "Goodnight Irene." He died October 17, 1972.

Hank Williams (1923–1953)

Hank Williams, Sr. is remembered most for his contribution to country and western, but as others of his peers, Williams had an influence on folk and rock music as well, from Bob Dylan to the Byrds. He died in the backseat of a car on New Year's Day, 1953, of a drug overdose and heart failure. He was wasted away to a near-skeleton, the subject of his own monologue recording, "Too Many Parties and Too Many Pals."

Larry Williams (1935–1979)

"Bony Moroni" and "Short Fat Fannie" are two of the hits Williams is most remembered for. He was a successful singer in the late fifties and early sixties. Unfortunately, he also ran a highly successful Hollywood prostitution ring. In 1979, he was shot—either by his own hand or by a member of a crime syndicate.

Paul Williams (1939–1973)

Soul music's most popular male vocal group in the last twenty-plus years has been the Temptations. Paul Williams, an original member of the group, profited from the group's success of more than 15 recordings in the top 10. However, success wasn't enough for Williams. In 1971, he quit the group, claiming medical reasons. On August 17, 1973, he was found dead in his car, the victim of murder or suicide.

Chuck Willis (1928–1958)

Willis earned the title "King of Western Swing" early in the fifties, but also influenced both rock and blues. Some of his crossover hits included, "C. C. Rider," "What Am I Living For?" and "Hang Up My Rock and Roll Shoes." Suffering from a stomach ailment, he unfortunately delayed necessary surgery, and subsequently died on the operating table at the age of 30.

Alan "Blind Owl" Wilson (1943–1970)

A Boston native, Wilson joined Bob Hite's successful bluesy rock band, Canned Heat, in 1967. Canned Heat was quickly recognized as the leader in blues/rock in the late sixties. The vocalist died in Hite's backyard in September 1970, from accidental drug poisoning.

Jackie Wilson (1936–1984)

Singer Jackie Wilson was once billed as "Mr. Excitement." He suffered a heart attack and collapsed on stage in 1975 during a performance with Dick Clark's "Good Ol' Rock and Roll Revival" in Cherry Hill, N.J. He slipped into a coma, and emerged a year later, incapacitated. Among Wilson's hit songs were "Lonely Teardrops," "Higher and Higher," and "To Be Loved." Wilson again entered the hospital on January 8, 1984, and died 14 days later at 49 years of age.

Dennis Wilson (1944–1983)

Dennis Wilson, the only real surfer of the sixties success, the Beach Boys, gave his own eulogy in 1965: "They say I live a fast life. Maybe I just like a fast life. I wouldn't give it up for anything in the world. It won't last forever, either. But the memories will" (*People*, January 16, 1984). He was 20 then, and certainly must have thought he had plenty of time—maybe not forever, but plenty of time. Fewer than 18 years later, his lifeless body was pulled from the marina he'd loved. Wilson had squandered millions of dollars on friends and good times during his brief life. He had married five times, and his last marriage was to Shawn Love, the 19-year-old daughter of his first cousin and fellow Beach Boy, Mike Love. She bore his fourth child, which was born a year before their marriage. He'd been known for his alcohol problem, and used drugs as well. Several days before his death, he had checked into a detox unit. The doctor who ran the program told *People* magazine that Wilson was "drinking about a fifth of vodka a day and doing a little coke [cocaine]" (January 16, 1984). Wilson's body, clad only in cutoff jeans and a face mask, was found in 13 feet of bone-chilling 58-degree water. Friends said he had been drinking heavily. Authorized biographer Byron Preiss quoted the dead surfer/singer: "The Beach Boys created a safe place for people . . . a place for people to go and kind of drift and enjoy themselves" (*USA Today*, December 30, 1983). How tragic that Wilson never found that safe place.

Chris Wood (1944–1983)

Chris Wood was the flute and saxophone player for the British rhythm-and-blues group Traffic during its heyday in the late sixties. He died of liver disease.

A Living Wage

Rock and roll, with its propensity for destructive lifestyles—drugs, promiscuity, alcohol, odd living situations, and even odder hours—has claimed more than its fair share of casualties. (In fact, a good number of the deaths listed here as accidental or caused by common ailments, were actually due to either drug- or alcohol-related problems, making the picture even more grim.)

A common thread that runs through nearly all of the deaths we have just reviewed is the element of tragedy. So many lives cut short—wasted. And yet, that's not the real tragedy. The real tragedy is that there is no evidence these people knew the true meaning of life. While here on earth they pursued happiness, even chased it headlong, but the real joy that was available to them is probably lost forever. Naturally, we can hope the "stubbornness of their hearts" ended as they approached the close of their lives, and that they accepted Christ into their lives. But the evidence shows the chances are slim. Those who curse God in life tend to curse Him in death as well, and "foxhole conversions," while dramatic, are rare.

If you have been chasing some of the same rainbows, and still haven't found the source of real happiness, Chapter 15 can help you find it. Turn to that chapter now, if you have been searching. Otherwise, it's time to move on to the last of our four critiques of rock music: the graphics. And as they say on television, "The scenes you are about to see are not meant for young viewers. Parental discretion is advised." Unfortunately, most of these albums and videos can be found in the bedrooms of 10-year-olds.

10

Graphics

It's been said that a picture is worth a thousand words. Modern merchandisers have always applied that principle to their packaging, and rock merchandisers are no different. They carefully design album covers so the pictures serve a twofold purpose: to "hype" or sell the record, and to provide an instant glimpse at what the buyer will receive for his money. Why, then, do so many album covers depict life's seamier side and promote the bizarre and the occult? What are rock music album covers saying?

God tells us we are to hate sin, and Ephesians 4 exhorts us to put off the "old man" (our sinful unregenerate nature) and put on the "new man" (our revitalized spiritual nature). Is exposing ourselves to the pornography and spiritualism prevalent on rock music albums putting off the "old man"? Do we show hatred for sin when we have smut-covered record albums stacked beside our stereos? Can occultic symbols affect us? Will they harm our relationship with God?

Nearly everyone, from the artist to the consumer, would agree that album art is important. Though the maxim "You can't judge a book by its cover" may hold true for books, the cover of an album gives the consumer a preview of the contents. It is the final sales tool employed to push the product, and it is very carefully designed.

First, the artist listens to the record, then to other recordings by the same group. Then he discusses the recording with the producers and the performers, trying to get a feel for what the group is trying to say. Then he "roughs" sketches of possible covers. Once the preliminary work is done, he again meets with the producers and the group until a consensus is reached. The final art or photography is carefully scrutinized. An album cover is not a quickly plastered together product. It is rather a carefully planned statement of intent and content.

The selection of album covers we have included is fairly representative of the market today (We have chosen not to reproduce some of them because they contain nudity). We could have shown scores of other covers representing each of the themes which seem to saturate rock music: nihilism, commercialism, rebellion and violence, hedonism, occultism and alcohol/drug abuse.

As you examine them, ask yourself, what do they really promote? What is the real force behind the dark images portrayed in rock music's album covers? Do I want to, by purchasing these, promote the causes and themes visible in the album art?

1. Quiet Riot's *Metal Health* became the first heavy metal debut album to reach the top 10 since Led Zeppelin's in 1969. Well-received songs from this album include, "Cum Feel the Noize," "Danger Zone," and "Let's Get Crazy." Vocalist Kevin DuBrow said of the LP, "On this *Quiet Riot* record, we said, '[expletive deleted] it with this pop [expletive deleted], we're going ballsy.' "[1]

2. Formed in England in 1975, the Hot Rods is sometimes referred to as an English version of the Ramones, the seminal punk rock group from the U.S. which created a musical upheaval in Great Britain. Eddie and the Hot Rods plays basic three-chord rock and roll, loud, hard and depressive.

1

2

3

4

3. The suicide rate among 15- to 19-year-olds has increased 200% in the last two decades, and as many as 500,000 teenagers attempt suicide each year.[2] Almost everyone has suicidal thoughts from time to time; acting on those thoughts, however, is a different matter. If a teenager is feeling depressed, unloved, or possibly has trouble communicating, it sometimes doesn't take much to trigger an actual suicide attempt. The despair and hopelessness sung about by groups such as the Suicide Commandoes has been known to incite such an attempt.

4. *Circus* magazine says if there were a school for heavy metallurgists to earn their diplomas, Iron Maiden would be on the faculty—with studs, leather and demonic posturing. Formed in 1977, this heavy metal prototype gained popularity when its single "Running Free" hit the charts. The chained, demented soul depicted on Maiden's *Piece of Mind* album, combined with the nihilistic lyrics, leads one to wonder if he is a reflection of the performer's own interior condition.

5. Vincent Furnier—a k a Alice Cooper—is the master of the macabre and an old hand at media hype. He struck gold in 1970 with the album *Love It To Death,* followed by *School's Out,* which came wrapped in disposable women's panties. As his stage shows became more gruesome, he attempted to prove his normalcy by chumming with Mr. Showbiz Establishment, Bob Hope. Constantly upstaging himself, however, proved trite, and Cooper seemed to lose favor with his young fans. He has, however, sold more than 60 million records. And his latest come back, *Da Da* has received good reviews.

6. For some time after its 1975 debut, Blondie was a fashion-setting, trendy, New Wave band led by blond sex symbol, Debby Harry, and her boyfriend, Chris Stein. Although the band has always insisted Blondie is a group venture, it is Harry's trampy, commercial appeal and sexually suggestive stage

5

6

manner that has gained media attention. The band exploited her image of liberated sexuality with a poster of Harry in a see-through top, and a caption that reads: "Wouldn't You Like To Rip Her To Shreds?"

7. In Blondie's biography, *Making Tracks*, vocalist Debbie Harry claimed she created the "pin-up" girl image, a character who "was primarily having fun. . . . Even if she was getting ready to jump off the Empire State Building, Blondie was going to have fun on the way down."[4] When that image failed to stir further record sales, Harry tried a new approach, hence the gruesome look on her solo album, *Koo Koo*. Explaining the shift, she said: "It's partially so I can maintain my sanity. . . . I mean, God forbid anybody should take it seriously."[5]

8. KISS—the personification of crass commercialism gone to a costume party—was one of America's best-selling bands in the seventies. Eleven of KISS's 18 albums have been certified gold, and 6 have been certified platinum. Their stage shows have included antics such as Simmons' fire-breathing and blood-vomiting, as well as vivid sexual demonstrations and sado-masochistic enactments of their lyrics. *The Rock Who's Who* says of KISS: "A virtual rock industry themselves, KISS merchandising includes T-shirts, comics, jewelry, and films . . . as well as albums. . . . Universally attacked by critics, KISS nonetheless endeared themselves to legions of prepubescent fans."[6]

9. Good-bye greasepaint! In a commercial move designed to attract a new following, KISS adopted a relatively well-washed look in October 1983, a move planned to coincide with the release of the LP *Lick It Up*, as well as an appearance on MTV—sans cosmetics. Though they now look like the average Joe, only taller, they say their music will remain as distinctive as ever. Paul Stanley, one of the group's originators, told *Circus* magazine why he liked KISS's brand of hard rock: "It appeals to you on a very low level. There's a lot of animal in all of us, and you're a lot healthier if you let it out."[7]

7   8

9

10

11

12

10. Move over KISS, here comes Motley Crue! No sooner had KISS washed off the makeup and traded in the studded leather, than Motley Crue rose up to fill the "void." In 1983, Canadian customs officials confiscated Crue's truckload of chains, spikes and leather as deadly weapons.[8] Undaunted, the group has pushed on, with two successful LPs—*Theatre of Pain* and *Shout at the Devil*. Still, the group contends they're not in it for the money—Mick Mars: "I need mucho chicks, I'm always horny"; Nikki Sixx, formerly of L.A.'s Ratt: "We're not in it for the money, we're in it for fun—and the chicks"; and Vince Neil: "I'm obsessed with sex, fast cars and faster women."[9]

11. Steven Gaines, co-author of *The Love You Make*, the Beatles' biography, said of Paul McCartney: "Of all of them, Paul was the only one who really had show business in his blood. . . . [For Paul] it was a rush, it was fun, it was power. I think he knew . . . how to manipulate the press."[10] One music reviewer called McCartney's *Pipes of Peace* album a leap "into a vat of shmaltz." Yet, McCartney has always had a flare for turning love into money. The inside

cover of the album reads: "In love all of life's contradictions dissolve and disappear." As one reviewer said, "I believe it, but I believe it more when it's less glossy."[11]

12. Though supposedly lovesongsters, the Beatles were not past using a little violence and slick humor-feigning-child-abuse to sell an album. On the original album cover of *Yesterday, Today and Tomorrow*, they were featured in butcher's coats, surrounded by decapitated baby doll bodies. Ironically, the album was not condemned by the general public, but was recalled after protests by meat packers. Today the cover is valued at several hundred dollars. Album cover infamy came later, when the Beatles released *Sgt. Pepper's Lonely Hearts Club Band,* which is covered with allusions to drugs, and *Abbey Road,* with its 25 subtle suggestions that McCartney was dead—both were nothing more than sales gimmicks.

13. Today, 70% of violent crimes are committed by youths under the age of 17. According to Judas Priest's musicians, however, their concerts do the public a "service" by draining "some of the aggression out of the systems of their audiences. So they put on elaborate, violent stage shows," according to *Hit Parader*.[12] The band likes to view itself as an inspirational model of "controlled decadence." However, one of its albums was advertised with the headline: "I scream. You scream. We all scream for vengeance. And for Judas Priest, revenge is sweet!"

14. This, and other heavy metal LP covers, portraying grisly, ritualistically violent scenes, prompted music columnist Bill McAllister to conclude: ". . . the packaging of many heavy metal albums is the ethical equivalent of yelling fire in a crowded theater: Because a few idiots insist on expressing themselves so crudely, innocent people could be victimized."[13]

13
14

15

16

15. Since the formation of AC/DC in 1974, Malcolm and Angus Young (Angus shown here getting his battery charged!), Cliff Williams, Phil Rudd, and Brian Johnson (who replaced the drug-wasted Bon Scott) have built a reputation as the ultimate people's band. *Hit Parader* magazine says these men will go to any lengths to please their fans. Bon Scott, the group's original lead vocalist, once said, "Our subject matter is what any kid out on the street might experience in a day's living."[14] Yet, with songs and albums presenting subjects such as "The Jack" (an ode to VD), *If You Want Blood*, "Beating Around the Bush," "Dirty Deeds Done Dirt Cheap," and "Gimme A Bullet," one can't help but agree with *Circus,* which says it's a "wonder their LPs didn't come in plain brown wrappers."[15]

16. Though this album cover once again deals with AC/DC's desire to create an electrifying performance, there is a not-so-subtle use of subliminal sexual stimulus, in that the lettering of the title, designed specifically to stand out from the rest of the lightly sketched drawing, forms not just the word "flick," but also a slang word for intercourse. According to media expert Brian Wilson Key, subliminal sexual messages of this type are often used, visibly or undetectably, to snare the consumer, and ultimately sell the product.

17. The treatment of lust as love is Ted Nugent's "thing." On the album *Cat Scratch Fever,* the theme of sadomasochism (gaining sexual pleasure through pain) becomes obvious once the album is opened to reveal Nugent being scarred by a woman's long nails. About his song, "Violent Love," which has been banned on some AM stations, he said, "Man, I write these songs so quickly it's incredible! The ideas just flow outta me."[16] It's not so surprising when you read in Scripture, "For out of the overflow of his heart [a man's] mouth speaks" (Luke 6:45, NIV).

17

18

19 | *Jungle! Jungle!* album cover depicts Annabelle Lwin reclining nude, with fellow band members, beside a lake.

20a

20b

18. "Nothing could have prepared us for the liberating lewdness of *Dirty Mind*," says *Rolling Stone*. Yet Prince had used songs about incest and oral sex to sing his way into the top 100. He was nominated in several categories for the American Music Awards, and his *1999* LP was chosen one of the top 10 albums by *Rock* magazine, who said of the recording, "[It] put funk in the mainstream and sex on the turntable."[18]

19. Since Annabelle Lwin left BowWowWow in 1983, they seem to have much less Wow in their collective Bow. According to *Rock* magazine, however, the group goes on, as does its original female vocalist.[19] Lwin first joined the group at the invitation of rock manager/exploiter Malcolm McClaren, who promptly asked the 14-year-old to strip for the cover of their debut album.

20. Alice Cooper was the first rock act to achieve widespread popularity *because of* an intentionally encouraged distasteful image," says *The Rock Who's Who*.[20] His group was also the first to dupe the unwitting media into promoting its negative image for profit. His *Muscle of Love* album (the title song is about masturbation), which went gold, came in a plain brown cardboard cover. However, inside was a scene depicting "The Institute of Nude Wrestling," and the band supposedly living the good life of sailors on shore leave. Cooper's much-publicized tours have been the biggest money-making ventures of rock history.

21. A late seventies "hard rock" band, Foreigner quickly became known for its top singles records, platinum-selling LP's, and biting, sexist tunes. Foreigner issued this album, *Head Games*, in 1979, and it was a bestseller instantly, with singles hits, "Dirty White Boy," "Head Games," and "Women." The obviously frightened teenybopper on the cover has good reason to be, as Foreigner sings that women belong "in the back seat." The album title is an obvious reference to oral sex.

22. The Scorpions released this album in West Germany, with title and lyric content graphically displayed by the cover art. Though the LP was later denied release in the U.S., due to the blatant child-pornography, the States are hardly exonerated. In 1977, up to one-third of U.S. pornography profits came from "kiddie-porn," with an estimated 1.2 million children involved in its creation.[21] Not surprisingly, the largest group of rape victims fall between the ages of 10 and 19 years.[22] The Scorpions could have used the demented Marquis De Sade's words for an endorsement: "Do not all passions require victims?"

23. Mick Jagger of the Rolling Stones seems to be unconcerned if his daughter becomes a sexual victim. He's been quoted as saying he wants his daughter to have sex "at an early age."[23] He also openly admits he entices his audience

21

22

Virgin Killer album cover depicts a nude, preadolescent girl in a pose suggesting sexual victimization.

Undercover album cover depicts a strategically covered nude woman.

23

24

25

26

"much the same as a girl's strip tease dance."[24] On the album *Undercover,* co-Stone, Keith Richards, says, "There's a lot of blood on this one. It's a very gory album."[25] That gore, says *Rock* magazine, includes the "stomach-churning saga of a man who hacks up his girlfriend, eats her, makes reference to *The Texas Chainsaw Massacre,* then turns around and proclaims 'I want to sing/I want to dance . . . and make some love.' Arrgh."[26] The Stones seem to have an endless supply of this sort of lyric, as they've signed a $25 million contract with CBS records that will not expire until the band members are in their fifties.

24. Many of Queen's album covers are too sexually graphic for display here. *Body Language,* which makes use of a nude body design, was censored by many retailers.

25. Black Sabbath has endured longer than any other heavy metal act, and

27   28

has become one of rock and roll's all-time favorite concert acts, though it has
lost two of its main vocalists, Ozzy Osbourne and Ronnie James Dio. This
album, *Sabbath Bloody Sabbath*, is covered with satanic symbols the group
is known for: the "lightning flash" letter (sometimes called the Satan sign,
and used in the AC/DC logo as well), the number 666 (which stands for the
Antichrist), and the demon-like creatures hovering over the naked human
about to sell his soul to Lucifer.

26. Journey has produced some 10 albums in its 10-plus years, incorporating
a commercially-oriented style and a reputation for million-sellers. On each
of its earlier albums has appeared a beatle, known in Egyptology as a scarab,
representing the soul and reincarnation.

27. Journey's *Frontiers* was the fifth best-selling album in 1983, and includes
Journey's renowned hard-rocking sound. It's different from its predecessors,
however, in that the cover of the LP does not contain the usual scarab. Instead,
there's a graphic which Columbia Records' publicist described as "a little blue
fellow called 'The Ally.' "[27] Only the band knows the significance of the new
mascot.

28. New Jersey-born Gary Wright helped form Spooky Tooth, a British pro-
gressive rock band best known for the tune "Evil Woman." After the group's
dissolution in 1974, Wright shifted from the frenetic scream-vocals of his
Tooth days, to the other-worldly, mystic style evidenced on this *Dream Weaver*
album. The change brought the singer a gold record, but it also demonstrated
his belief in astral projection (out of body experiences).

29. Uriah Heep was launched in 1970, a stylistic offspring of Deep Purple
and Led Zeppelin. Its first album, and most subsequent offerings, have been

29 30

31 32

skewered almost unanimously by rock critics, but the group has maintained its popularity with fans. Many of its recordings contain occultic references and the cover representation of a demon on this album could hardly have come out of someone's imagination. Researchers of ancient civilizations have found the same demonic art, the same type of devil head, depicted in bygone cultures.

30. Earth, Wind and Fire is one of the first black rock/soul bands to crossover into the white market, and by the late seventies its brand of danceable, brassy music was producing a number of hit tunes and albums. While the group espouses a hopeful attitude toward brotherhood and happiness, it exhibits, through lyrics and album covers, that its means to those commendable ends often include the use of the occult and spiritism. Each one of its album covers bears some (if not several) occultic symbols, as shown on the cover of *Spirit*. It depicts pyramids, the supposed energy and life-force producers in the occult.

31. Alice Cooper, whose stage act has earned him the title of the "Grand Old Man of Rubber Chickens (Rock and Roll Branch)" by the *Who's Who in Rock* almanac, uses many grisly symbols on his albums. *Billion Dollar Babies,* which has one of the mildest covers, enjoyed advance sales of over one million dollars. It includes the song, "I Love the Dead," an anthem of necrophilia.

32. Mick Jagger of the Rolling Stones once said, "We're moving after the mind, as are most of the new groups." When the Stones dried up musically, in the sixties, and nearly went bankrupt despite revenues that topped $350 million, the group tried a new tack. Though its records were still drenched in drugs and sex, occultism began to be used as well, hence *Their Satanic Majesties Request* (shown here), *Beggar's Banquet* and *Goat's Head Soup.* By 1981-82, the band's revenues may well have topped $100 million—not counting record sales![28] Now in mid-life and supposedly respectable, the Stones have power, riches and a new generation of fans.

33. Named Singer of the Year in 1982 by *Billboard* magazine, Ozzy Osbourne helped promote his early records by biting the head off a dove in front of the CBS Record executives and biting the head off a bat at a concert. This album, *Speak of the Devil,* shows him supposedly consuming human flesh; others portray him in heavily occult themes.

34. Though born into poverty, Ozzy Osbourne got an early break in the music business—tuning horns in an auto factory. When he first started singing in a local band, he supplemented his income with petty theft and shoplifting. Eventually, he was caught, convicted and imprisoned for three months.[29] After the prison stint, Osbourne formed Black Sabbath, and eventually branched

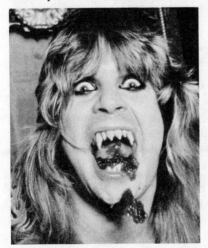

34

33

35a

35b

36

37

off with his own band. *Bark at the Moon,* Osbourne's LP which proclaims
"Ozzy Unleashed!" on the cover, leads one to wonder: which is worse, his bark
or his bite?

35. Led Zeppelin defined the term "heavy metal." With nine chart-topping
albums, it reigned over metal music until 1980, when its crazed drummer,
John Bonham, died of alcohol abuse. During that time, Zep's greatest hit was
"Stairway to Heaven" (1971), a mystical ballad which reflected the band's
general interest in mythology, as well as guitarist Jimmy Page's deeper dabbling in the occult. *Presence* became Zep's first certified platinum award-
winner in 1976.[30] The album is virtually blank on the outside, but opens to
reveal 15 or 20 common life scenes—home, school, or business—each including an oddly-shaped object as its focal point. The object's design is supposed
to symbolize the force that enabled the band to so profoundly affect audiences—a power simply referred to as a "presence." Robert Plant has gone on,
following the group's demise, to carve out a lucrative solo career with two
gold albums and sold-out concert dates.

36. No longer recording or touring, but still selling many records, the Doobie Brothers' name was conjured up during a pot-smoking session. One band member recalls, "We were passing around a joint—a 'doobie' [slang term for a marijuana cigarette]—and someone said, 'We're all doobie brothers.' We were called 'Pud' before that."[31] The album cover pictures a partially smoked joint.

37. Drugs have been the subject of cover art and lyrics since rock and roll was born. Ray Charles sang "Let's Go Get Stoned"; the Beatles recorded "Lucy in the Sky With Diamonds"; Peter Tosh sang "Legalize It" (marijuana); AC/DC sang "Have a Drink on Me"; KISS recorded "Cold Gin"; and Pink Floyd extolled drugs in "Comfortably Numb." Though drug overdoses caused the deaths of Al Wilson (Canned Heat); Gram Parsons and Gary Thain (Uriah Heep); Vinnie Taylor (ShaNaNa); Keith Moon (The Who); Lowell George (Little Feat); Dennis Wilson (Beach Boys); Tommy Bolin (Deep Purple); Elvis Presley; Janis Joplin; Jimi Hendrix; and scores of other talented rock stars, drug use continues to be a part of the rock scene, and is praised in the music and depicted on album covers. This album photo reveals a young man giving himself a heroin fix.

Images of a Dark World

The covers you have just seen are but a miniscule sampling. There are so many more covers, some too perverse to show, that graphically portray rock's dark world. Nazareth has produced an LP cover displaying various occult symbols, alongside a depiction of Christ hanging upside down on a cross. Alan Parson Project's album cover of *Eve* shows three women dressed in black wedding veils. A close look at their faces, however, confirms all three have the scabs of syphilis on their otherwise beautiful faces.

The original cover of *Mom's Apple Pie*, by the band with the same name, featured "Mom" holding a pie with one slice removed. Hidden among the apples was a drawing of a vagina. After retailers protested, subsequent copies showed the slice bricked up with barbed wire around it, and tears in "Mom's" eyes.[32]

Boz Scagg's *Middleman* LP cover and content were so perverse that the *Los Angeles Times*—the second largest newspaper in the country—refused to promote and advertise the album. The letters of the title of James Brown's *Sex Machine* are formed with the bodies of nude women. Inside the jacket of Van Halen's top 10 LP, *Women and Children First*, looms a giant poster of barechested David Lee Roth tied up in chains. Explains Roth: "The picture got such an intense reaction that we said, 'That's rock 'n' roll.' Anyway, it's always been one of my sexual fantasies to be tied up."[33]

Moody Blues promotes the cause of Transcendental Meditation on its cover of *In Search of a Lost Chord*. Besides artwork depicting reincarnation, the back cover includes instruction on TM and on the origins of Hinduism and the mantra. Cat Stevens, who has since left music to follow his Eastern religion-of-choice, once depicted a Buddha on his album cover.

Sex seems to be the most effective sales device. Even romantic rock/folk-singer Judy Collins succumbed to its use. On the cover of *Hard Times For Lovers*, she features a nude photograph of herself. When questioned about the photo, her reply was, she'd never done it before—so why not?[34]

The same mentality must have infected the performer/marriage partners, Lindsey Buckingham/Stevie Nicks and John Lennon/Yoko Ono. The former wedded duo of Fleetwood Mac (Buckingham and Nicks) posed in the nude on an album bearing their names as title. Likewise, Lennon and Ono display both front and back nude portraits on their *Two Virgins* LP, which was rather inappropriate since Lennon was still married to his first wife at the time.

These covers, and the many others like them, graphically display the dark world of rock music, with all its sin and error in full view. Don't make the mistake of thinking these things cannot affect you, for the Scripture says, "The eye is not satisfied with seeing, nor the ear filled with hearing" (Eccles. 1:8, RSV). In other words, your eyes can never see enough to be satisfied and your ears can never hear enough. Therefore, if you are filling your eyes and ears with garbage, you'll want more garbage. But if you are concentrating on good, healthy, upbuilding sights and sounds, you'll want all the more, and the result will be inner growth, rather than corruption. The decision is a personal one, however. The world provides more than enough ways to tempt your eyes and ears. It takes conscious, personal effort to avoid those potentially harmful influences.

PART THREE

Suicides and Subliminals
Concerts and Questions

If what you have been reading troubles you, we understand. It is very difficult for a "born and bred American" to divorce himself from rock and roll, for it has grown from obscure beginnings to become part of the culture of the country. John Denver once said, "Rock music is a greater influence over the souls of men than primitive Christianity." While it's obvious Denver was speaking as one who seems to know little about Christianity, he certainly knows his music—and he definitely has a point. Rock music has dominated the lives of many people, sometimes proving deadly.

In the the last four chapters, we have seen where rock music's negative influence is most obvious—in the lyrics, lifestyles, goals and graphics. But that's not the whole picture. There are three more areas of influence that, while not as obvious, as easily documented, or as prominent, are nonetheless worth investigating.

Suicides: There is increasing evidence that rock music is guilty of murder. Teenage suicide is a growing problem, and we have discovered that many suicidal deaths can be linked to rock music.

Subliminals: Although we are much more concerned with overt messages on rock music, we believe you have a right to know some of the latest documentation indicating that subliminal messages have been recorded for years on a wide range of rock recordings.

Concerts: Rock music has also proven itself deadly in another form, the rock concert. Hundreds of people have died, and literally thousands injured, through drug- and violence-related incidents at rock concerts. Though the mayhem goes on, parents and law officials, alike, have continued to ignore the evidence.

Following these three informative chapters, we'll give the answers to the questions people most often ask us. You may be asking some of the same questions, so you deserve clear answers—some may surprise you.

11

Don't Fear the Reaper

The Suicide Fantasy

At this moment, 10% of America's high school students may be toying with thoughts of suicide.[1] In fact, "there are more youngsters thinking, obsessing, and worrying about suicide than ever before," writes Dr. Michael Peck of the Los Angeles Suicide Prevention Center.[2] More than 5,600 young men and women under the age of 25 took their lives in 1982, the most recent year with figures available; suicide was the second leading cause of death in that age group, surpassed only by auto accidents (some of which were probably also suicides). The annual suicide rate among 15- to 19-year-olds, nationally, has increased 300% since 1955. It is estimated that as many as half a million suicide attempts are made each year. Girls attempt to kill themselves more often, but boys are four times more successful, probably due to more violent, decisive methods.

Suicidal thoughts, studies have shown, are not uncommon. Almost everyone has entertained brief thoughts about suicide at one time or another. On one college campus, 70% of those questioned had considered suicide at some point in their lives.

What, therefore, tips the balance, causing a young person to choose death instead of life? Naturally, the answer is as varied as the number of suicide victims, but certain key factors are present in a large number of cases, and one of those factors is the influence of rock music. Says *Cornerstone* magazine, "When teenagers start to plan suicide they have entered the world of unreality. Thinking that death will bring them peace, many begin to fantasize and romanticize about their death."[3] This is when young people are most susceptible to the lies rock music promotes, lies promoted by rock's lyrics and goals.

The onset of suicidal thinking seems to follow a pattern. First, something goes wrong. The problem might be the pain of a family move, or the breakup of a romance. Second, there seems to be no one who can really help. The person may feel betrayed or ignored by the people important to him. This leaves him wide open for hopelessness to set in, and that is when rock music is most likely to have a major affect, by convincing him death is the only answer to

153

his pain. Naturally, drugs can compound the music's affect.

Experts give dozens of reasons for the rise of the suicidal trend among the young, including the breakup of traditional family units (only about 38% of the country's young people now live with both natural parents), competition at school, the absence of religious beliefs and training, the lack of parental guidance and support, and the increasing violence in society.

Lack of parental supervision is also a contributing factor. One-sixth of our children are now living in single-parent homes, usually headed by a woman; and even in intact families, nearly one-half of the mothers are working, so no parent is at home much of the time.

In *Psychology Today,* Dr. U. Bronfenbenner points out that coming home to an empty house is probably one of the key problem areas, ". . . whether the problem is reading difficulties, truancy, dropping out, drug addiction, or childhood depression. . . ."[4] Compounding the affects of any one or a combination of these factors is the unlimited access a lone child has to rock music, via radio, his own stereo, and, more recently, MTV.

Many parents relax a bit when their children reach the age of 11 or 12, thinking the good parenting they provided during the "formative" early years will get their children through adolescence. Unfortunately, the opposite is likely to be true. When Bronfenbenner was asked what age he considered most critical in the development of human potential, he replied:

> The junior-high school years. . . . Nowadays, they're the most critical in terms of the destructive effects on a young person's development. . . . This youthful stage is just as critical as the earlier childhood stage. Both are entry points into the problems of people not caring. Right now, the junior-high school is often a disintegrating, alienating world.[5]

Without parental supervision, without structure, without the critical viewpoint of an adult, who can filter, censor and redefine the lies and half-truths with which much rock music bombards its young audience, a child in trouble is particularly vulnerable.

If rock music tells him life is cheap and the answer to his problem is to die—who is there to deny it? If rock music says the end of a romance is the end of the world, who will reassure that the pain will lessen? If a child is wrapped in a world of fantasy, nightmares, violence and nihilism, what reason will he have for hoping anything better awaits him in the real world? If he is told by his rock heroes that drugs remove the pain, and alcohol will make him adult—and everyone is doing it—how can a parent provide needed bolstering against the pressure?

If a teenager has listened to his favorite rock star sing to him six hours a day or more, telling him the solution is suicide, how can any parent, who averages approximately two minutes of conversation with his child each day, convince him life is worth living?

Rock Music—Wanted for Murder

Rock music, though only one of many influences, has often been the deciding factor that pushes someone over the brink to choose suicide. The following case histories are horrific proof.

In Plano, Texas, a happy young man named Bruce, full of verve and energy, developed what friends described as a "darker side" after he saw the movie *Pink Floyd—The Wall*, about a rock singer who builds a wall around himself to shut out a world he views as hostile. The teenager began wearing rebel-style leather jacket and boots, as did his best friend, Bill. One night, in a scene reminiscent of *Rebel Without A Cause*, Bruce and Bill staged a drag race with another boy. Before the race was over, young Bill was dead. Acting as a signalman, he'd been accidentally side-swiped by one of the young dragsters.

Following the accident, Bruce kept to himself, telling friends he would see Bill again, "some sunny day"—a line from one of Pink Floyd's songs. The day after Bill's funeral, Bruce was found dead in his car. The engine was running and in the car's cassette player was a Pink Floyd tape, spun down through its last song, "Goodbye Cruel World."[6]

Six days after Bruce's death, another boy in the same town took his life by carbon monoxide asphyxiation in the family garage. He, too, died listening to music. According to *Newsweek,* his car radio was blaring.[7]

A young man, in severe despair, committed suicide while listening to John Lennon's song "Cold Turkey," according to *Shofar* magazine. The song, the magazine reports, didn't necessarily make him take his life, but presumably added to his depression. The song describes the horror of one who is trying to escape the entrapment of drug addiction, and includes the mournful cry, "I wish I was a baby; I wish I was dead."[8]

A 16-year-old young man, who had recently moved from a big city to a small midwestern town, felt he needed to "act tough and look tough" to maintain his big-city image—which included listening to heavy metal, nihilistic groups such as Blue Cheer, Black Sabbath, Led Zeppelin and Grand Funk Railroad. Maintaining the image also led him into drugs, and eventually, into deep depression. Finally, with Black Sabbath's music wailing, he put a shotgun to his chin and pulled the trigger. Miraculously, the young man lived to tell the story, and you will read more about him later.

An Indianapolis youth, 14 years old, fell deeper and deeper into the use of drugs; his mother claims this was due to the urging of rock music. The ensuing depression eventually caused the young man to attempt suicide. Though this young AC/DC fan shot himself in the head, he too, lived to tell about it.

Another young man, who had become a sixties buff, shut himself in his room for a week after the murder of John Lennon. According to a schoolmate, the recluse was "really confused and depressed after that."[9] One night, shortly afterward, the young man went home and shot himself in the head.

156

Described by his parents as a sensitive boy who spent hours in his room listening to his "heroes"—KISS, AC/DC, Tom Petty, and the Cars—Steve Boucher began showing signs of trouble around the age of 13. His parents, however, chalked up the defiance and smoking to "normal teenage rebellion." Eventually, with songs like "Highway to Hell" and "Shoot to Thrill" echoing in his brain, Steve took the hunting rifle he'd inherited from his grandfather, held the barrel to his forehead, and pulled the trigger. He died beneath the poster calendar of AC/DC, who sing, ". . . you're only young, but you're gonna die. . ." ("Hell's Bells"). This story is described in detail later in the chapter.

It's not surprising that KISS states on the back of its *Destroyer* album, "We're back to destroy your minds and you know we're destroying your minds and you love it,"[10] or that Kevin Cronin of REO Speedwagon once said, "Living on the brink of disaster at all times is what Rock 'n' Roll is all about!"[11]

The number of songs recorded every year with lyrics that can destroy the minds of young people and shove them to the brink of despair and ultimate disaster is incredible. Some examples: the CH3's album *Fear of Life;* Pink Floyd's "Drug Abuse" (". . . balanced on the biggest wave . . . you race toward an early grave . . ."), as well as "Goodbye Cruel World"; Ozzy Osbourne's *Diary of a Madman* LP, and "Suicide Solution" from the *Blizzard of Oz* album; AC/DC's "Hell's Bells" on the album *Back In Black,* in addition to "Shoot to Thrill" (". . . put your head up to me, pull the trigger, really do it now, shoot to thrill, way to kill . . ."); Black Sabbath's "Killing Yourself to Live" (". . . you don't care if you don't see again the light of day . . ."); and Blue Oyster Cult's "Don't Fear the Reaper."

The list of songs is both endless and pathetic. At a time when a young person has lost all hope for living, when he needs an encouraging word, a vision for a better future, and a reason to go on, he gets from his rock music "friends" pain, despair, misery, and, many times, the inducement to take his own life.

Is this music truly affecting young people? Does it actually entice them to commit the ultimate act of despair—suicide? Let's look more closely at the life-and-death situations of two of the young people whose suicide attempts were reportedly linked to rock and roll and see.

You Can't Hold On Too Long

Steve Boucher was a normal thirteen-year-old kid—somewhat quiet and sensitive, but obedient to his parents and average in school. Then, around 1978, when KISS became very popular throughout the country, Steve became interested in rock music. Before then, his parents recalled, he had listened mostly to soft ballads, and hadn't been very involved in music. As he entered the world of rock, Steve also became defiant and began to stay in his room for hours at a time listening to his music, even going to sleep by rock "lullabies."

His parents assumed Steve's trouble was normal teenage rebellion, and hoped it would soon pass. Instead, his fascination with rock music grew.

Steve's mother, Sandee Boucher, describes that time in Steve's life: "KISS was his first group . . . his heroes. It bothered me, but I thought it was just a gimmick that would run its course and then die out. You know, we had Elvis Presley. . . ."

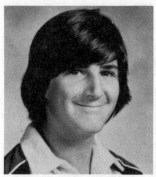

Steve Boucher

Instead, from his infatuation with KISS, Steve "seemed to just graduate on to harder stuff—worse things." Soon, his mother relates, Steve exhibited an obsession for AC/DC. "He had it written on everything, his notebooks, his schoolbooks. He was making up a T-shirt and it had AC/DC on it. . . ." His walls also were covered with KISS and AC/DC memorabilia; then the family moved to a new home and Sandee Boucher put her foot down.

"When we moved I didn't allow him to put them [posters, etc.] on his wall. But he came to me with an AC/DC calendar and it was awful," Sandee recalls. "He wanted to put it above his bed. I said, 'Steve, put a nice picture there.' [But he said] no. If he couldn't have that, he didn't want anything." Finally, his mother allowed him to hang the offensive calendar behind his door. "And he did, and he died right underneath it—right underneath the calendar."

Of course, if the Bouchers had been aware of the content of the music in which their son was absorbed for most of his waking hours and even while he slept, they would probably have vetoed or at least curtailed it. However, as typical parents, they had no idea. When Steve played his music, his dad usually reacted by telling the boy to turn it down and shut the door. "I didn't like the noise," George Boucher admits. "I didn't like the music, and I couldn't care less about what the words were."

Sandee even encouraged the use of headphones—"That way I didn't have to hear it." Even so, he often had the volume turned up so loud that, even though he was in his room with the headphones on, his mother could still hear the music.

Sometimes, Steve would come to his mother with one of his records and ask her to listen to it. "He really tried hard to get me to condone it," Sandee recalls. "He would say, 'Listen to this—even you would like this.' But I would just say, 'Steve, I don't like this. Go to your room and listen to it—I don't like it.' "

Therefore, the Bouchers didn't realize that KISS's LP's were filled with songs about drugs and rebellion, and that AC/DC sang of revolt and self-destruction. Sandee says, "I did read something on the album cover of one of the records, and thought, *Isn't that awful.* It was advocating a lifestyle that was promiscuous—sex—but I didn't do anything about it."

Neither parent recognized the connection between Steve's actions and his music. They even saw the Peters brothers on a news program, but the truth about rock didn't get through to them. "I remember, I was fixing supper," says Sandee, "and saw these 'fanatics,' and they were having a bonfire and burning records. I said, 'Look at those fanatics. That's censorship. That's awful.' At the time I thought it was silly—that it [rock] was harmless music and that [burning records] was censorship." She adds quickly, "I don't remember Steve saying anything. He was interested and he stood there watching."

So the Bouchers didn't interfere with Steve's preoccupation with rock music, even though bad went to worse. They didn't know it then, but their 14-year-old son had begun smoking pot. Eventually, Sandee found matches in his pocket, and accused him of smoking cigarettes, which he readily admitted. In fact, he even seemed relieved to have his mom aware of it, and he promised to stop. However, they never discovered their son was using drugs until he had died.

The month before Steve's suicide, he began to slip. But with no insight into the depth of his problem, his parents didn't catch the tiny signals and cries for help that a person contemplating suicide often sends out. When Steve asked his dad about insurance, Mr. Boucher thought it was simply an "innocent question." Steve spoke to his sister about suicide—75% of people who have successfully committed suicide told someone they were thinking of doing it—but Steve's sister agreed to tell no one.

George Boucher explains, "The last week [of Steve's life] we think he was staying up late at night, smoking marijuana. And he was very tired going to school—listess, dull. I think he had resigned himself that he was going to do it. . . . I'm sure he had considered it for at least a month.

"He inherited a 30-30 hunting rifle from his grandfather, and that night [Friday, March 27, 1981, at 7:03 p.m.], he propped the gun against the floor, and leaned over it, and put the barrel to his forehead."

George and Sandee Boucher were not at home that tragic evening, though their daughter was. She heard the gun blast and knocked on her brother's bedroom door. Of course, there was no reply.

Sandee recalls: "It was several hours that she waited for us to come home. I was going to get ready for bed when she came to me and said, 'Mom, there was a loud noise in Steve's room, and he didn't come out and he didn't answer when I knocked.' I knocked on his door, and then opened it, and I found him lying on the floor. I think our daughter had gone in there, but because of the horror of it, she'd blocked it out of her mind."

Following Steve's death, his parents sought answers. Though suicide can never fully be explained or understood, the Bouchers at least wanted some clue as to Steve's thoughts before his death. They searched in vain for a suicide note or any papers that would shed some light on the mystery. Eventually they began to play tapes Steve had personally recorded, hoping to find a message.

George says, "He had made tapes off the radio, and we were just listening to them and waiting for a break in them—waiting for him to come in and say, 'I hate you. I'm going to kill myself,' something like that.

"Then we started noticing things coming on the lyrics. It was the first time I had ever realized what he was listening to."

The Bouchers noticed that if a song had made a particular impression on Steve, he had recorded it several times so he could replay it often. Some of the groups of which he had multiple tapes were AC/DC, Tom Petty and the Heartbreaks, the Cars, and KISS.

"The one that stands out in my mind the most," says Sandee, "is the AC/DC song 'Shoot to Thrill.' He had recorded it twice and had the album. It goes, 'Are you willing? Keep it coming, and put your head up to me. I'm gonna pull it, pull it, pull the trigger. Super thrill, way to kill . . . I've got my gun and I'm ready and I'm gonna fire at will. . . .' "

"I don't know which album it's from," George adds, "but the one [most outstanding] to me says, 'Nobody knows how I feel/I'll get my revenge from the grave. . . .' "

Another song that apparently made a strong impression on Steve says, ". . . you wish that it were over, you never slow down/You're looking for kicks with nothing around/You can't hold on too long (it's all right). . . ."

"It's the repetition of this," Sandee says; "it's just pounding it in. And it's the way they emphasize the words—'it's *all right*' to give up."

"Anyone would have to be a fool to think that it had no influence," adds Steve's father emphatically. "We're not saying that he killed himself *only* because he listened to music, or to lyrics like this. But if it was in his mind, and he already had this suggestion. . . . [The music] gives suicide credibility—it promotes it, encourages it and advertises it."

"I read some of the lyrics to several people and they said that it amounts to murder," says Sandee.

George agrees completely. "I think that they [rock musicians and artists] should have the same limitations for what they can record on music as printed material is liable for. This is anti-church . . . it's a kind of cult. It's advertising hell—trying to sell hell."

The Bouchers are certain that rock musicians and their music are pulling down the moral values of America, but believe it is possible to combat that effect—if parents "have the courage to interfere when needed and the courage to stand up for your own convictions."

"If a child was running for the road," Sandee adds, "and a car was heading down on him, the parent would get the child out of danger. Also, if a child were reaching for fire, the parent would grab his hand and keep it away from fire. Music is as dangerous. We have an obligation to screen it , . . and get rid of it if it's dangerous."

"I'm a firm believer that saying yes does not necessarily prove love," Sandee says. "I think it shows more love to take the risk and say no."

What about a child who insists the music doesn't affect him, who says, "I've never tried to commit suicide, I don't smoke dope. It's not going to affect me"? What would the Bouchers say to that parent or teen?

Sandee: "Its so subtle . . . and it changes us whether we are aware of it or not. It makes it acceptable—it changes whole value systems. . . . I found phrases of these songs going around in my own head—I was singing them! And I know better!"

George: "We've dug into this a little bit since, and I'm convinced that they [rock musicians] are trying to push their own values. A lot of singers have a certain lifestyle, and they promote it with their music. They're trying to have other people copy them."

Sandee again: "And it influences the kids because they look up to them as idols. They're looking for a role model. They see the rock stars doing it, and it makes it acceptible."

John Tanner Lives to See the Light of Day

John Tanner's tale has a happier ending. "I'd been getting really depressed," he told us in the all-too-familiar story, "and had been feeling sorry for myself for a couple months or so. I had finally decided that I was going to commit suicide and get it all over with, instead of having to go through a life of 'misery.' So I loaded up my shotgun. . . . At about 5:15 p.m., I just put it up to my chin and told God I was 'coming home' and pulled the trigger."

It was January 15, 1975, and John, a resident of north central Minnesota, was 16 years old. He heard the hammer hit, but never heard the shot that should have killed him. He was thrown back six or seven feet by the shock of the blast, and knocked unconscious for a few minutes. When he came to on his bed, he was thrashing about and dazed, but couldn't believe he was still alive.

John Tanner's entire face had been blown off by the shotgun blast. "I thought I'd pull the trigger and then I wouldn't feel pain," John explains. "I was conscious for three hours after that, until they got me to the University of Minnesota. . . ."

The slug from John's gun had entered his head under, and slightly behind, his chin, and had emerged directly between his eyes. His jaw, nose, tongue, the roof of his mouth, and all but three teeth were gone. Life-saving procedures were begun immediately, and once John was in stable condition, the painful, slow process of reconstructing his face was begun—a process that has required over 20 surgeries in 10 years, at a cost of over $300,000.

Why did a young man of 16, living in relative comfort in a small, middle-American town, feel driven to suicide? John says: "I just lost my sense of worth through listening to a lot of acid rock and smoking pot. . . . I didn't really appreciate anything anymore. I started looking at the negative side of things. It just built up inside me."

Having recently moved from the "big city" of Minneapolis, John had been out to impress the small-town crowd in his school. To look and act tough, he listened to the "macho" music heavy metal bands produce. Innocently, his older brother gave John a stack of albums he no longer desired—including several by Black Sabbath, Blue Cheer, Led Zeppelin, and Grand Funk Railroad. They were just what John wanted to enhance his new image.

"I was 14 or 15 then and I just started liking Black Sabbath and was into them pretty heavily." The music, John says, directly relates to his quick entrance into drug abuse. "As far as I'm concerned," he says, "there's a definite connection, because the musicians that put out rock music are on drugs—probably heavier than most people are—and they know what sounds good when you're under the influence of a narcotic, and that's what they play. They are more after a feeling of a moment—what makes you feel good for the time being."

Many groups play music that is best understood, and in some cases only makes sense, when the listener is on a mind-altering drug. And, of course, while in the suggestible frame of mind that drugs induce, the lyrics are free to wreak havoc on the listener's subconscious. That is why drugs and rock music are often accomplices in the suicide conspiracy.

For John, the thoughts of suicide weren't instantaneous, though other areas of his thinking saw a rapid change when rock entered his life. He says, "I started getting more rebellious right away. I started disobeying what my elders had told me to do, and I started losing interest in things I should have paid more attention to—out of rebellion. The depression came on more gradually."

The depression did come though, and soon thoughts of suicide began to plague John—thoughts he insists came directly from his music. "I think from being real dedicated to Black Sabbath—because they are really depressing—that I got from them a real deep depression, and I'd say that's where the suicide stems from."

The sort of suicidal lyrics that brought John Tanner into a self-destructive frame of mind include the song "Killing Yourself to Live" (from *Sabbath, Bloody Sabbath*), which John can quote by heart: "The execution of your mind, you really have to learn/You're wishing that the hands of doom could take your mind away/And you don't care if you don't see again the light of day." This song suggests suicide is the only way to cope with problems, but John Tanner has discovered he *did* want to see "the light of day," and now he hopes others will learn from his mistakes so they won't have to suffer or cause others suffering as he has.

Other songs which greatly influenced young John Tanner were "Sweet Leaf," a song about pot which John played a great deal, and "Snow Blind," a tune dealing with the theme of cocaine. John says he received his earliest thoughts about using drugs from listening to rock music lyrics such as these.

More directly influencing his thoughts of suicide were songs such as Black Sabbath's "After Forever," from the album *Master of Reality*, which says,

"Have you ever thought about your soul, can it be saved? Or perhaps you think that when you're dead you just stay in the grave. . . . When you think about death, do you lose your breath?. . . I'll be prepared when you're lonely and scared at the end of our days. . . ." Another song on the same album is called "Into The Void," which was also instrumental in John's deathly decision: "Leave them to their future in their graves/Make a home where love is there to stay/Peace and happiness in every way. . . ." It implies a person should somehow escape life, and be free to enjoy a new dimension—another life somewhere.

"I listened to that LP a lot before I shot myself," John admits, "and I was already pretty depressed. I listened to what they sang, and I took it very sincerely. I'm sure it had a pretty good-sized effect on my . . . thoughts."

John, in desperation, finally decided to end his life, to find the "peace and happiness" his favorite group kept telling him he could find "at the end of his days." He lived in the country at the time, and owned a 12-gauge shotgun. He put a slug into the gun and set it against the chimney in his room. There it sat for three days as he struggled with his decision.

"I was getting more depressed, especially after I decided to do it. I wasn't thinking realistically. Then the day I shot myself, I skipped out of school and stayed in my room and listened to albums all day." John says he listened to Black Sabbath and Grand Funk Railroad that day, especially Black Sabbath's *Paranoid* album. By 5:15, the music had done its work. John Tanner was "psyched up" enough to pull the trigger.

What good came out of such a tragic event? John says, ". . . now I know that nothing is worth getting that depressed over—*ever*. And I know that I'm going to heaven, someday, because after I shot myself, I was lying on the floor and still conscious, and I accepted Christ. He saved me from dying then—and several times in the hospital afterward—so I know that He's real. I know, too, that He's helped me with my . . . attitude so that I think more maturely now, and so that I can help other people."

The people John would most like to help are teenagers who are still under the deathly influence of rock music. "Look at what people like me have had to go through because of drugs, drinking, rock and perversion." Though John is aware of the pressures young people face from their peers, and the cost of going against the crowd, he warns, "It [rock music and the lifestyle—and death-style—it promotes] really catches up with you, and you pay for it mentally as well as physically. I can remember a lot of times of torment that were just mental since [the suicide attempt]. It hasn't been easy, and I . . . can see now that if I had just listened to my mother and father—even though they seemed old and 'corny' at the time . . . I'd be in a much better position now. I wouldn't have wasted nine or ten years of my life, and I'd have a skill by now. I'd have something of a little more meaning than just a mangled . . . face."

To kids who think rock music couldn't affect them the way it did John, he admonishes, "*Everything* you come in contact with affects you one way or another. Rock music," he says, "can definitely influence a young person to try drugs. They start listening to it. Then pretty soon, they'll start hanging around with people that are doing drugs of some sort—marijuana probably. And that's where it starts. That's what I started with, and then that just led to acid and other kinds of drugs and drinking.

"American people just don't see how bad things are anymore," John contends, and stresses that the answer for young people is to ". . . get rid of their albums and tapes and whatever. Quit doing drugs, quit drinking—or anything that pollutes your body, because that will affect your mind. Get control over your mind because you're the only one who can. Start controlling yourself in a positive manner so that you don't end up depressed." Part of that positive picture, John says, is to "pay more attention" when they hear about Christ, and get to know Him personally as John has.

"Even if you don't end up trying to commit suicide, it's no fun being depressed, so that's a good enough reason as any. . . ." John Tanner should know—he put his mind in the hands of doom, but thanks to God, he lived to see the light of day.

How to Help a Person Considering Suicide

We hope the evidence presented thus far has convinced you that rock and roll music can be hazardous to your health, and that you will take precautions to protect yourself or your teenager. If you're a parent, that means, as the Bouchers have poignantly advised, bravely standing up for your convictions and sometimes saying no. It also means learning how to offer alternatives. If you're interested in more ideas, Chapter 16 should help.

If you're a teenager, protecting yourself means checking it out: check the music you like, its lyrics and album covers, its artists' lifestyles and goals. And if you find anything that, as John Tanner says, pollutes your body or affects your mind, get rid of it! That's easier said than done, but Chapter 15 might help you make the right decisions.

Beyond that, however, we are concerned that you may know someone who is seriously contemplating suicide. For teenagers such as Steve Boucher, and some of the others mentioned here, it's too late to change anything. However, if you know a person who is feeling lonely or depressed, there is still time. Here are some ways you can help him.

1. *Be willing to talk.* You don't need a psychology degree to lend an interested ear. One of the biggest problems connected with suicide is lack of communication. A common myth says if you talk to a person about suicide, you'll put the thought in his head. That's simply not true. Listening to the fears and thoughts of a depressed person helps him see that someone understands. "It provides a link of human contact," says Rose Wall, a crisis intervention counselor in Los Angeles.

2. *Ask the person "feelings-oriented" questions,* such as: "Have you been feeling down?" or "Has something been on your mind? You haven't been your

usual self." If the person opens up a little, try to get more specific. "Whom are you mad at?" "What made you so down on yourself?" "Are you thinking about doing something—such as suicide?"

3. *Take the person seriously.* Even a young child doesn't like his feelings being made light of. It is another common myth that those who talk about suicide don't actually go through with it. Eight out of ten suicides clearly indicate their intentions to someone. If you are that someone, ask him how he intends to do it. Get details. Listen, be supportive—then get help.

4. Whether you're a concerned adult, a teenaged friend or a parent, if you discover a potential suicide victim, *connect him with a competent, trained professional* who can counsel him out of his suicidal feelings. There is always help available, including suicide prevention "hotlines" (check your directory), mental health clinics, and suicide prevention centers. However, for the young person, the closest line of help is through his parents, teachers, school counselor or pastor. Even if the person balks at the idea of telling his parents, *someone* needs to know. And it's not betraying a confidence, in this case, to tell an adult. It's the most loyal act a true friend could perform. This is one situation where silence is not golden.

5. Once the immediate trauma is over, try to help the person find healthy fun and entertainment. *Tell him the facts you know about rock music*—how it can affect the mind. Pass along a copy of this book; or put him in contact with the Truth About Rock information service at P.O. Box 9222, St. Paul, MN, 55109, where up-to-date documentation is available; or bring him to a seminar in your area.

If Your Are Seriously Considering Suicide

As a teenager, you're probably discovering that sorting out life's problems and finding answers isn't always easy—and sometimes is downright painful. It may be hard to believe right now, but the pain will pass. Sometimes, though, we all need someone to help us do the sorting. You need to take the responsibility to find someone to talk to—an adult—someone who can help.

If you don't think you can talk about it with your parents, find a youth leader, a pastor, a teacher, or a neighbor. If you can't bear to tell someone you know about your problem, at least contact a crisis service. The counselors maintain your anonymity, and they'll help.

Remember, though, more than anything, Jesus Christ wants to help. He's there with you even if you can't feel His presence in your desperation and confusion. He's there loving you—no matter who you are or what you've done.

Do you recall the apostle Judas? Though he was one of Jesus' closest friends, Judas betrayed Him. We can learn from that example.

"Until the last," writes William V. Rauscher in *The Case Against Suicide,* "Jesus tried to bring Judas into the love of God. Jesus did not reject him, nor did He expose him as a traitor, but He knew.

"God is always trying to win us to himself even to the last moment, before it is too late. It was the potential of the man that interested Jesus when He chose Judas. Jesus sees what can be."[13]

And Jesus sees what you can be. Jesus knows what it is like to hurt and He knows what it is like to be tempted. He's been lonely, rejected by His friends, and laughed at by the people who knew Him best. He knows you. He knows what you're going through. And He knows what you can be.

If you don't know Jesus personally, or if you've been running from His comfort and care, ask Him into your life and begin to obey Him. And then seek out a church or a youth group where you and your relationship with Jesus can grow. (One factor that keeps kids from committing suicide is involvement in an ongoing youth group. Psychiatrist Mary Giffin, co-author with Carol Felsenthal of *A Cry For Help*, says "Church groups are especially positive in this regard. When kids belong to a group with a common ethical value, they tend not to turn to suicide.")

Do as John Tanner so urgently recommended: get control of your mind—you're the only one who can. Seek out help and you, too, will someday believe, where there's life, there's hope.

12

The Subject Is Subliminals

"Say, say, say what you want/But don't play games with my affections."
So goes the 1983-84 hit by Michael Jackson and Paul McCartney. Even the
legendary superstars of rock music want people to "tell it like it is." No hidden
games, no secret messages, no sham, no deception. And yet, one of the most
controversial elements in the rock music industry has been the issue of messages hidden within the music.

Does backward masking exist? Can subliminals actually affect the listener? Who is going to the trouble of concealing those inside-out missives on
records? Should a person be concerned?

In the early eighties, accusations were hurled at certain rock groups,
alleging they had laid subliminal messages on recording tracks in hopes of
influencing listeners to take drugs, worship Satan, or simply buy more records. The technique, sometimes called backward masking, has been fairly
well documented on albums by the Beatles, Rolling Stones and Pink Floyd.

Though we are much more uneasy about audible, straightforward messages than any covert communication on rock and roll recordings, and though
we do not want people running out and buying records to confirm the examples
of substimuli listed below, the Bible does warn that we should beware so Satan
can't take advantage of us (1 Pet. 5:8). Therefore, some investigation seems
prudent.

The "subliminal" is the subconscious or deepest part of the mind. Though
scientists know the subconscious mind exists and can measure many of its
functions, there is no simple dividing line between it and the conscious mind—
the threshold between the two shifts constantly. Then, too, each person is
different and even the same individual perceives differently at different times,
so studies of the complex human mind's functions are difficult, and findings
are often hotly debated.

One of the debates concerns subliminal stimulation, which can come in
many forms—words or pictures flashed so quickly we don't consciously remember them; words "masked" by electronic tricks so we don't consciously
hear them; or pictures or symbols placed within a work so we don't consciously
recall seeing them. They are all, according to media expert Dr. Wilson Bryan

Key, "purposely designed . . . with the motive of soliciting, manipulating, modifying or managing human behavior."[1]

The concept of a computer and its programmer provides a fair analogy of the way the brain perceives these secret messages. Our conscious mind is like a computer programmer, who can make value judgments, picking and choosing the data he wishes, and determining right from wrong. The subconscious mind, however, is similar to a computer, which has no power to reason. It simply stores information. Our subconscious mind also is a databank, unable to make value judgments.

William Yarroll, a neuro-scientific researcher with the Applied Potential Institute in Aurora, Colorado, studies the thought processes of the brain. He says that at the base of brain is the "reticular activating system"—or in laymanese, an editing device. This system acts as programmer to the brain, screening out unwanted or unacceptable information. However, when bits of information are presented to the mind in a covert form, such as by backward masking, they circumvent this screening procedure. Why?

According to Lloyd H. Silverman, adjunct professor of psychology at New York University, two brain centers deal with outside stimuli. "One center is responsible for registering a stimulus, and the other for bringing it into consciousness. The first center is far more sensitive than the second, so that a very weak stimulus [such as low-volume words hidden below the music] will register in the mind, but it won't come into consciousness." Since the mind doesn't need the information for the moment, it puts it in a holding pattern before it reaches the conscious level—before the receiver (you) is aware of it.[2]

Before we examine how all this affects human behavior and just where rock and roll fits into the picture, let's take a short look at the history of sneaky stimuli, a history that began at the same time as rock music.

Big Brother Eats Popcorn

In 1956, one of the first attempts at subconscious mind control was organized by James Vicary and his Subliminal Projection Company. After applying for patents, Vicary sought out clients for a device that would flash on a movie screen, every five seconds for just 1/3,000th of a second, a message such as "Hungry? Eat popcorn," or "Drink Coca-Cola."[3] A Fort Lee, New Jersey theater employed the device during a six weeks' screening of *Picnic*, and concession sales increased dramatically—popcorn by 57.5% and Coke by 18%![4]

The next year, the Precon Process and Equipment Corporation was formed. Its stated purpose was to place subliminal messages in movies, taverns, and on billboards. The officers of the company included a psychologist, and a neurologist with engineering training. The company claimed to have doubled, by subliminal methods only, the consumption of a beverage advertised on location. They later applied for and received a patent.[5]

Also in 1957, it was discovered that a Chicago radio station had been selling subliminal advertising space at $1,000 for 400 messages aired over a four-month period.[6] Results, however, were not made public.

Other subliminal message experiments were attempted during the fifties and early sixties, in the States, by university professors and abroad by the British Broadcasting Corporation, but results were inconclusive.

During this time, however, a Louisiana researcher in medical electronics, Dr. Hal Becker, was developing a device called a tachistoscope, which he planned to use, according to *Science Digest*, for flashing subliminal public service announcements, such as "Drive Safely," during television shows.[7] The device, which flashed images at 3- to 10-second intervals, was capable of introducing a message to the brain without the recipient's awareness. Becker's work, and that of other researchers, essentially went underground, however, in the wake of public outcry.

New Yorker magazine first blew the whistle on the secret messages, claiming "minds were being broken and entered." *Newsday* also picked up the battle cry, calling subliminals "the most alarming invention since the atomic bomb."[8] Surprisingly, however, though legislation was proposed, no laws were passed. Eventually, complaints dwindled and the whole issue seemed quite dead by 1970.

Research continued quietly, however, and several attempts were made to technologically manipulate people's minds. *Advertising* magazine reported rather matter-of-factly that Toyota Motor Sales, USA, was using subliminal images to enhance its commercials.[9] Then, in 1973, a toy manufacturer inserted the words "Get It" in a television commercial for a game called "Husker Du." Suddenly the FCC decided things were getting out of hand and warned its stations that the use of such techniques was "contrary to the public interest." Though the commercials' subliminals were discarded before the effect could be measured, the FCC said, "Whether effective or not, such broadcasts are clearly intended to be deceptive."[10]

In 1974, a Canadian broadcaster uncovered the use of subliminals once again—this time on both the Voice of America and Radio Moscow. It seems we don't want someone to play mind games with our kids, but it's all right to do it with someone else's children—in the name of freedom, of course. Nevertheless, the United Nations launched a study which concluded, "The cultural implications of subliminal indoctrination is a major threat to human rights throughout the world," and further, the modification or even elimination of a culture was possible through subliminal stimuli.[11] The United Nations, it seems, was not happy with Big Brother's progression from popcorn to propaganda, and quickly condemned the use of subliminals on international airwaves.

Consequently, hidden messages are supposedly no longer a threat in radio or television advertising, or propaganda. However, that same sly seduction is still possible in stores, movie theaters, salesrooms, and musical recordings. And once again, Dr. Hal Becker has come to the forefront with a device he mysteriously labels the "little black box."

Actually, the device is an updated version of his tachistoscope, using an endless loop cassette player which is capable of receiving, mixing and broadcasting material from two separate sources. Furthermore, it adjusts one of those sources so it is perceivable only subliminally. The box has been used since 1978 to scramble messages of honesty-inducement with Muzak-like melodies. Blended into the background music of at least 37 stores, thus far in the U.S., are Becker's little reminders: "Be honest—do not steal—I am honest—I will not steal." The words vary slightly, but the message remains the same, 9,000 times each hour. According to Becker, the system saved one company more than half a million dollars by reducing its theft losses a whopping 37% over a 9-month period.[12]

This same device—utilizing both audio and video tapes—was recognized by the New Orleans Medical Society as a successful aid for a weight reduction program Becker and his partner, Canadian behavioral scientist Louis Romberg, have operated for years. And a Toronto real estate agency uses the "black box" to inspire its sales personnel.[13] Even professional football managers utilize Becker's silent coaching to augment pep talks.

Then, in late 1983, a small Michigan firm, Stimutech, brought the mind-bending business into the computer age. Its home computer kit, Expando-Vision, consists of eight cartridges and a home computer-to-television interface. Depending on the program of his choice, the user can flash goal-oriented messages across his own television screen at the rate of 1/30th of a second every 2 1/2 minutes.[14] The messages—sort of an electronic string-around-the-finger reminding the user he is lovable, or successful, or confident—are designed to help him lose weight, quit smoking, control stress, increase productivity and a number of other tasks.

This personal use of subliminals seems acceptable. After all, the subject is both aware of and receptive to the message. But other uses of subliminals have surfaced lately, which are not so healthy. For example, *The Exorcist* is one of three films known to contain substimuli. Images of blood, ghosts, and death masks were concealed to enhance the over-all sense of horror the film created. Warner Brothers, producer of the movie, was sued in 1979 by an Indiana teenager who fainted during the film and broke his jaw. His lawyer insisted the fleeting death mask was "one of the major issues of the case."[15]

Another movie, *Texas Chain Saw Massacres,* was selected as the outstanding film of the year by the London Film Festival the year it was released. Its producer, Tobe Hooper, not only admitted that subliminals were used to enhance the effect of the movie, but also that "subliminal perception is a killer. The capacity of the unconscious to take information and run with it is unlimited. We flatter ourselves by thinking we are in control of our thinking."[16]

Big Brother Meets the Beatles

In the recording industry, the Beatles were known as innovators—the first to employ sophisticated multiple tracks; introduce psychedelics into the music; produce a "concept album"; and elevate album covers to an art form. They were also the first rock group proven to have laid reversed vocal tracks onto a record album.

On their 1968 double album, *The Beatles,* commonly known as "The White Album," the Beatles hyped their "Paul is dead" sales gimmick with a backward masked message. In the song "Revolution Number Nine," over and over at the end of the recording are the lyrics, "number nine, number nine, number nine. . . ." If that portion is played in reverse, it was discovered, the real message comes through: "Turn me on, dead man," accompanied by piano playing; another portion of the same record, played backward, reveals crowd noise and then someone screaming, "Get me out!" The gimmick worked far better than ever imagined, and soon fans were scrambling for the record just to ruin their needles by playing it backward!

Messages on other groups' albums were found as well, some employing the backward masking trick, others recorded at too low a volume to be consciously heard, or recorded forward at very high speed. Many messages obviously have been inserted intentionally, while others remain a mystery.

In his book *Media Sexploitation*, Key mentions that Blue Swede's "Hooked on a Feeling," a 1974 remake of the B.J. Thomas hit, was the first rock record found to have obscenities embedded in the background.[17] The tune, which was the only real money-maker for the Swedish group, featured a seeming "tribal chant" in the background, which *Who's Who in Rock* describes as "oddly captivating."[18] That background phrase, which sounded something like "ooga-chock-a, ooga-chock-a," was responsible for the dismissal of five disc jockeys who, according to Key, played the record, then pointed out what obscenities were being spoken in the background.[19] Once again, however, it was the Beatles who had pioneered the art. Soon subliminal messages—some just nonsense—were discovered on a number of their early recordings, including "Girl," recorded in 1965; "Baby, You're A Rich Man," recorded in 1967; "I Am a Walrus," also 1967; and a number of others.

Electric Light Orchestra also entered the subliminals game in 1974, when they produced *Eldorado,* which *The Rock Who's Who* says firmly established the group as stars.[20] The album, which eventually was certified gold, is embedded with several backward messages, including, "Christ, you're the nasty one, you're infernal" (meaning hellish, hateful or abominable), and "He's there on the cross and dead" (inferring that Jesus is dead and there is no resurrection).

That group had another hit recording the following year with *Face the Music*, a misleading title since the main message of the music is recorded backward. On the cut, "Fire Is High," before the lyrics begin, a "secret message" is recorded which, played backward, clearly says, "The music is reversible, but time is not. Turn back . . . turn back . . . turn back. . . ."

Pink Floyd, that cheery underground purveyor of loneliness and depression, earned its first certified platinum award album with *Animals*, released in 1977. In the song "Sheep," from that LP, there is a distorted rendition of the Twenty-third Psalm embedded forward on the sound track. A portion of the mocking "prayer" says, ". . . with bright knives he releaseth my soul. He makes me to hang on hooks in high places . . . we shall raise up and then we shall make the bugger's eyes water" ("bugger" is a slang term for sodomite—homosexual, or a contemptible person with whom sodomy is committed).

In an even more obvious attempt to sell records, Pink Floyd's next release, *The Wall*, has the following message backward masked into the song "Goodbye Blue Sky": "Congratulations! You've just discovered the secret message. Please send your answer to: 'Old Pink,' in care of The Funny Farm, . . . [the address]."

Styx, the group from Chicago, which sports a mythical name and occultic connections, features the occult backward masked on at least one of its songs. "Snowblind," on their *Paradise Theatre* LP, when played in reverse says, "Move Satan in our voices." In addition, the group gave its *Killroy Was Here* album a label warning it contains secret messages, presumably as a sales gimmick.

Cheap Trick, another Illinois group, lived up to its name with the album *Heaven Tonight* (1978). The tricksters recorded The Lord's Prayer at 1/8th speed, then overlaid the song "How Are You" so the listener would consciously hear only a faint, chipmunk-like chirp in the background. Why the Lord's Prayer?

A possible explanation is found in Mike Warnke's book, *The Satan Seller*. Warnke says that often in occult worship, participants chant the Lord's Prayer, either forward or backward, as subtle mockery of God.[21]

Blue Oyster Cult also used the 1/8th-speed gimmick to record the message, "Furthermore, our father who art in heaven–Satan," on the cut, "You're Not the One," from their *Mirrors* LP released in 1979.

Satan is also the subject of a song on the album, *Raunch-n-Roll*, by Black Oak Arkansas. The backward masking on the song, "The Day When the Electricity Came to Arkansas," says, "Satan, Satan, Satan, he is god, he is god, he is god." Following that is what sounds like demonic laughter, then the chanting of prayers similar to those used in satanic worship.

Jefferson Starship sings the song, "A Child Is Coming," on its 1970 LP, *Blows Against the Empire*, and tells us everything is getting better with this "child," but the little urchin is never identified—at least played forward. Play the tune in reverse, however, and the message is clear: "Son of Satan."

Anyone—rock fan or not—has probably heard the very popular song by Queen, "Another One Bites the Dust." It was often played in ball parks across the country when a player struck out. Played on an echoey, schmaltzy organ, the tune perhaps added a touch of humor, but the original recording has imbedded in it a message that isn't funny. Repeated four times is the backward masked message, "Decide to smoke marijuana, its fun to smoke marijuana, decide to smoke marijuana."

The Rolling Stones jumped into the mind-bending business with their *Some Girls* album, released in 1978, which became their best-selling record—over four million copies. The title song on that album included the racist, sexist line, "Black girls just wanna get [expletive deleted] all night." When the radio stations across the country refused to play the song because the offensive word was one of seven that the U.S Supreme Court has declared "dirty," they simply backward masked the word on the song so the new version sounded like "humped." The song was still offensive, racist and sexist, but legal. Naturally, radio stations quickly got wise to the scam and had a heydey with it, which only served to boost sales further.[22]

Following *Some Girls'* success, the Stones wallowed in a mire of bad press and drug problems for some time and enjoyed no outstanding hits. Then in 1980, they returned to the forefront with *Emotional Rescue,* and then *Tatoo You.* Both records went platinum and were followed by a successful tour. The song "Tops" on the *Tatoo* LP includes a backward masked "love song" which says, "I love you said the Devil."

The devil surfaces on a number of albums by both Led Zeppelin and the Eagles, as well. On the Eagles' LP, *Hotel California*, the title cut played forward says, ". . . this could be heaven or hell. . . ." However, when played in reverse the message revealed is: "Yes, Satan, he organized his own religion . . . it was delicious . . . he puts it in a vat and fixes it for his son and gives it away. . . ."

Led Zeppelin has hidden backward communication on at least two of its recordings. On *Houses of the Holy,* the lyrics heard forward are: ". . . is the word that only leaves you guessing. . . ." Played backward, one hears, "Satan is really lord." The band was at its subtly satanic best, however, with the *Led Zeppelin III* LP, a critical and record-breaking success. Of the LP's hit single, "Stairway to Heaven," Robert Plant said, "Stairway gets the best reactions of anything we do."[23] The song tells of a woman's climb up the stairway to heaven. "There are two paths you can go by," the song tells us, and ". . . you know, sometimes words have two meanings." Played backward, the listener can hear one of those meanings, and it tells of one path: "There's no escaping it. . . . Here's to my sweet Satan. No other made a path, for it makes me sad, whose power is Satan." Elsewhere on the backward side, according to David A. Noebel, it says, "There was a little child born naked . . . now I am Satan," and "I will sing because I live with Satan."[24]

The real lies on this recording are in the forward version, however. First of all the song says the woman is "buying a stairway to heaven." That's impossible, since heaven can't be earned or bought—it's a free gift. Satan would just love people to fall for that falsehood. Likewise, the song claims "there are two paths to go by, but in the long run there's still time to change the road you're on. . . ." Don't you believe it! The time to choose the narrow path that leads to heaven is today. Don't think you can wait until you're old. Those who live cursing God most often die cursing Him as well, because their hearts become callous—"hardened" as the Bible puts it—and God's invitation can no longer penetrate.

This record, as many others, proves that even without subliminal stimuli, the lies can be heard loudly and clearly. The audio masking of secret messages *is* there, however, and in sufficient numbers to make one want to know who are doing it, why they are doing it, if it does have persuasive powers, and what should be done about it.

Big Brother Meets the Peters Brothers

Dr. Israel Goldiamond, a psychology professor at the University of Chicago, says it is very difficult to say something forward and have it make sense when played backward:

> Words are not spoken one at a time—you speak in bursts of several words between breaths, with valleys and hills in the sound energy levels coming out of your mouth. . . . The effort it would take to say something in English which would mean one thing forward and another backward is incredible![25]

And yet, cases apparently exist. Perhaps the genius of satanic influence has been a factor in some albums. This would explain the many times that words spoken forward say something else entirely when played backward. Other instances can probably be credited to the power of suggestion—people hear what they expect to hear—or to coincidence or misinterpretation. Still enough clearly intentional cases have been documented to warrant consideration.

Why backward, you might wonder. One explanation can be found in Aleister Crowley's book, *Manual On Magic*. Crowley said his followers should train themselves to think backward. It was one of the ways, he believed, they would get insight into the coming world. He encouraged them to practice writing, listening, speaking, and even walking backward. Strangely enough, the brain seems able to handle backward images with ease. According to Yarroll, the creative, right hemisphere of the brain does the work. He claims document forgers have used this principle for years, making good, handwritten copies of a mirrored image, drawing, letter or signature.[26]

Likewise, the study of hypnotism has also shed some light on the brain's ability to pick up backward stimuli. According to Key, "Many people in a hypnotic trance can fluently read upside-down, mirror-image texts, suggesting that the brain can perceive information despite seemingly incomprehensible distortions."[27]

Whether Satan-created or simply Satan-inspired, subliminal stimuli certainly have the "Satanic Seal of Approval," for one never hears of secular rock albums promoting secretly the gospel of Christ—or even wholesome thoughts, such as, "Eat all your vegetables, Maynard," or "Would it hurt to visit your grandmother once in a while?" Instead, the messages are always negative, and seem to fit into rock's six categories of error, defined earlier: nihilism, commercialism, rebellion, hedonism, satanism and drug abuse.

Some incidences of rock music subliminals are, no doubt, the work of the rock stars, their producers or technicians. One reason is, as Mick Jagger said, "Satanism sells records."[28] Another reason, which explains why so many of the messages seem to make no sense: they are simply a gimmick to sell records. After all, it's time-consuming and expensive to perform technical tricks on records, and seasoned businessmen such as the Beatles and the Rolling Stones would not use subliminals just for amusement. Those seemingly nonsensical words provoke an emotional response in people, and are therefore promotional tools.

According to Vance Packard, author of two best-selling books describing the games admen play, *The Hidden Persuaders* and *The People Shapers*, certain words are charged with highly emotional overtones—words such as whore, raped and bitch were given as examples.[29] Others known to create a quick response are sex and death.[30] Such emotion-provoking words, the studies show, can visually be flashed twice as fast as neutral words and still cause a response. They are that powerful. When used subliminally, either by audio or visual masking, those words can powerfully affect the consumer.

Advertising people are now beginning to apply this same technique to TV commercials. Electronics specialists, together with psychologists, have created a computerized, voice-compression device that speeds up commercials by as much as 40% without distortion or comprehension loss. Amazingly, the new, jack-rabbit-style commercials are remembered far better than their tortoise-slow counterparts.[31]

Meanwhile, one of the world's largest advertising agencies, says Packard, forecasts that by 1990, many TV messages will be coming at us in three-second blasts, combining words, symbols and other imagery. "The messages will be almost subliminal," Packard predicts.[32]

This sort of evidence makes it easier to understand why many supposedly nonsensical messages appear on rock records. They are quick, power-packed "flag" words to grab our subconscious' attention. But just for the sake of argument, let's discard all but the intelligible, obviously intentional subliminal messages. Though these are admittedly few in number, the question still remains, can they influence us?

The answer is highly contested, but most testing does show an affect on behavior and opinions. Let's look at some of the opinions from respected people and publications.

Wilson Bryan Key: "Subliminal technology sells records by the tens of millions each year in North America. No one apparently knows or understands as yet, however, the consequences of this sensory bombardment upon human value systems."[33]

Family Health magazine: ". . . Dr. Becker's little black box apparently *is* producing results. . . . It does seem to alter the behavior of *the young and the impulsive. It does seem to change minds. . . "*[34] (author's italics).

Science Digest: "Shevrin [psychologist at the University of Michigan, and active in subliminal technique research] . . . has been probing electronic responses to subliminal stimulation and has discovered brain-wave 'correlates' that show the brain responding 'differentially' to subliminal messages." In other words, he has discovered electronic impulses registering responses to messages received unconsciously.[35]

Psychology Today magazine: Dr. Silverman (mentioned earlier), the magazine says, believes subliminal messages affect emotions and can change a person's behavior. He uses a technique called "subliminal psychodynamic activation" to help people read better, lose weight or quit smoking. His series of studies, spanning 10 years, have proved remarkably successful.[36]

Art Linkletter, following the drug-related death of his daughter in 1969, blamed "secret messages" in rock music for "encouraging young people to take part in the growing problem of drug abuse."[37]

Ira Appleman, assistant professor of psychology, Loyola University: "The effects of subliminal manipulation are small and controversial. It's hard to study. How do you know whether something was subliminal or not? Subjects may be unwilling to tell you."[38]

St. Paul Dispatch: As a result of findings that rock records contain subliminal messages, California Assemblyman Phillip Wyman has proposed a state law requiring records containing subliminal messages to bear a warning label. Wyman answers his critics, who contend he is attempting to legislate morals, by saying, "I don't care, as a legislator, what the message is."[39] His concern, Wyman contends, is that the recording may be influencing behavior. A committee has recommended full-scale hearings on the subject.[40]

Saturday Review editorial: "Nothing is more difficult in the modern world than to protect the privacy of the human soul."[41]

Perhaps now the dilemma is more obvious. How do we measure something we can't hear? How do we test subliminals' effects on people objectively? After all, we can't follow them around forever. How do we even legislate something so difficult to isolate, so impossible to find agreement on, and that no one in the media—especially the music industry—is willing to admit is being done?

On this issue the questions outnumber the answers. So, what's a person to do? Well, in most cases, a simple look at the album cover or lyric sheet will be enough on which to base a solid judgment. Then, too, a look at the lifestyles of the artists and any intentions they have espoused can also help. After all, if a rock star's life is a mess, he probably has nothing good to say, forward or backward.

Whether or not we accept the belief that backward masking registers in our mind and affects our future behavior, we must agree that listening repeatedly to records promoting values which we detest does basically the same thing. Whether the messages are hidden or not, they *do* stay with us.

Consider Lot. He was a righteous man, living with his godly uncle, Abraham. He knew right from wrong, and further, he desired what was right. However, years spent in Sodom changed Lot. Though he still desired what was right, his judgment was affected by the moral garbage dump in which he lived. When angels of the Lord came to destroy Sodom, and were nearly attacked by the men of the city who desired them for homosexual relations, Lot offered instead his own virgin daughters for his neighbors to gang rape! It wasn't that Lot didn't love his daughters, or that he desired them harmed. He simply no longer knew right from wrong. For too long he had been "oppressed by the sensual conduct of unprincipled men" (2 Pet. 2:7, NASB).

We do not fall in a moment. "Sin," according to Dr. D. G. Kehl, of Arizona State University in Tempe, "has both an accumulative and a domino effect. Satan plants subtle suggestions, often subliminal ones; he influences an attitude; makes a 'minor' victory—always in preparation for the big fall, the iron-bound habit."[42] David was a man after God's own heart, and Samson was a warrior of the Lord, and yet, each fell into wrong-doing because he allowed himself to remain in questionable surroundings where, as Lot, he was open to subliminal messages. The Bible warns to beware, "lest Satan should get an advantage of us" (2 Cor. 2:11). If we aren't careful, Satan can rob us also of the joy of a Christian way of life, as well as our salvation.

We have researched this subject of subliminal stimuli and backward masking because we're concerned about you. The facts and opinions here are not, in any way, meant to imply that everyone who listens to a song containing sub-stimuli will smoke dope or worship Satan. However, we hope you are convinced it is possible that many in the rock music industry are "playing games with your affections" and that you'll seek out music guaranteed to contain no sham, no deception.

13

Concerts: Hazardous to Your Health

In a Knoxville, Tennessee, theater, an 18-year-old woman was stripped and sexually abused by a gang of youths in the aisle during a rock concert. Though hundreds of people were watching, they ignored her pleas for help. "They were just like animals," she told a reporter later. "Everybody was smoking marijuana."[1]

At a stadium in Cincinnati, Ohio, 11 people were asphyxiated, some while still standing, others while being trampled, as a crowd of rock fans pressed to enter The Who's concert. Lead singer, Pete Townshend, said of the incident, "We're not going to let a little thing like this stop us. . . . We had a tour to do. We're a rock 'n' roll band. You know we don't [expletive deleted] around worrying about 11 people dying. . . . When you go on the road you put an armor around yourself."[2]

An "armor"-less 15-year-old Tampa, Florida, youth received serious burns over 35% of his upper body when he tried to mimic a KISS human-torch concert stunt. He had filled his mouth with lighter fluid and exhaled across a flaming acetylene torch.[3]

The more extreme heavy metal bands evoke not only rebellion but violence at their concerts, and sometimes their behavior is extreme. Jason Flom, an A & M Records talent scout, reports the kids in a heavy metal concert in Tampa, Florida, were standing in front, banging their heads on the stage.[4]

Robberies, rapes, car thefts, stabbings, gang fights, rioting—and even assaults upon fans by rock stars themselves—all occur with frequency at rock concerts. Violence at rock concerts is such a common phenomenon that it seems practical to print the following warning on all concert tickets: WARNING: THE SURGEON GENERAL HAS DETERMINED THAT ROCK CONCERT ATTENDANCE IS HAZARDOUS TO YOUR HEALTH.

I Guess That's Why They Call It the Blues

"Heavy metal" seems to have derived its name from the apocalyptic William S. Burroughs novel, *Naked Lunch*. In the 1959 book, the expression was a synonym for torture. Rock critics first borrowed the term to describe groups such as Black Sabbath and Grand Funk Railroad.[5] Since heavy metal groups

178

tour more than any other kind of band, their nihilistic, "torturous" music is inflicted on rock fans more at concerts than via AM radio (although that is changing), creating an environment both hypnotizing and tremendously negative.

The outrageous antics and wild stage designs lend themselves to that environment, producing an overwhelming effect. The musicians grimace and writhe as if possessed (sometimes a definite possibility). Strobe lights and smoke machines create an eerie, otherworldly feeling, and the earsplitting volume makes communication virtually impossible.

"We take the kids away from their parents and their environment," Grand Funk's drummer, Donnie Brewer, boasted of the group's phenomenal concerts, "to where the only reality is the rhythm and the beat."[6]

Enrapt by the sights and sounds, the young fan, who averages about 15 years old, is in a most suggestible mental state—open to the messages of the music.

The Who was once in the forefront of nihilistic, on-stage violence, ending many of its concerts by destroying its equipment, as if life ended when the concert was over. The celebrated British quartet, whose influence was perhaps nearly as strong as the Beatles and the Rolling Stones, soon saw others following its auto-destruct showmanship, most notably, the Plasmatics.

During her normal two-hour performance, Wendy O. Williams of the Plasmatics will systematically sledgehammer a television set, splinter an electric guitar, and explode a car.[7] Total abandonment from reality is the aim of all this wreckage; as Rolling Stone Mick Jagger put it: "The only performance that really makes it is one that achieves madness."

Devo has another philosophy. It seems the group wants to give its fans a good time by making them feel miserable. "We've read the studies of sound," said one of the techno-video funk artists. "We'd love to make everybody show up at our concerts in diapers, and then have them [expletive deleted] in their pants. And we'd hose them all down at the end."[8] A similar synth-rock group that capitalizes on the nihilistic is the Tubes. With songs such as "Mondo Bondage" and "Mr. Hate," vocalist Fee Waybill and his female counterpart enact scenes of rape, murder and revenge, as well as plenty of striptease and sex. The display was described by one critic as "anything but cathartic or instructive."[9]

Can these assaults on young rock fans' sense of hope and well-being actually cause damage? Can attitudes and antics on stage persuade concertgoers? After a cranium-pounding at a Ted Nugent concert, one critic said, "Those kids would do anything for Ted. If he told 'em to jump off a cliff, they'd probably do it, no questions asked."[10] Though still trying to maintain their boyish image, the Beatles admitted once, "Our music is capable of causing emotional instability, disorganized behavior, rebellion, and even revolution."[11]

In 1978, a California music therapist confirmed the Beatles' theory when he administered an emotional stability test to 240 school children, ages 10 to 18. While the children took the test, the therapist played rock music. The results were then examined by a psychologist who was unaware of either the group tested or the circumstances under which testing took place. He concluded the test had been given in a mental hospital. While one test is perhaps not grounds to claim conclusive evidence, the results are, nonetheless alarming.[12]

Steve Glantz, a Detroit concert promoter, seems to think KISS has a similar effect on its fans. "It's almost like Hitler-Rock," says Glantz of the overpowering atmosphere of KISS concerts, "because the audience—because of the beat—they're mesmerized by the music. I mean they have the audience hypnotized. They could say, 'We're going out there and lifting up this building,' and they'd just go lift it up. That's the kind of control they have. That's why their following is so strong and so indestructible."[13]

Rock stars exert a tremendous power over their fans. Ozzy Osbourne got a chance to see just how strong that pull is when he decided to shave his head to enhance his image. *Hit Parader* magazine says fans did likewise, just to prove how devoted to him they were. Osbourne said of a concert, " . . . there were 25 kids in the front with shaved heads, smiling and pointing to their heads when I looked down at them. . . . It's a good thing I didn't have my leg amputated."[14]

It shouldn't come as much of a surprise. David Lee Roth of Van Halen notes, "I've always looked at Van Halen as a role model for kids. We're anti-heroes, and that suits me fine." He added with a grin, "I've always been a problem child. It's just that now I'm getting paid for it."[15]

At the age of 14 or 15, most young people become exposed, for the first time, to significant trauma—boyfriend/girlfriend troubles, death or divorce in the family, or possibly a move—and they don't have the experience necessary to realize the pain is a temporary thing. Rev. Don Smith, a Methodist youth director in Plano, Texas, where teenage suicide has reached epidemic proportions, says, "They are so impressionable and have such a need to be popular. If suicide is seen as something everybody in trouble is doing, I worry about them."[16]

Young people have enough pressures in their lives without subjecting themselves to an environment that is hopeless and nihilistic. Psalm 146 consoles with the message that the person who is happy is the person whose help and hope depends on the Lord—but that song of strength can be drowned out by the negative influence rock music possesses, an influence felt perhaps most strongly at a concert.

All You Need Is Cash

The commercial value of rock concerts is undeniable. Obviously, there would be no concerts if the people involved made no money. However, in their search for that profit, rock promoters and stars are willing to go to any extreme. When rock began, that extreme translated into the "duck walk" of Chuck Berry and the pompadoured gaudiness of Little Richard. Elvis Presley took the extreme further when he added his animal-like, sexual antics, earning him the nickname "Elvis the Pelvis." The Beatles added a new dimension to rock concert history when they introduced psychedelia to the music, and the Rolling Stones added to the one-up-manship by demonstrating open rebellion in their shows. Flower power and free love were the next elements added to hype rock concerts, though Frank Zappa was quick to admit, "The whole hippie scene is wishful thinking. They wish they could love, but they're full of [expletive deleted]."[17]

As if to drown out the truth of Zappa's statement, metal madness blasted off to produce wrap-around sound. Even that wasn't enough, however, and new aberrations were added. There were glitter rockers, monster rockers, country rockers, disco rockers, Satan rockers, and punk rockers. In the eighties, rock has diverged in a number of directions, but words such as nasty, crude, bawdy, androgynous and pornographic seem to describe most of the sensationalist gimmicks.

Most rock celebrities and hopefuls would go to virtually any extreme and use any gimmick if they thought it would promote them to star status. Most rock stars are playing for the money, and there's plenty to be made. Some of the current top concert attractions are the Police, the Grateful Dead, Jackson Browne, Journey, Black Sabbath and David Bowie. The Police have been clearly number one, having grossed an average of $1,066,600 per concert for just three of the many concerts they played in 1983.[18] The live music business grosses in the billions, not to mention the souvenir-merchandising business which has become an industry grossing hundreds of millions.[19] To make that kind of cash, most rock music hopefuls will be as bizarre as necessary to build an image and a following.

Grammy Award-winning producer Michael Omartian, who has produced albums for Christopher Cross, Donna Summer and Rod Stewart, knows the music industry inside and out. He said in a recent TV interview with CBN News correspondent, Steve McPheeters:

The bizarre is so much a part of a stage persona as opposed to a lifestyle. . . . That's what disturbs me more than anything. . . . These people who get off the stage become like anybody else, and yet they portray, to vulnerable people all over the place, this image that [says], "Do whatever you want to do. It doesn't matter. There's nothing to live for anyway. Let's just go get crazy."

And yet, they walk off and they've got their accountants taking care of their money very carefully—to make sure that they're secure for the rest of their lives. And they've got their whole home situation as secure as possible because they don't want to be vulnerable to craziness. So the very thing that they're advocating is the very opposite of their lifestyle offstage.

The overwhelming majority [of rock stars] care mostly about the money that will be derived from success. And I feel like it's easier to cater to the base nature in all of us than to try to put something inspiring and positive into you, because that requires thought. The baser things of our very nature require no thinking.

Undeniably, many rock personalities are simply pawns in the money game—exploiting the latest craze in hope of finding success. But do young people have to be duped in the process? Bernie Leadon, former singer and guitarist with the Eagles, says many groups employ "shock rock" only to attract the attention of teens, and he fears some groups may be too drugged to realize the dangers involved for both themselves and their following—much less to care.[20] This, the Bible says, is a sign of the end times: "Evil persons and imposters will keep on going from bad to worse, deceiving others and being deceived themselves" (2 Tim. 3:13, GNB).

Since teenagers have more spending money than ever before, they have become an attractive market. However, each of us has a responsibility to spend money wisely. Matt. 6:19–21 says we should concentrate our time, energy and money on what is really important and of eternal value, "For your heart will always be where your riches are" (GNB). It's an attitude that will keep us from buying rock's phony, commercialized image, as well as the concert tickets.

Rebellion and Violence: Rock Concert Companions

We've already discussed the concert in which Mick Jagger sang "Sympathy for the Devil" while an unarmed man was beaten and stabbed before the stage by toughs Jagger had hired for "security." That infamous event was fully covered by the media, but we seldom hear of other violence inflicted on fans by rock music promoters and artists.

Elton John highlighted a two-week, sold-out engagement at London's Hammersmith Odeon by throwing a piano stool across the stage and hitting a woman in the head. Although the injury was accidental, her boyfriend attacked the singer in retribution.[21]

Concert-goers do enter at their own risk, however, and violence does often explode. At a concert in Ontario, California, hard-guy rocker, John Cougar Mellencamp, launched into an obscenity-laced talk with the promoter and then threw a drum set into the audience. His outburst injured two girls and he quickly left the stage.[22]

Molly Hatchet, known for its after-hours violence, even fills intermissions with battles. Singer Danny Joe Brown "beat the [expletive deleted]" out of a professional wrestler during the break in one of the group's Jacksonville concerts. Unruffled, Brown went back onstage for the second show.[23] "We prefer to do our [expletive deleted] kicking on stage," says guitarist Dave Hlubek, but Brown warned the punks at England's Reading Festival: "I hope nobody starts spittin'—I'll beat the [expletive deleted] outta somebody who does that in fronta me."[24]

Tempers often flare when violence is so prevalent. Freddie Mercury, Queen's lead vocalist, says, "We row about everything, even the air we breathe.

We're the bitchiest band on earth, darling. We're at each other's *throats*. One night Roger [Taylor] was in a foul mood and he threw his entire bloody drumset across the stage. The thing only just missed me—I might have been killed."[25]

Another flare-up occurred in Montreal when Pink Floyd played before 80,000 people. The band sensed trouble coming when they just couldn't "connect" with their fans, many of whom were stoned or drunk. The audience repeatedly set off cherry bombs and there were several beatings with beer bottles. Finally, Roger Waters recalls, he "found himself spitting on a guy who couldn't stop yelling. It was a real war."[26]

Aerosmith's tough-minded manager, David Krebs, says, "None of my groups will ever play Cincinnati again. The last time Aerosmith played Cincinatti somebody was shot."[27] The band's Steve Tyler added that fans also tore up seats and set them on fire, and former Aerosmith guitarist Joe Perry's hand was injured by a cherry bomb, thrown from the audience.[28]

Fans at a Neil Young concert in Louisville, Kentucky, went wild in the convention center when Young was forced to leave the stage, due to illness, after performing for about an hour. As he collapsed in his dressing room, they ripped chairs from the floor and threw beer cups on stage.[29]

The Beach Boys actually brought down the house in Salina, Kansas. A frenzied, sellout crowd at that city's Bicentennial Center stomped, screamed and clapped so loudly that ceiling materials and lighting fixtures fell in the auditorium's hallways.[30] And yet, Neil Young and the Beach Boys are, by rock standards, quite mild—and so are their fans.

In speaking of more fanatic bands, an article in *Time* magazine said some bands seem to play as though possessed. "The music itself is animated by excess, insists on, and receives, a response in kind." Using The Who as an example, the article went on: "Who audiences are some of the most fiercely loyal, and some of the wildest in rock. Abandon is the aim, and to reach that, The Who act in concert with the audience."[31]

A former security guard at New York's Nassau Coliseum says Black Sabbath provokes the most violent fans, and Milwaukee promoter, Randy McElrath, agrees: "Yeah, their crowds are a high-risk type situation." Defining a People's Rock audience, says McElrath, depends upon with what they're "abusing themselves. . . . " The fans who come to see Sabbath and Blue Oyster Cult, he says, are "a pretty heavy-drinking crowd. . . . They're a real rowdy crowd, one of your rowdiest."[32] The people who clamor for heavy metal tend to aggregate into boisterous mobs, often more interested in booze and petty violence than in the music.

When Black Sabbath played in Wisconsin's 12,000-seat Milwaukee Arena in 1980, bassist Geezer Butler was knocked unconscious by a flying bottle. The ruckus that ensued after the group left the stage resulted in 150 arrests, and the city was put on its first riot alert in 20 years.[33]

The band has developed such a notoriety for violence that citizens groups have formed against it. One successful group in Savannah, Georgia, started a letter-writing campaign against the band's appearance, and eventually per-suaded the promoters to cancel the concert. "It looked as though more people didn't want them than did," the promoters told *USA Today*.[34]

Ozzy Osbourne, who does his best to crank up his fans to the excesses for which his former Black Sabbath buddies are known, appears to be walking on the edge at all times. He says he gets "a thrill" from his dove decapitation stunts, and that he enjoys throwing offal at the audience (about 25 pounds of calf livers and pig intestines are dumped on the audience each night). "The freakiest thing of all," says Osbourne, "is that the kids *ask* to be thrown it."[35] He hasn't said who asked him to urinate onstage, or who enjoys his trampling little puppies to death. The audience violence which often accompanies his performances, as does his old group's, Black Sabbath, is not altogether con-demned by Osbourne. "Let them get rid of their aggression in a [concert] hall," he says, "and they're not going to be outside mugging some old lady for her purse."[36]

If that's so, then why do so many rock stars hire Hulk-sized bodyguards? Frank Zappa, who employs an ex-policeman, says with more honesty than Osbourne displays, "You get a lot of very strange people at any rock concert and the drugs people use at the moment increase the risk of a crazy, violent attack."[37]

Michael Jackson's lawyer, John Branca, voiced the same concern: "I worry all the time. . . . The Who had riots. With a tour of this magnitude [Jackson's 1984 summer tour], it's got to be planned with perfectionism to make sure it's conducted smoothly." According to *Rolling Stone*, the "extraordinary scope of Michael's popularity magnifies tenfold the problems presented by an av-erage rock tour. . . . In fact, one promoter has dubbed the Jackson's outing 'the Nitro Tour: At any moment, the whole thing could blow up.' " The mag-azine quoted another fearful promoter:

> I'm just very, very concerned from a safety standpoint, because I know . . . when these little kids come there with their parents or by themselves, they're going to make a beeline for the front of that stage, and I don't wanna see any little kids get trampled. . . . I could not guarantee the safety of those in front of the stage. I don't think anybody can—if they do, they're liars.[38]

Larry Larson, Jackson's tour coordinator, doesn't seem bothered, how-ever. " . . . I know that the Jacksons are going to generate a tremendous amount of enthusiasm," he says. "But . . . the Jacksons do not have a history of cre-ating riots." *Rolling Stone* pointed out, however, that "the last time the Jack-sons played New York City, dozens of youths were arrested after a chain-snatching spree inside Madison Square Garden." When the possibility of kids getting trampled was suggested to Larson, the magazine says he shrugged it off: "Well, you can get run over by a truck while walking across the street. We all have certain risks in life."[39]

Judas Priest band members excuse the excessive violence, claiming their fans want it and deserve it. Guitarist Glenn Tipton says, "When our fans pay to see us, we owe them a show. Judas Priest is the best rock and roll band around and we'll do anything to prove it." Teammate Rob Halford agrees: "We make fans believe we live the lives we sing about. Sure, there may be a few unsavory things in our music, a bit of tension and hostility, but that's what the world's about these days."[40]

Motorhead's lead singer, Lemmy Kilmister, sees it the same way:

> They [the fans] know what to expect when they come to our show, 'cause we're gonna give it to 'em full blast. . . . I think we're developing the same kind of following over here [America] that we have back home: a real street-level group of kids who come to our shows and buy our records to blow off a little steam and have a good time. . . . For us the bottom line will always be the thousands of kids with their fists in the air fighting to get to the front rows at our shows.[41]

The Chicago *Tribune* sees it differently. It says this sort of frenzy-producing atmosphere is nothing more than "selling our youth shoddy music, shoddy ideas." After quoting Pete Townshend—"The whole purpose of a rock concert is for people to forget themselves, to lose their egos in the crowd, and to disappear"—it reminds its readers to remember the eleven who were lost forever at one of The Who's concerts. "Never mind," the article concludes caustically, "if they trample or are trampled to death in the process."

A Lust for Entertainment, or Entertainment for Lust

Grand Funk Railroad, those grandaddies of the seventies rock bands, were, as *Who's Who in Rock* describes, "totally and irrevocably 'hype,' all sound and fury, signifying nothing."[42] In 1970 alone its "sound and fury" sold 10 million records, and in 1970–1971 it grossed $120 million. In the summer of 1971, Funk filled Shea Stadium with 55,000 young teens, grossing over $300,000 for that concert alone. The group walked on stage with clenched fist salutes, while the scoreboard spelled out a sexual expletive. Then, lead guitarist Mike Farner greeted his adolescent audience by saying, "You're the best [expletive deleted] audience in the whole world."[43]

Sexually explicit language, no matter how offensive, is perhaps the least harmful prurience abounding at most rock concerts. The performers' behavior is worse. *Circus* magazine chose Pat Benatar Best Female Vocalist in 1981; and in 1984, she took top honors in the American Music Awards, and has won at least four Grammy awards. Despite her excellent voice, it is her sex-pot image that gets the press—and brings young fans to her concerts. "Audiences were bogged over," *Circus* says, "by the singer's shift of moods—purringly seductive on the verses, blood wringing on the chorus."[44]

When *Rock* magazine interviewed "the sexy songstress," they quoted her as saying:

> I've always enjoyed playing live before an enthusiastic audience. When I look directly in the eyes of the audience and I know they're getting off on my music, I feel I can perform all night. At times like that, I truly feel like I'm making

love to my entire audience. . . . Sometimes I look out and I see lust on these teenage boys' faces.[45]

Benatar has been frightened at times by the intensity of the response she provokes. Once while touring Europe, she refused to do an encore because the audience worried her. "The whole crowd was mostly men, and they were all yelling obscenities. . . . I said, ' . . . I'm not going out there, they're nuts.' Sometimes I'd rather be androgynous."[46]

That sort of reaction probably wouldn't phase Debbie Harry who has said, "I've always thought the main ingredients in rock are sex, really good stage shows and really sassy music. Sex and sass. I really think that's where it's at."[47] Another time Harry stated, "I just dance around and shake . . . I wear tight clothes. I wear short skirts—try to look hot. . . . If someone's undressing me with their eyes, that's not an offense to me."[48]

Writer Cheryl Lavin describes Tina Turner's act in much the same way: "[She's] the high-priestess of 'raunch and roll'; the woman who rubs up and down against the microphone, letting it nuzzle her ear; the one who wears lingerie on stage most women wouldn't wear to bed."[49]

"I feel the music business is sexless, except on stage," says 1984 Grammy winner Chaka Kahn. "It's like making love. . . . I'll look a guy in the eye sometimes, and shake at him. . . . I can feel some eyes undressing me. . . . They can undress me with their eyes—it's alright because I'm [expletive deleted] them anyway."[50]

The Plasmatics specializes in sexually suggestive songs and onstage destruction. "Everytime we play," giggles Williams, "I have orgasms—especially on 'Butcher Baby.' "[51] Describing one of her concerts, *Creem* magazine reported, ' 'Wendy is wearing tight black pants and an almost non-existent bra. . . . Later in the set she will exit the stage briefly and return nude to the waist, except for strategically applied gobs of whipped cream."[52]

Patterning its style after the Plasmatics, Missing Persons, an L.A.-based group, trades on synthesized sounds and sex appeal. Fronting the group is Dale Bozzio, a former Playboy bunny who has been described as a "punk Joan Rivers." Though she claims no desire to lead young kids into drugs, anarchy or "stupid things like devil worship," her group sells sleaze without a twinge of conscience.

Rolling Stone magazine says of the blond-and-pink-haired Bozzio:

Dale wears bikini tops made of clear-plastic bubbles with plastic-tubing straps, and uses cut-up posters or records for her tiny bottoms. It was Dale's body, plastered on the cover of the band's homemade and self-distributed first EP, that probably caught radio programmers' eyes back in 1981."[53]

Sound magazine quotes Dale's husband/drummer Terry Bozzio on the subject of sex: "There's been sexuality in rock and roll since the beginning . . . Dale, I'll admit, wears uniforms that flaunt it."[54]

Image is all-important in the rock music industry, and no one promotes image better than Duran Duran (named after the villain in the 1968 Jane Fonda movie, *Barbarella*). The group is making musical history with its top-10 hits, promoted on MTV in what *USA Today* describes as "sexy mini-melodramas shot in such exotic locales as Sri Lanka and Antigua." The group is often compared with the Beatles, due to its members' good looks and hysterical fans. Bassist John Taylor, 23, says, "I play the role of being a rock star on stage. When the music works, the audience and the performer often feel like they're having an orgasm together."[55] At least the Duran Duran group seems to respect its fans.

David Cassidy is another story. In an interview laced with obscenities, he spoke mockingly of his female fans, who, after his concerts, leave behind "thousands of sticky seats."[56]

A David Cassidy clone, brother Shaun, gets thousands of pieces of mail each week, and backstage security is heavy at his performances, which *Circus* magazine says "regularly drive stadiums full of pre-teen girls into ecstasy." Says Shaun, "You'd be amazed what is flung at me on stage."

"It's extremely sexual," agrees Hedy End, managing editor of *Sixteen* magazine. "Girls want to get as close to their idols as they can. And it's healthy.... It helps them get over the bumps of growing up."[57]

Adam Ant agrees with that assessment of young audiences. "Audiences have a psychology. When you go on, there's a very sexual feeling.... When you're getting hot, sweaty, sticky, and moving about, it's the closest thing to making love, really. It's a lust for entertainment, a lust for escapism."[58]

"People want the outrageous," insists Rick James, and according to *Us* magazine, he does the best he can to accommodate their demands. "He juts like Jagger and struts like Stewart, wielding consummate power over his audience," the magazine says, and the audience screams, "We want Rick to funk us up!" over and over again. James says with a shrug, "I'm still a juvenile delinquent. I haven't gotten out of it, only perfected it."[59]

Of the strutting, Rod Stewart says, "If I can't jump around, what's the use in doing the shows?"[60] In an interview with *Hit Parader*, Stewart remarked:

> We had an amazing experience the other night. At one point I had about 15 brassieres around my waist. I've never seen so many brassieres thrown up on stage—they just kept coming, and I stuck them in my trousers. I had them all around—that was a really good concert![61]

Van Halen's David Lee Roth doesn't get much lingerie thrown at him—his audiences are mostly male. Onstage, Roth alternates between telling his fans how great he is, and how great they are for being smart enough to like him—according to *Us* magazine. Roth says of his critics, "The worse they write about us the better I like it.... Van Halen music does make me feel very sexy. I get to act out all my fantasies."[62]

One of those critics, Pete Bishop of the Pittsburgh *Press,* wrote:

> The overriding aspect of last night's Van Halen concert ... was the obnoxious,

disgusting exhibition of singer David Lee Roth. . . . The bad language flowed from his mouth more freely than beer at an Oktoberfest. . . . The *coup de grâce*, however, came during "Ain't Talking About Love" as Roth appeared in black leather pants with cutouts up the outside of each leg and two big cutouts in the rear with a large tassel down the middle—and no undies. Imagine paying 12 bucks to get mooned—that's *not* entertainment.[63]

James Morrison, the Doors' former golden-haired sex symbol/exhibitionist, was known for his erotic performances as much as his surreal lyrics preoccupied with sex and death. By 1968, the Doors had three gold albums and had become an enormous concert attraction, largely due to Morrison's theatrics. In March 1969, Morrison was finally arrested in Miami, Florida, and charged as follows: "Morrison did lewdly and lasciviously expose his [genitals] . . . did simulate the act of masturbation upon himself and oral copulation upon another . . . [and] did unlawfully and publicly use and utter profane and indecent language."[64] Many subsequent concerts, according to *The Rock Who's Who*, turned into outrageous fiascos due to Morrison's antics. Morrison, wasted by drugs and drink, eventually left the Doors and, shortly thereafter, died under mysterious circumstances.[65]

James Morrison, however, did not invent sexual excess on stage—nor was he the worst offender—though possibly the most publicized. Queen's tours have featured transvestites, strippers, snake charmers and even a naked woman who smoked cigarettes between her legs![66] Jimi Hendrix's trademark was his exhibitionist technique—he would pluck the strings of his guitar with his teeth, sensually fondling the instrument. Then he'd vividly pantomime copulation, with the guitar as his sexual partner. In a review of a 1967 Hendrix live appearance as the opening act for the Monkees, writer Lillian Roxon said of the guitar sex affair, "Even the little girls who had come to see the Monkees understood what this was about."[67]

Jethro Tull's Ian Anderson is known for his manic, sexually explicit stage antics, which often utilized both his flute and the sound system. The concerts were often bizarre and loaded with sexuality and vulgarities, but it was Anderson's fondness for grabbing his loins and talking about how his "microphone stand had an erection" that enhanced the group's popularity.[68]

In a typical Prince concert, too, sexual display is rampant. Prince, called by *Rolling Stone* the most influential music man of the eighties so far, often strokes the neck of his guitar, feigning masturbation; pantomimes sexual foreplay; performs striptease routines leaving little to the imagination; and, with a series of gasps and shudders, simulates orgasm.[69]

Iggy Pop, formerly Iggy Stooge, formerly James Osterberg, earns the dubious honor of being the most disturbing and provocative on stage. Says *The Rock's Who's Who*:

Over the years, his notoriety grew with deeds such as threatening and vilifying audiences, cutting himself with broken bottles, pouring hot wax over his body, intentionally smashing out his teeth, and throwing up, even urinating on audiences and allowing ardent fans to perform fellatio [oral sex] on him.[70]

In 1977, following two critically acclaimed albums, *The Idiot* and *Lust for Life,* Iggy Pop regrouped with the Stooges and returned to the live and lewd shows he was known best for, often accompanied by his mentor, David Bowie, and former bassist of the Sex Pistols, Glen Matlock.

The Apostle Paul could have had a rock concert's wanton hedonism in mind when he wrote: "But mark this: There will be terrible times in the last days. People will be lovers of themselves, lovers of money, boastful, proud, abusive, disobedient to their parents, ungrateful, unholy, without love, unforgiving, slanderous, without self-control, brutal, not lovers of good, treacherous, rash, conceited, lovers of pleasure rather than lovers of God—having a form of godliness but denying its power. Have nothing to do with them" (2 Tim. 3:1–5, NIV).

Dante's Inferno Is Coming to Your Home Town

As pointed out previously, 1 Sam. 15:22, 23 declares that rebellion and arrogance are related to witchcraft and idolatry, and are equally repulsive in God's eyes. If the two are equal, then it is logical to conclude they frequently appear together, and it seems rebellion can lead to witchcraft.

This was the case for the people of Judah. Isaiah warned them that because they had rebelled against God, and because they had sought the occultic wisdom of Egypt over the wisdom of God, they were headed for disaster. But they replied, "Don't talk to us about what's right. Tell us what we want to hear. Let us keep our illusions. Get out of our way and stop blocking our path. We don't want to hear about your holy God of Israel" (Isa. 30:10, 11, GNB). The outcome of their rebellion was the practice of pagan religion. Are there parallels in the rock music world?

Think about it a moment—when Iron Maiden storms onto the stage, amidst hellish flashpots and blinding lights, what is the first sign they display? The clenched fist of rebellion. When black-caped Ronnie Dio cranks up the amplifiers on a set that looks like Dante's Inferno—all smoke and fire and a huge devil as a backdrop—what do his raw-lunged vocals most often proclaim? The spirit of alienation. When Twisted Sister or Ozzy Osbourne or Motley Crue—or any of the many rock groups that slam the one-two punch of rebellion and occultism in the faces of their audiences—charge onstage, how do the fans respond? They shake their fists to the music, scream the lyrics, and many times participate in open violence. It is no accident that signs of Satanism or occultism in the stage show so often go hand in hand with signs of rebellion in the audience.

Meat Loaf (or Mr. Loaf, as the *New York Times* insists on calling him), possibly the world's largest rock singer (6'2", 260 pounds), sang lead for Ted Nugent's Amboy Dukes before his "lucky" break came with a role in the cult movie, *Rocky Horror Picture Show.*[71] At about the same time, a songwriter who is fascinated by the supernatural and science fiction—Jim Steinmen—

linked up with Loaf to create an album. The result was *Bat Out of Hell*, produced by another dabbler in mysticism, Todd Rundgren. Loaf admits that when he goes on stage, he gets possessed.[72]

United Press International reported that KISS bass player Gene Simmons was "disgusted" with accusations by religious leaders that the band is "satanic." KISS had been greeted by protests from religious leaders in many cities during its 1983 100-city, 6-month tour.[73]

Although Simmons claims the group isn't satanic, former KISS catman, Peter Criss, describes the concerts as nearly insane. Says Criss:

> I was fed up with ducking bottles and M-80s and getting hit in the face with cigarette lighters. Also, there were four really heavy egos involved in KISS, and it was getting to me that I was becoming Peter "The Cat" 24 hours a day and was losing Peter Criss the person. I felt I had to make a change to preserve my sanity.[74]

Criss has just given us a good description of the rebellion and arrogance the Bible warns is the first step toward the occult and Satanism. But there's further proof.

Producer Bob Ezrin described KISS as "symbols of unfettered evil,"[75] and its fan magazines call it "fire-breathing demons from rock and roll hell."[76] KISS sings songs for its 14-and-under crowd such as "God of Thunder" and "Hotter Than Hell."

Gene Simmons implies demon worship when he lewdly extends his tongue—an ancient pagan symbol he has continued to use, despite the discarding of the hellish makeup and costumes. He also repeatedly gestures the *Il Cornuto,* the traditional Sicilian sign (forefinger and little finger extended, other fingers curled into a fist) used among Black Arts practitioners to ward off "the evil eye."

All this in an environment that is, according to Simmons, ". . . totally by design . . . loud enough that you can't think and you can't hear. We *are* the environment. . . . There's too much going on onstage visually, for you not to look at us. You just have no choice."[77]

Simmons has just described perfectly a captive audience. Although the group doesn't seem to take itself too seriously—more like comic book anti-heroes—and though its members deride accusations that their act exudes demonic overtones, it is obvious that even if their pre-pubescent fans had the necessary maturity and information to know the difference between a hoax and the real thing, given the overpowering environment of a concert, they would not be able to think it through—or to turn away!

Joe Cocker, a talented rhythm-and-blues singer, is best known for his use of grotesque contortions during a performance. Of his spasmodic, wildman delivery, Cocker was quoted by *Time* magazine as saying that when he sings rock music, something "seizes" him.[78]

When Black Sabbath formed in 1968, it employed the use of loud noise and occultic phenomena to amass a following, and in the process, was inundated with letters and objects from people deeply involved in the supernatural. As a result, the group has had to avoid almost all contact with its unpredictable fans. It must have seemed a small sacrifice, however; for when the press picked up on hints that the group was composed of active warlocks, the Antichrist image sold a mountain of vinyl—including *Paranoid, Sabbath Bloody Sabbath,* and *Heaven and Hell.*

A Minneapolis concert by the group was described as follows:

> . . . Dio [Ronnie James Dio, now promoting his own band] marched up and down the stage clothed like Dracula in a cape, his voice filling the arena, his hand perpetually flashing the traditional Italian hand gesture to ward off the evil eye. . . . During the second half, the stage was shrouded with black cloth. Eerie music seeped through the P.A. and lights blinked to represent lightning. Some fans yelled, "We want you," imitating the voice of Orgar, the demonic Uncle Sam who may be the first cartoon figure on a pinball machine to be a subculture hero. Others held high a banner reading, "We sold our soul for rock 'n' roll."[79]

Ritchie Blackmore was formerly of the mystical, heavy metal band, Deep Purple, a group he formed in Hamburg, Germany, in 1968. He carried with him that same mysticism and doom when, out of boredom, he left Deep Purple to form Rainbow. Blackmore likes to record his music in a supposedly haunted 17th-century castle, and his interest in Black Magic has been the inspiration for much of his music—including "Yoga for Health," "Stargazer," and "Tarot Woman."[80]

The moody singer, who dresses in black, says that during his live performances he astral projects to float above his audiences. He also takes part in séances in a misdirected effort "to get closer to God."[81]

John McLaughlin has claimed out-of-body experiences similar to Blackmore's. McLaughlin, an incredibly talented guitarist, has been part of at least 10 different groups, but is most well-known for his Mahavishnu Orchestra, which he founded following his conversion to the philosphy of Bengal mystic, Sri Chinmoy. That group's *Birds of Fire* LP established McLaughlin's popularity. He joined forces with another Sri Chinmoy convert, Carlos Santana, to produce *Love, Devotion, and Surrender,* which sold enough copies to be certified gold, despite its mystically obsessive nature.[82]

No longer a disciple of Sri Chinmoy, but still evidently involved with mysticism, McLaughlin formed Shakti in 1976, and The One Truth Bank in 1979. What is the inspiration for all of this Eastern-dominated music and does it lead to satanic involvement? McLaughlin himself said, "When I let the spirit play me, it's an intense delight. My role as musician is to make everyone aware of his own divinity."[83]

That clearly indicates McLaughlin is on the wrong road. However, he further clarified his involvement in the occult when he described to *Circus* magazine his concert experiences: "One night we were playing and suddenly the spirit entered into me, and I was playing, but it was no longer me playing."[84]

Through the brief examples noted here, we've viewed the way rock stars have promoted the occult in their concerts. Some have dabbled in it, some have supposedly "played" with it, and others have virtually immersed themselves in it. No matter what the occult involvement, however, its use is most frequently an attention-getting device. Unfortunately, just as a puppet doesn't know it is attached to and dependent on its master, rock stars too often fail to realize there are strings attached to occultic practices, and a very powerful master puppeteer pulls the strings.

A Gathering of the Tribes

Gracie Slick, the former sex symbol of the psychedelic sixties, is now a middle-aged rock and roll survivor. Many of the young people she sang to at places such as Woodstock and Altamont were not so lucky—they have become victims of drug and/or alcohol abuse, and unlike Slick, didn't pull out in time.

Now in a solo career, she claims to have beaten both drug and alcohol dependency. Of those psychedelic sixties days, Slick remembers a scene that wasn't pretty: "The Jefferson Airplane and I stayed on the stage all night long taking drugs and wondering how we could avoid going to the bathroom," she says of Woodstock, a festival which, through media and song hype, has taken on idyllic, mythic qualities. "I don't know where Joni Mitchell was when she wrote the song 'Woodstock,' but . . . to me Woodstock was a lot of helicopters, drugs, mud and an endless sea of smiling faces."[85]

The Grateful Dead were around in those days as well. Its spokesman and "resident guru," Jerry Garcia, described the group's popular sound, acid rock, as "music you listen to when you are high on acid."[86] The Dead was known as the band that stood for rebellion and drugs, and its fans were heavy dopers. A typical concert was often sotted with LSD as well as pot, and Dead's followers have appropiately been dubbed "dead-heads." Describing a Dead concert, an article in *Us* magazine stated, "Wine-filled goatskins, marijuana and assorted other 'party favors' are passed through the crowd."[87]

KISS concert-goers prefer another poison. After lead vocalist/guitarist Paul Stanley introduces the song, "Cold Gin," with a brief discourse about tequila and vodka, he poses a question to his young fans. What is it, he asks the screaming crowd, that one really needs to "get down and dirty": On cue the teenyboppers scream back in delight, "Cold gin!" "What?" he bellows. "Cold gin!" the crowd (some a decade away from the legal drinking age) squeals back as KISS explodes into the number.[88]

The hard rockers of Van Halen caused a stir with a similar incident at a Cincinnati concert. "They thought I was aiding and abetting the crowd by telling them to smoke and drink," explains Roth. "But people were just having a riotous good time."[89]

USA Today describes one of Van Halen's concerts:

On stage, Roth—typically clad in tight leather pants and open vest—has more moves than a striptease artist. His concert chatter has him happily playing the role of host to an arena-sized frat party. "I often tell people attending a Van Halen concert to put some cotton in their ears, have a few beers and enjoy the party," says Roth. Roth, who claims he's "recreational director for the immoral majority," describes rock 'n' roll as a "gathering of the tribes."[90]

Journey, formed by two former Santana members, Neal Schon and Gregg Rolie, emerged from the drug-oriented West Coast scene about 1979, and has recorded such hits as "Lovin', Touchin', Squeezin'," and "Any Way You Want It." Speaking of its fans, Journey manager Herbie Herbert reports they generally show up at their concerts with "a pill and a joint."[91]

Elton John's shows are typically drug-centered too. At a concert in New York's Central Park, sponsored by Calvin Klein jeans, thousands of marijuana joints were passed around by teenagers who had come to listen to the bespectacled rocker.[92]

Ted Nugent's fans are also categorized as drug users. Vincent Ford of *Hard Rock* magazine writes, "Ted Nugent's audience is hard rock oriented. They are more than likely young teens flipped out in an aura of pot-smoking, cheap wine, beer, and quaaludes."[93] Although "King Gonzo" does not advocate drugs personally, his Amboy Dukes' *Journey to the Center of Your Mind* is a drug anthem that *Rolling Stone* named to its Psychedelic Top 40.[94]

People magazine describes a Quiet Riot concert in these terms:

Onstage the group relies on punch and pose when playing for its largely adolescent audiences. [Kevin] DuBrow, 28, augments screaming vocals with a self-styled "demented cheerleader" routine, guzzling from a bottle of Jack Daniel's and occasionally hoisting bare-chested guitarist [Carlos] Cavazo, 25, to his shoulders. . . . The chemistry has worked to produce a nightly avalanche of lingerie onstage, plus sales of almost 4 million records.

Offstage, however, another side of the group emerges. "Even DuBrow," the article goes on, "whose 'Let's get craaazeee!' yell and wide-eyed mugging spark Quiet Riot concerts, is not as crazy as he seems. His Jack Daniel's bottle actually contains cold herbal tea."[95]

Do the fans know whether the liquid in the bottle is the real stuff or not? Probably not. So while DuBrow makes sure he doesn't get drunk, he encourages his young fans to do so. "Down the line when someone mentions Quiet Riot," he muses, "I hope they'll think of a great party they went to once."[96]

Some of those parties don't turn out too "great," however; in fact, *most* of them don't. An article in *Circus* magazine describes the first day of a California concert that was attended by over 250,000 spectators:

By 6 p.m. Saturday over 700 people were treated for OD's, MD's [mixing drugs], and other medical problems. . . . Over half the drug overdoses were caused by PCP [angel dust]. Initial reports said two people had died from drugs mixed with alcohol, but Ontario police have confirmed no deaths occurred. There were, however, an unaccountable number of car lootings, two robberies, two rapes and a stabbing reported.[97]

Aerosmith's concerts have traditionally been places reeking with the sickening sweet aroma of marijuana. In fact, the band (once billed as Rolling Stones sound-alikes) even paid $3,650 to bail out 52 of its fans who had been jailed for drug possession at one of its concerts.

The effects of drug abuse often catch up with rock and rollers, however—sometimes right on stage. That's what Billy Joel once related in an interview. He claimed he had walked onto the stage for a performance and was too doped to be coherent. He insists he has since cleaned up his act.[98]

Those singers of "White Punks on Dope," the Tubes, suffered from even greater embarrassment (and pain) when one of their satirical characters, "Quay Lude," simply couldn't remain on his feet. Seemingly under the influence of alcohol or drugs, Quay Lude, described by *Circus* magazine, "staggers through a wall of speaker cabs, collapses, is rescued by roadies and tended by nurses."[99]

In a chapter entitled "Parents. . . . You Just Don't Know," the author of *The god of Rock,* Michael K. Haynes, describes the following scene at a rock concert he and his son attended as paramedics:

> The decibel level of the music was so loud that it shook the ground. The crowd was so worked up that they were hurting one another as well as themselves. The medics couldn't get to the ones who needed help; the heat was unbearable; the nudity was rampant; the drugs filled the air and the noses of the youth; the language was so vile it was an outright curse; the aid station was crowded with nice-looking young people who couldn't handle all or a part of the above; and we had only gotten to the second act [Ozzy Osbourne]!
>
> . . . I thought of the reported deaths at this type of concert. I thought of the hospitalization . . . of the overdoses, the pregnancies, the illicit sex, the nudity, the outright punishment of human beings that I had just witnessed. . . . Why is it that this has been going on for years and parents and churches are still in the dark? Either Satan is plenty shrewd, or we are just plain dumb.[100]

14

The Yeah-But Quiz Game

Almost anyone who has been a teenager knows the Yeah-But Quiz Game. The object of the game is to construct rebuttal to the opponent's (usually a parent) statement that refutes, confuses, or sidetracks him. However, the "opponent" does have one advantage over the youthful challenger: he was once a teenager, too, and has a few strategic Yeah-But responses worked out in advance.

During the years since our Truth About Rock seminars first began, we have heard literally thousands of Yeah-Buts, and have been involved in a few heated debates that rivaled the Yeah-But Quiz Game for excitement. Most questions we brothers field, however, come from sincere, honest seekers of truth, concerned about one aspect or another of the rock music issue. The following is a sampling of the most frequently asked questions. We hope our answers to these questions will settle any Yeah-Buts that may have come to your mind.

Are you saying rock and roll will send me to hell?

No one and nothing can "send" you to hell. The devil can't send you to hell, your friends can't send you to hell, movies can't send you to hell, nor can any kind of music send you to hell. The only person who can send you to hell is *yourself*. What other people and things *can* do, however, is provide an occasion to sin, and it is unforgiven sin which can keep you from an eternity in heaven. As an occasion to sin—something that can cause both temptation and confusion—rock music can trip you up, cloud your thinking, and misguide you so you miss heaven, and that is where rock's danger lies.

Why haven't you included documentation on my favorite group?

The music scene today changes at an unbelievable rate. This week's stars were maybe unheard of last month. And today's hottest flash could be as cold tomorrow as a Minnesota mosquito in December. Sometimes magazines and newspapers avoid the latest sensation for fear the material will be out of date before it hits the newsstand. Most publishers, therefore, wait to see if a musician's popularity lasts a while before interviewing him. Then, too, many groups don't allow interviews at first because they fear negative publicity.

Our list of groups and stars, therefore, is not all-inclusive, but it does not need to be. What you need is a consensus of what most rock groups stand for and the criteria necessary to judge any particular group for yourself. Remember, the Bible says "ye shall know them by their fruits" (Matt. 7:16). Many musicians have been in the business so long that the evidence of their corrupt fruit is overwhelming, while others are still trying to cope with sudden success. Nonetheless, both veterans and rookies exhibit the fruit of their work in the same ways—through their lyrics, lifestyles, goals and graphics. If a favorite group or musician is not included in this book, simply use the criteria we have established and judge for yourself. Remember, though, your decision is between you and God—a personal decision that you must "own." Others can help you discern, but ultimately you must decide.

Why have you said nothing about the beat in rock music? Isn't it "demonic"?

If you've ever heard the old champagne bubble-maestro, Lawrence Welk, strike up the "boys in the band" for a lively, instrumental pop music number, with "and-uh-one-uh, and-uh-two-uh...," you'd never think there was anything demonic about rhythm!

Seriously, though much has been made of the syncopated beat of rock music, a look in any music dictionary will tell us that syncopation is nothing more than accenting a beat that is normally unaccented. Sometimes that's the afterbeat (usually in rock music), and sometimes it involves anticipating or delaying a note. Though syncopation prevails in rock music, it's found in other styles as well—including ancient Jewish folk songs.

Thus, beat or rhythm, whether syncopated or not, is not intrinsically evil. While rock music may use a more driving beat than other styles, all music uses rhythm. Rhythm is part of nature; it is all around us and it is God-created (the universe itself moves in rhythm).

Though music can strongly affect people, and researchers are still learning the physical and psychological affect it can have on people, it doesn't have the ability to just "take over" and drive people to frenzies. More often, any frenzied behavior is likely to be caused by the lyrics in the music or the environment of a concert, combined with the intent of the rock star and the carefully-staged way he incites his audience. Consider crooners from the forties, such as Bing Crosby and Frank Sinatra. They weren't singing music with a driving rock beat, but they knew how to "send" their audiences of swooning bobby-soxers. It was the intent, the lyrical content, and the concert atmosphere that had those girls screaming—not any "jungle beat."

Though the beat of a tune can rouse, uplift, relax, energize, drag down, or even disturb, such emotions have nothing to do with demons. Emotions are feelings and feelings can be controlled. Some people trace the beat in rock music to African roots in an attempt to prove some sort of "witch doctor" presence in the music. Stories are sometimes told of African natives who, upon hearing a missionary's kids play rock music, fearfully wonder why *bwana* is "communicating with demons." Other tales tell of African visitors to this country likening rock music to their witchdoctor's tunes back in their tribal home.

These so-called "proofs," that a demon is somehow in the beat, are, in our opinion, merely coincidences. In these cases, the listeners, simply and mistakenly, had associated something in their culture with a similar thing in Western culture. It is the same as if we would watch someone giving honor in the old Japanese manner of bowing. We Westerners might ask, "Why are you groveling in such a humiliating manner—don't you have any pride?" But to the Japanese it is a sign of reverence and respect—a very good thing.

The temptation is to tie our culture to our faith—if we don't like the sound of it, we tend to think it must be wrong. As Steve Lawhead says in *Rock Revisited*:

> That rock and its "evil beat" originated with the slaves of Africa is a racist notion which will not stand up. . . . To lay the origins of a music condemned for its savagery and immorality at the feet of one racial group shows a narrow interpretation of history. Worse, it is an insidious form of prejudice and racism, one into which many people have unwittingly fallen.[1]

The Bible, remember, says nothing about rhythm. How, therefore, can we make a ruling regarding God's view of rhythm if He hasn't bothered to discuss it with us? As Jim Krupa writes in his article entitled "Principles for Evaluating Christian Contemporary Rock Music, "I have never found any Biblical support for the belief that songs which emphasize rhythm are to be shunned by godly people." As listeners, then, we should be much more concerned about a rock song's words than its beat.

What makes you think a rock star's lifestyle will have an affect on me?

If you don't believe your favorite rock stars affect your attitudes and actions, look around you. Where did the nostalgic fifties craze get its start? Why was America suddenly wearing dance clothes and legwarmers? Why did every girl under 20 start wearing loose-fitting, baglady dresses and slashed up sweatshirts? Why do boys and girls sport lookalike hairstyles? All of these styles were inspired, and sometimes created, by rock stars or their managers. The way many people dress indicates rock music's pervasive influence in that and many other areas of life.

Gene Simmons told us in an interview, he has discontinued his fire-blowing stunt because a young man was killed emulating the rock star in 1983. If Simmons is concerned about kids killing themselves because one used his favorite KISS star as a role model, it seems reasonable to assume other supposedly less-dangerous antics KISS promotes (both on and off stage) might be mimicked as well. Gene Simmons and other rock celebrities like him claim their lives are a private matter—but not when they glamorize their lifestyles through the press and through their music lyrics and stage banter.

"Can't you take a joke?" some people will remark. "Don't you know these rock stars are only hyping their images?" Of course, that is often the case—but what 10-year-old can tell the difference between reality and stage hype? If rock groups truly appreciate their fans, as they say they do, and sincerely have the fans' welfare in mind, they would not promote sex, Satanism, drugs and violence. Instead, they would help idolizing youngsters build character, strong values and productive lives.

Why do you talk about taking a militant stand against rock, and fighting "a war" on rock music? Is that the Christian way?

Jesus Christ, the Son of God, once stood in the marketplace and viciously challenged the religious leaders of the day. He called them a den of snakes and empty tombs—whitewashed on the outside and rotten on the inside.

That's a fairly good description of many of today's rock stars. The media makes them out to be glamorous, much bigger than life, and, sadly, many of them start to believe the myth themselves. They exude the image of the American dream fulfilled—happiness and contentment—but it's just white-wash. A quick look at previous chapters on lifestyles and goals quickly reveals the inside story. Behind the glittering money and the glamorous escapades, few are really happy. The real story shows lives filled with divorce, drugs, mental problems, premature death, and agonizing quests for happiness.

Even superstar Michael Jackson admits, despite the adulation of millions of fans, and even the support of a close-knit family, he is lonely. "Even at home, I'm lonely," he says. "I sit in my room sometimes and cry. . . . I some-times walk around the neighborhood at night, just hoping to find someone to talk to. But I just end up coming home."[2]

In an excerpt from *Michael!*, author Mark Bego says, "One minute he's the sexy, spinning singer emotionally lacerating his fans with sass and as-suredness, the next he is lonely and dejected and doesn't know what direction to turn."[3]

In admitting his problem, Jackson probably could have done his young fans some good—everyone can relate to periods of loneliness—if only he'd had the right answer. But his answer to the emptiness in his life is to stay as much as possible in a fantasy world. "I love to forget," he says of his penchant for pretending. "That's fun to me. I love it so much. It's escape. . . . Especially when you really believe it and it's not like you're acting. . . ."[4] Sweet dreams are *not* made of this; sooner or later a person has to come down from the clouds.

We have no personal animosity against Michael Jackson or any rock star—we love each of them just as God does. But today's teens are searching and they deserve better answers than rock stars are giving them—and that angers us. So just as Jesus took a militant stand against the hypocrisy and error He saw in His day, we have taken a stand against one of the most formidable shapers of the character and conscience of today's youth—rock music. And whether a star flagrantly attacks moral living or is just sadly misguided, his error must not go unquestioned. Jesus didn't take a backseat in His day, and neither should any of us—parents or teens.

Our Constitution and Bill of Rights guarantee freedom of speech. Aren't you talking about censorship? Aren't you trying to legislate morality?

Many laws on the books legislate morality. In fact, to some extent, every law does. At one point in history the constitutional right to private property was pitted against the moral right of a black person to be served in a restaurant. More recently, a company's constitutional right to hire whomever it wished was at odds with a woman's moral right to have equality in the work place. And even more recently, the right to freedom of speech was contested when a student newspaper published an editorial demanding someone kill the President of the United States. The President's moral right to life took precedence over the paper's right to free speech, because historically our individual freedoms have only been guaranteed to the extent they don't impinge on another's freedoms.

Consequently, "kiddie porn" movies that show bondage, rape and death of youngsters are illegal; even though the Constitution gives movie producers certain freedoms, they are not free to produce films violating a child's freedom of choice. Is this legislating morality? Perhaps in a sense it is; however, it is also constitutionally and historically permissible.

Unfortunately, however, "kiddie porn" rock songs that sing about bondage, rape or death have thus far escaped the same scrutiny. Likewise, although there are obscenity laws governing what can be spoken over the public airwaves, anyone can strap on a guitar, call himself a music artist and *sing* four-letter words—producing hit records and videos that air in heavy rotation.

We are not suggesting that anyone's freedoms be taken away, only that existing laws be properly enforced to halt the obscenities and indecencies in rock music which are now being allowed airplay. One of those laws is U.S. Code Title 18, Section 1464. It declares: "Whoever utters any obscene, indecent or profane language by means of radio communications shall be fined not more than $10,000 or imprisoned not more than two years or both."

If that law were properly being enforced, it would deplete much of rock's powerfully harmful affect on young people, because a good portion of the music now being played would never pass inspection.

In order to facilitate stricter enforcement of the laws which could be used to regulate rock music, we further advocate the rating of rock records by the manufacturer, so that their purchase can be monitored by parents—on whom the ultimate responsibility lies for the care and upbringing of today's youth. Along with a rating system—one similar to that now employed voluntarily by the movie industry—should come prohibition of sale of any obscene, indecent or profane record to a minor, unless parental permission is received. As with the movie industry, this system would not be a perfect one, but at least it would help stem the tide of corruption flowing unchecked from the rock music industry today.

Finally, we're not trying to tell people what they can or cannot listen to. We are only trying to tell the average American there are some very negative things happening in rock and roll—and does he know about them? Or want to support them?

Why don't you say anything about the noise level of rock music and how it can hurt people's hearing?

Our ears, scientists have proven, are such sensitive instruments that they operate as well as—and in some cases, better than—the most advanced electronic sound detectors. The ear is designed to detect sounds that displace the fluid around the stereocilia (the finger-like appendages to the inner ear hair cells) by less than a billionth of an inch—ten times smaller than a single atom![5] God has created a masterpiece, and it's a delicate system that needs protection.

Most ear doctors would agree that anything over 90 decibels on the sound scale is dangerous to our hearing. And many groups play much higher—often at 120 to 125 decibels (only slightly under the noise level at a busy airport on a clear day). Lemmy Kilmister of Motorhead once told *Hit Parader* that his group wanted to see "blood comin' out of everyone's ears, if possible. Nothing dangerous, just enough to let us know they're having a good time."[6]

That sort of "good time" has left many rock stars and fans with impaired hearing. However, we haven't stressed the hearing-loss issue because, frankly, it falls on deaf ears—young people don't seem to care. As Ted Nugent, who is now partially deaf in his left ear, once said, "But . . . it's a small price to pay."[7] In other words, the immediate gratification and fun is supposedly worth the suffering that will come later. Unfortunately, many young people, with all their future ahead of them, tend to think the same way. It's a shortsighted view and one we lament; after all, we each are the stewards of our bodies and should take good care of them.

Even more dangerous than the level of noise, however, is that many teenagers apparently need constant sound. A sizable number of teens seem very uncomfortable with both silence and conversation. They use electronics—radio, TV and recordings—to build a cushion around themselves, avoiding the labor and pain of learning how to relate to others and coming to know oneself.

Granted, the teen years are sometimes tough, and everyone needs a little "space" now and then, but hiding in electronic solitude only prolongs the agony—sooner or later we all must learn to communicate. Doesn't it seem more inviting to spend troublesome times in the company of friends and family who love us and want to help us than to spend those days with companions whose goal is to put "blisters in eardrums," as Kilmister once put it?[8]

I don't listen to the words, I just listen to the music. How is rock music going to affect me?

Seventy percent of young people buy a recording because of the tune or beat, not the lyrics, and they come to our Truth About Rock seminars claiming they don't listen to the words. And yet, when snatches of tunes are played during a seminar, and then cut off, the same kids continue singing the words they weren't even aware they knew. Is this mindless mimicry? We doubt it. The Bible says as a man thinks in his heart, so is he (Prov. 23:7), and since music is such a spiritual medium—one that can pass the intellect and enter what is called "the heart"—it has an even greater potential for persuasion.

During the 1984 Super Bowl, sponsors eagerly paid up to $345,000 for a mere 30 seconds of air time because they were willing to bet they could influence your buying behavior. Likewise, quiz shows receive thousands of dollars in giveaway prizes from sponsors, in exchange for a brief mention of the manufacturer's names by a speed-reading announcer. Do they think it's worth it? Of course, they do. They know those few seconds of time are priceless because they are persuasive.

Now consider the average teen, listening to six hours of rock music a day, with probably a little TV video rock thrown in on the side. He is a pretty tough nut to crack if he spends that many hours immersed in music and yet remains unaffected.

Some liberal souls believe a child can be permanently harmed by glimpses of stereotyped role models in a first-grade reader; yet, those same activists naively think hours spent, a few years later, under the pervasive influence of rock's messages—immorality, pornography, violence and Satanism—are not going to affect that same child.

Do you listen to, or study closely, the commercials that pop up on your TV screen every 15 minutes? Probably not, and yet chances are you can complete these slogans: "Reach out, reach out and . . ."; "Hold the pickles, hold . . ."; and now for an oldie: "Oh, there's something about an . . ." Chances are, if you're over 30, you got all three (the ads were for Bell Telephone, Burger King and Aqua Velva). That's the power of the great American jingle: a message set to music. And that is also the power of rock music.

Why do you give information on groups such as the Beatles or the Doors—groups that aren't even together anymore?

It's important to note the groups that were on the leading edge of what was once happening in rock music because characteristics of rock music are passed on like genes in a family tree. What Elvis did affected the Beatles, the Stones, and virtually every group that's ever laid down a guitar lick. Likewise, the Beatles and the Stones have influenced groups that followed them, and today's bands will affect future rock and rollers. It's helpful, therefore, to analyze the roots of rock and roll, as well as the particular style or group which happens to be the latest rage.

Of equal importance is the fact that the music of the big stars lives on long after they are dead. Elvis' estate is making almost as much money as ever; the Beatles are selling more records today than they did in their heyday; and the Doors' old tunes are still being sold in large volume.

The Rolling Stones sang the bawdy "[I Can't Get No] Satisfaction" back in 1965; and in 1984, a Rolling Stones video, including "Satisfaction," was nominated for a Grammy Award. The Everly Brothers scored hit after hit from 1957 to 1962, then broke up in 1964. Their legacy continued, however, as hit recordings of their songs appeared regularly, covered by other stars; and then, in 1984, the duo reunited and may produce another string of gold records.

A complete list would cover many pages. Not only do rock stars' songs survive, but their words do as well. With the media covering every facet of rock stars' lives, and the press ready to gobble up every "pearl" from their mouths and record it for posterity, their intentions, lifestyles and even their most personal opinions and actions are publicized long after they pass away, affecting and infecting new generations of impressionable young people enamored by the hype.

Rock stars don't really believe everything they sing about. Aren't they just trying to make up lyrics that rhyme?

Perhaps that's so—at least that's what Electra Asylum Records' Joseph Smith would like us to believe. However, if music composers don't believe in what they write about, the only other motive is money. Do you want to be a victim of hype, simply swept along by another person's hunger for possessions and fame? And what of the moral responsibility of both the artist and the music industry? George Forell, author of *Corporation Ethics: The Quest For Moral Authority*, says, "The social irresponsibility of corporations is . . . the resulting defect of the men and women who have worshipped the golden calf of idolatry."[9]

The music industry needs to become less concerned with rhyme, rhythm, and songs that sell, and work to provide the very best in entertainment for young people—music that is uplifing and inspiring. There should be songs that build strong morals in young people and teach them to be good citizens; music that will help stem the divorce rate by teaching about real love, not lust; tunes that will help end child abuse and wife battering by showing how men can be men and not bullies; melodies that derail the tendency toward teenage rebellion, and advocate respect, communication and character.

Instead, the music industry seems content to give us role models with perverted, distorted views, who heartily sing their assaults upon Christian value systems—all for want of words to rhyme with love, peace or joy? Incredible.

Who are you to say what is right or wrong? Doesn't an artist have a right to freedom of expression?

We admit some of the distortions that rockers sing about may be accepted values in certain areas of society—such as the fantasy world of Hollywood or the pro-homosexual climate of San Francisco. But to grant today's philosopher—the rock musician—total freedom to preach whatever "gospel" he or she wishes on our public airwaves, without concern for the negative effect it may have on impressionable listeners, is foolishness.

There is no stated "artist's freedom of expression" clause in the First Amendment. Instead, we have laws such as the Federal Communications Code, listed earlier, which spell out fines and prison sentences for those broadcasting perversion to minor children. And there are many more arguments for judicial sanctions against the use of obscenity in the media—including common law, nuisance doctrine, trespass, constitutional notions of privacy and due process, health considerations and existing federal regulatory authority.[10] It's time some of these statutes were utilized to bring the recording industry back to moral responsibility. If you are interested in joining the fight to stop pornographic music from being sold to minors or played on the public airwaves, note the petition in Appendix 2 of this book.

Are you advocating the confiscation of records that promote any view differing from yours, e.g., a song about Buddhism? Isn't that Fascist?

We do not advocate the confiscation of *any* record, for *any* reason. We are simply saying, if a record includes a song which promotes any religion, or talks about drugs, or sings four-letter-worded odes to promiscuity, the album jacket should clearly say so. A label could be affixed which reads: "Notice: this record contains a song which could be construed to promote _____." It would provide parents a buying guide so that they can be better informed about their children's music purchases, and would give teenagers a basis on which to judge the music to which they listen.

Why do you pick on rock music, when country, "easy listening" and Broadway music, for instance, contain many of the same problems?

When our seminars began, our congregation, Zion Christian Center, was a very young parish with a median age of 21. Rock, therefore, was a major issue in the lives of most of those young people. Few, if any of them, were listening to six hours a day of Wayne Newton, Roy Acuff or "Fiddler on the Roof." They, and the young people toward whom we now direct the seminars, were at a highly impressionable age and were feeling the detrimental effects of rock music in their Christian walks.

Also, in the last 15 years, rock artists have become much more militant, more blatant, about their moral values. They openly advocate and promote "alternative lifestyles," whereas 20 years ago, they wouldn't even have been caught smoking in public because they were so concerned about its affect on their fans.

We are not saying *all* rock bands advocate harmful or morally-degrading lifestyles, but enough of them do, and blatantly so, for it to be of major concern.

Why do you burn records?

First of all, we don't burn records—the former rock fan decides to burn his own records. It is a personal decision, not one that anyone makes for him— especially not the Peters brothers. Furthermore, the records which are burned are from the listener's own collection, not records he has purchased for the occasion.

We advocate burning—or if the local fire codes prohibits burning, then destruction by another means—because burning is scriptural, as explained in Chapter 4. Three instances in the Bible refer to burning as a means of disposal of objects which hinder the believer in his walk.

Even Jesus said, if your right hand offends you, cut it off, and if your right eye offends you, pluck it out (Matt. 5:29, 30). That's pretty strong language, but He didn't mean we should literally dismember ourselves. He was saying figuratively, "If there's something near and dear to you which is causing you to sin—get rid of it."

That is the purpose of the burning. If you own records you think are a problem for you, that are harming your life, do whatever is necessary to get rid of them. One excellent way is burning. It is not only a graphic declaration, but keeps you from reneging on your commitment. It's similar in many ways to a chain-smoker flushing his last pack of cigarettes down the toilet. He doesn't keep the pack around, just in case he loses his resolve. And, if he's convinced smoking is harmful to life, he doesn't give or sell the pack to someone else so the cigarettes can blacken that person's lungs. Burning is a scriptural means of ridding yourself of a bad influence in such a way that it becomes difficult to go back on your intentions, and keeps others from falling into the same trap as well.

Often, our burnings are likened to the unfortunate, deplorable confiscation of personal books by the Nazi regime. However, nothing could be further from the truth, for the Nazis themselves decided what was acceptable and what was not. The Nazis stole the personal property and the Nazis burned it. We, on the other hand, stress that ridding yourself of the evil effects of most rock and roll is a *personal* decision, one even a youngster needs to make on his own. Parents, of course, should be a guiding force in all areas (and the very young need more parental authority exerted over them).

Still, the decision to give up rock music ultimately rests on the shoulders of the listener. Why? Because rock's influence is so pervasive. It is all around us and it takes a conscious effort at times to avoid it. Hauling a teenager's records out to the dump won't end the problem if he doesn't agree with the decision—not when there are radios, rock videos, rock music movies, etc. (not to mention friends' record collections).

I listened to Elvis and Jerry Lee Lewis when I was a kid, and I'm all right today—I'm a good parent, spouse, citizen and church-goer. Why didn't rock music affect me?

Some people listen to bad rock songs and this music has little effect on them, just as some people can drink a beer or play a game of poker and not have it change their lives. But how many thousands of others are affected? Do we really want our children to play rock and roll Russian Roulette? The law of averages says, sooner or later, someone is going to get hurt.

In addition, rock music is so much more blatant and immoral today, as a quick flip through this book's chapters on rock's history will show. What was done with innuendo, or behind closed doors, 20 years ago is not only openly discussed but proudly and publicly practiced today. Why should we allow immoral and profane people to become the heroes and role models of our nation—leaders for our young people to worship and follow?

Look back at the lives of people like Elvis Presley and Jerry Lee Lewis. Mild though their songs may be, by today's sunken standards, their lives are models of unhappiness and pain. Presley died with 14 different drugs in his system; Lewis, though still alive, is on his sixth marriage. Just on principle alone, why should we put these people on a pedestal?

But shouldn't parents allow their children to experience the worldly view of life so they can eventually face the world unafraid?

Even though Jesus was the Son the God, He wasn't ready to face Satan until He had fasted and prayed for 40 days and nights. Yet, we sometimes think we should allow our children liberal doses of the world—even though Scripture warns us Satan prowls about our world like a hungry lion seeking to destroy us (1 Pet. 4:8).

Prov. 22:6 says, "Train up a child in the way he should go: and when he is old, he will not depart from it." In other words, show him the positive. It doesn't say, "Show him all the ways he could possibly go, and when he is old he will be wise enough to figure it all out." Just as we wouldn't expose a child to a deadly virus, in order to make him strong, so also we shouldn't expose a child to immorality in hopes he will build the strength to battle it.

In this age of communication and electronic wizardry, we can rest assured a child is inundated with worldly philosophy; no one can escape it entirely. But who is giving him an alternative view? When children go outside to play, they inevitably end up with dirty clothes. As our teens and preteens struggle to grow in the midst of an immoral culture, they too, are likely to become spiritually soiled. They need parents who are willing to be "stronger than dirt," not parents who push them into the mud.

PART FOUR

Changing Your Tune

15

Free Indeed

Gene Simmons of KISS once told a *Circus* interviewer he stopped believing in God when he started asking questions. Simmons says, if there is a God who created the universe, "that would mean that this God has very nonhuman characteristics."[1]

Simmons makes a couple of wrong assumptions here. First, he stopped believing in God when he started asking a few questions. There is, however, nothing wrong with questioning one's faith. After all, how do we get to know a person better? We ask him questions: "Where do you come from?" "What's your opinion on this?" And once we are on friendly terms, we even begin to challenge his reasoning at times—to find out why he thinks as he does.

Building a relationship with God works much the same way. God doesn't expect or want us to rely on our parents' faith forever. He wants each of us to grow up, think things through, and know Him and accept Him personally. And inevitably, that will mean asking questions.

Sometimes, however, when questions of faith come to our minds, they can be unsettling. They can make us wonder if God is real. After all, if He were real, we wouldn't have doubts—would we? But doubts and questions are a natural part of the process of stepping back; of surveying the issue of faith, in general, and God, in particular; of coming to know and understand both with a personal conviction. It's part of maturing—an important part.

We must be certain, though, to ask our questions of someone trustworthy, preferably someone a little older and more mature in his or her faith. In that way, we'll avoid drawing false conclusions and using inaccurate information as Simmons did.

The second inaccurate assumption Simmons makes is that God has very nonhuman characteristics. The Bible says just the opposite: "Then God said, 'And now we will make human beings; they will be like us and resemble us' " (Gen. 1:26, GNB). If we resemble God, the reverse is also true—He resembles us, and exhibits many of the same qualities we do.

Simmons went on to question God's motive for wanting our praise: " . . . why would this God who is very non-human want to hear his name repeated—

209

'Thou art great, Thou art this, Thou art that'? . . . That's a really frail characteristic."[2]

Specifically *because* we are so self-centered, God has given us ways to remember Him and His blessings. For example, God told Moses His people should celebrate the Passover, so after they had entered the Promised Land, the Hebrews would be reminded yearly of their miraculous rescue and all that God had done for them on the way to the land He had given them. God knew that, without constant prompting, the people would eventually forget all the miracles, and thus forget Him. We are no different than those ancients. Without a means of jogging our memories, we would eventually lose sight of God and lose our way.

Simmons continued to challenge God's existence by questioning why God would be jealous of other gods, as the Bible says. "If He's hot stuff, the way God is supposed to be, why is He afraid. . . ? If I'm hot stuff, I'm not worried. I'm all-powerful. . . . At the end, they've got to come to me."[3]

Simmons doesn't realize, unfortunately, that God is concerned more with *our* welfare than His when He commands us to honor only Him. Of course, He is infinitely worthy of that honor, but also, He doesn't want us to waste time being knocked about by every false doctrine or new theology that blows our way.

Every religion on earth, with the exception of Christianity, puts its trust in what *man* can do for himself in order to earn salvation. Unfortunately, however, we all sin; left to our own devices, none of us would make the mark. (Some religions have even admitted this, and have invented the idea of reincarnation so we can "try, try again." Sad to say, even if we were not "appointed only one time to die," as Scripture says, we still wouldn't succeed on our own, because we all sin—none of us is perfect.)

Not one of us could ever earn salvation, no matter how many chances we would receive. None of us are worthy to be in God's presence, and in our sinful state we wouldn't be comfortable. We would certainly feel naked and embarrassed, much as did Adam and Eve who hid from God after they had sinned. They no longer wanted to be in His presence because they had lost their innocence.

Since we all fall short, there is only one way to obtain eternal happiness. God loves us so much He made provision through His Son, Jesus. Now, if God gave us His most precious Son as a gift, free and clear, why would He want us wasting time trying imitations while He offers the real thing? That is why He warns us, "So be careful how you live. Don't live like ignorant people, but like wise people. Make good use of every opportunity you have, because these are evil days. Don't be fools, then, but try to find out what the Lord wants you to do" (Eph. 5:15, GNB).

Gene Simmons surmises that God isn't "too worried about whether we believe or we don't or any of that stuff."[4]

On the contrary, God does care! In fact, "God loved the world so much that He gave His only Son, so that everyone who believes in Him may not die but have eternal life. For God did not send His Son into the world to be its judge, but to be its savior" (John 3:16, GNB). In other words, God cared so much that He sent "the very best." Can you imagine sending your own son to die for someone else and then not caring if that person believed he'd been saved or accepted your son as the one to save him? Of course not!

Finally, Simmons told the *Circus* interviewer he thinks we're on our own in this world, to "make our own mistakes, to get ourselves out of trouble."[5]

Simmons' statement does not match the picture of loving compassion and care Jesus reflected shortly before He died, when He declared God's love for Jerusalem (and likewise, for all of us): "Jerusalem, Jerusalem! You kill the prophets and stone the messengers God has sent you! How many times I wanted to put my arms around all your people, just as a hen gathers her chicks under her wings, but you would not let me!" (Matt. 23:37, GNB).

God's love, salvation, peace, joy, and all the good things that make life worth living, are for each of us—and free for the asking. Simmons was right about one thing, though: God does allow us to make our own mistakes. And the biggest mistake we could ever make would be not to accept His Son as Savior and Lord.

It's a decision we have to make for ourselves; no one else can make it for us. Parents can't accept Jesus Christ for us, and we can't get salvation on the basis of someone else's experience with Him. Neither can religion save us. We can go to church seven days a week and memorize all the laws of the church, but only when we each personally accept the Lord into our own life are we saved.

Is that a narrow viewpoint? Yes, it is. Jesus explains: "Go in through the narrow gate, because the gate to hell is wide and the road that leads to it is easy, and there are many who travel it" (Matt. 7:13, GNB). In other words, there is a *specific* way to enter heaven, but plenty of ways to get into hell.

Jesus then says, "But the gate to life is narrow and the way that leads to it is hard, and there are few people who find it" (Matt. 7:14, GNB). He is telling each of us not to expect the Christian walk to be an easy one, and also not to expect to see a great many others trying to travel the same road. So look around you. Are you traveling the same route as everyone you know? If so, you probably are going the wrong way.

Jesus also warned there are many who would lead us astray, even some who seem to know God. We have nothing to fear, however, because Jesus walked the road before us. He knows the way and He will lead anyone who wants to follow Him.

It's Up to You

If you have never accepted Jesus as your personal Savior, don't let fear stop you, especially fear of embarrassment from your friends. Kerry Livgren, a member of the group Kansas, experienced that kind of fear before he accepted Jesus. Livgren says:

> The last thing in the world I wanted to be was one of those fanatical born-again Christians. Because of my image of what Christianity meant, my concept of what Christians were like, and what it would mean socially, economically and personally for me to become one, the thought absolutely terrified me. And yet . . . it was something I really needed and wanted, but I didn't want to admit this.[26]

Livgren weighed the cost and realized that Jesus had given much, much more—His life—and so, Livgren did accept the Lord. And he's stayed with the band and been a powerful witness to the true meaning of Christianity among those he works with, as well as his fans.

If a member of a rock band can accept Christ and continue to function within the same setting (if God leads him to do so), but in a new way, certainly we can, too—without fear. The Bible says perfect love casts out fear. We don't have that love, but Jesus does and once He begins living within each of us, He can give us the confidence we need.

The first step is to admit our need—we're all incomplete. You may have asked yourself, "What's wrong with me anyway? Why am I so unhappy? What's life all about?" Such questions are symptomatic of the inner void each of us has. Life without God was never meant to work right. God intended that the troubles and questions we have would become so spiritually painful that they would drive us toward Him.

The second step is to realize sin keeps us from God's gift of life. Our sins separate us from God (Isa. 59:2). To some, that may sound strange or trite, because the world has just about erased the concept of sin. In fact, an extensive survey taken in 1984, in one of the mainline Christian denominations, revealed 30% of the people surveyed felt there was no such thing as sin. But no matter how we try to cover up or pretty up sin with fancy, psychological terms, the ugly consequences remain. Jesus didn't die for our "poor choices impacted by the socio-economic structures and lack of familial bonding under which we spent our early childhood development." He died for our sins.

Whether the modern world wishes to acknowledge it or not, we are slaves to sin and our bonds tie us down. Jesus, however, has purchased access to the Father, and He can set us free. "So if the Son makes you free," it says in John 8:36, "you will be free indeed" (RSV).

To be free from sin, and reconciled to God, all we have to do is turn from our independent, sinful ways, and ask for salvation. God sent His Son to die, paying the penalty for us. Now Jesus stands knocking at the door of our hearts, just waiting for each of us to invite Him in (Rev. 3:20).

Starting a New Life

Pray in your own words, or use the short prayer below:

> "Dear Lord Jesus, I know that I'm a sinner, and that I need your

forgiveness. Please forgive me and take my life and make me new. I want you to be my personal Savior. I turn from my old way of life and choose to serve you now. Thank you, Jesus. Amen."

If you just prayed that prayer, and meant it, then you have just made the most important decision of your life. You're a new person with a new lease on life, no matter what your age may be! Now live for Christ with all your heart, your mind, and your soul. Practically speaking, that should involve four important activities: Scripture reading, daily prayer, fellowship with other Christians, and a new lifestyle.

1. *Scripture.* In Heb. 4:12, we read, "The word of God is quick and powerful . . . a discerner of the thoughts and intents of the heart" (KJV). Today, in our media-packed world, we need all the discernment we can get in order to stay true to our commitment to the Lord. But the Word of God in Scripture can't cut through Jell-O if we don't *read* it. It has to become part of our normal thought life.

In many ways the Bible is similar to vitamins. Vitamins can be somewhat helpful if taken sporadically, but they provide the most benefit when taken every day—on a regular basis. In the same way, *daily* reading of the Word arms you against the attack of the deceiver, Satan, by providing a strong defense. Jesus was tempted by Satan while He was in the desert, and He used Scripture to fend off the devil. Likewise, when we find ourselves in a dangerous situation, Scripture is the "sword of truth" which can fight off temptation.

Don't delay. Find a version of the Bible you can understand—one that "speaks your language"—then spend a small amount of time every day studying it.

If you don't know where to begin, try one of the four Gospels, perhaps the Book of Mark. You don't need to spend hours at it—simply read a few verses or a chapter every day until it becomes a habit. Continue reading until that book of the Bible is finished, and then go on to another book, perhaps one of the Epistles—James is a good place to start.

If you're a beginner, don't try to start in Genesis and read straight through. Even Bible scholars can get bogged down by some of the more obscure passages of the Old Testament, so save those for when you have gotten a "feel" for the way God speaks through Scripture.

2. *Prayer.* In order to hear God speak to us, it's important that we precede Scripture reading with a brief time of prayer, asking for God's presence and insight.

A daily prayer time—be it 10 minutes or an hour—is essential to spiritual growth. Communication is the key to knowledge, and as a Christian we must make it a top priority to communicate with God, to know Him personally. If you have trouble getting started, there are a number of devotional books for young people that provide something to think about, as well as new insights and inspiration for daily living. A local Christian bookstore can help you select the right book.

A daily dosage of prayer and Scripture reading will go far in helping you to "not be conformed to this world but be transformed by the renewal of your mind, that you may prove what is the will of God, what is good and acceptable and perfect" (Rom. 12:2, RSV).

3. *Fellowship.* Since we're social beings, we need more than prayer with God and study of His Word, we need fellowship with other Christians to help us in our spiritual walk. Friends who are trying to live as we are provide healthy peer pressure. Without it, we are likely to trip up on the many lies the devil spreads in our path.

David Hope, another member of Kansas who has accepted Christ, says when he began his walk with the Lord, " . . . something was missing. . . . You've got to read the Word, and you've got to pray, but it's really important to get fellowship."[7]

Likewise, Mylon Le Fevre, who has played with a number of rock bands before coming to the Lord, and has gone on to form his own group, BrokenHeart, says although he had given his life to Christ, he suffered some very hard times without fellowship. He began reverting to his old lifestyle. Finally, a drug overdose in England left him unconscious in the hospital for 23 hours, and nearly cost him his life. Now he believes "getting in a strong fellowship is really, really important and to be under some strong teaching, straight out of the Word and not somebody's opinion."[8]

Eph. 4:11ff. explains how fellowship works and why it's so necessary to seek out a group of believers—whether a church with a healthy ministry to young people, a Christian club, a Bible study, or simply Christian school friends. The passage says each of us has been given a certain ministry, a function. Therefore, together, we form a whole, healthy unit—a body—in which we all may grow and mature, and eventually reach the full potential God sees in us.

4. *A new lifestyle.* Making wise choices as we walk the Christian path takes time, and sometimes pain, but nothing of true value comes instantly. It takes care, precision, and skill to turn a rough diamond into a beautifully-faceted and polished, precious stone. In the same way, we're "chipped away" by the Lord through our circumstances, to reveal the precious gem underneath. Each time we make a right choice, more of the "rough" exterior is removed and we become more capable of reflecting God's character.

The Christian walk isn't a one-time transaction, like buying some sort of life insurance policy. Instead, it's embarking on a new road. In fact, the word repentance actually means "turning around" and that is what God expects us to do—to turn around and follow Jesus, separating ourselves from the relationships and activities that once led us into sin. It means letting Jesus be our Lord, our "boss."

Glenn Kaiser, of the Christian heavy metal group, Resurrection Band, puts it this way:

> The Book of Acts shows the early church's emphasis. It mentions the title "savior" twice. "Lord" is included 111 times. Jesus is our Savior, but He is just as importantly our Lord. He demands action, not just a quick prayer.[9]

Let's face it, new beginnings are sometimes painful, but if you sense God is telling you to make some changes in your life, only you can do it. As Bono Vox (Hewson) of U2 once said, "Revolution starts at home, in your heart, in your refusal to compromise your beliefs and your values."[10] That is what God is calling you to, a revolutionary way of life. He wants you to discern not just what is good for your life, but what is the very best (Phil. 1:10), remembering that Scripture is not necessarily inspiring, but inspired, and commands us to do "everything in the name of the Lord Jesus."

Sing a New Song

You may soon find a need to change the music to which you listen. Can you honestly say your music inspires you to listen "in the name of the Lord"? Is it Christlike? Does it "teach and instruct in all wisdom"? Does it cause thankfulness for God's blessings to well up in your heart? That is what music should do for you, according to Col. 3:16. If you can't honestly claim your music is doing these things, then God may be calling you to "change your tune." As Reggie Vinson, a songwriter and performer with John Lennon, Alice Cooper, KISS and others, before his conversion to the Lord, says:

> If it isn't saying the Word, there's no purpose for it. You see, the devil is out to destroy your mind with music. He's out to drive you crazy and make you use drugs.... With young people he'll use rock 'n' roll. In gospel music, if you're not saying the Word, you're missing out on the whole purpose of what God is doing.[11]

And consider this: Listening to potentially harmful music, buying records, and going to concerts, even if it does not seem to affect you personally, is lending financial support to an immoral or harmful cause. In other words, you're giving added clout to a group which could be harming someone else.

In 2 Chron. 19:2, a prophet asks the king, "Do you think it is right to help those who are wicked and to take the side of those who hate the Lord? What you have done has brought the Lord's anger on you" (GNB). God is doing a serious work in our lives, and He doesn't want us wasting our God-given resources on activities which thwart His plan. There are grave consequences for those who do so.

Furthermore, each of us needs to question music's priority in our lives. Though good music can be entertaining and relaxing, we need to maintain a healthy balance. Dallas Holm, a popular Christian contemporary artist, says the devil's substitute for the joy of the Lord is entertainment.

> We are the most entertained society in the world, and our lives are so cluttered

with meaningless, worthless things. People just indulge in so much of no value. [For rock music in particular], I used to be hesitant to talk about things like this for fear that people would think I was nuts, but . . . if we Christians would just listen to what these people [rock artists] are saying and listen to what their desires are . . . there is no questions that we . . . should have nothing to do with it. . . . I don't think . . . you can listen to it and please the Lord or do yourself any good.[12]

If music is a major priority in your life—if you are spending hours a day listening to music—perhaps you should take your daily schedule before the Lord in prayer. If you are not to be conformed to this world, then it seems reasonable that for every hour you spend listening to the world—through music, television, films, magazines, etc.—you should grant at least equal time to the Lord, if not more! How can you hope to withstand the pressures of the world if you are spending six hours a day with the media and ten minutes daily with the Lord in prayer?

We do not necessarily suggest you indiscriminately toss out all rock music. We do, however, advise that you consider not only the amount of time and money you consume on rock music, and the impact it has on others, but also examine your motives for involvement with rock music before you made a commitment to Jesus.

If, for instance, you were heavily involved with rebellious or satanic forms of rock music; if you spent several hours a day listening privately to music; or if rock music was persuading you toward drug abuse, sexual promiscuity, suicide or rebellion, you should probably drop all contact with music for a time.

Since you have surrounded yourself for so long with a very destructive force, it will take time to "deprogram." For a while, even Christian contemporary music should probably be avoided. Instead, spend your free time submerged in the Lord—pray, read Scripture, indulge in times of quiet contemplation, find some constructive reading, wholesome entertainment, and good times with other Christians.

It may take a level of obedience you haven't attempted before to rid yourself of the often-harmful influences of rock music, but as Steve Taylor, a New Wave Christian rock singer, puts it, "[The Bible] says that we show our love for God not only by our emotions, but by our obedience. That's what love for God means—being obedient. . . . It's by being obedient, and not waiting for the Lord to zap us with a big high."[13] Taylor is right. The Lord loves those who demonstrate through their obedience a hatred of evil, and He promises to bless them because of their righteousness.

Upon This Rock

Any time we attempt to rid our lives of something (bad or good), we leave a void and can sometimes sense it. If rock music has been an important part of your life, and you now choose to discard most of it, expect to feel empty.

It's similar, perhaps, to the psychological withdrawal a former smoker experiences—he doesn't know what to do with his hands.

Christian contemporary music can help fill that void—that sensation of not knowing what to do with your ears—and there are bands to fit into every style, gospel to rockabilly, heavy metal to New Wave.

Don't be fooled, however. A Christian label does not necessarily guarantee Christian content. As you seek alternatives to the rock music you have chosen to discard, remember the criteria for judging a music group are the same whether the artists profess Christianity or are clearly anti-Christian. You need to check the four basics: the lyrics, lifestyles, goals, and graphics of any music you select to determine if it is "the best."

1. *Lyrics*. The words to a song are, of course, the most obvious tip-off to poor quality. Ask yourself if the lyrics honor Jesus, if they are scriptural. Would they help others find Christ? Music teaches, and if it is Christian music, it must be theologically correct. Furthermore, the words must be clearly stated and understandable. If you have any doubts, seek out advice. Remember, just as with a secular song, Christian musical messages can have incredible impact on the listener's life.

2. *Lifestyles*. Find out something about the Christian artists whose music you admire. Are they living lives sold out for Christ? Do they give concerts that edify God, not their own talents? Are their priorities in order? In short, is their lifestyle consistent with the Christian message? Christian contemporary music magazines are the best sources for this information.

3. *Graphics*. Until recently, most Christian music was packaged quite conservatively, with perhaps a nice picture of the group and an appropiate title. However, Christian music producers have moved forward to appeal to modern tastes, and album covers have become innovative works of art. Usually, the new graphics serve to better represent the particular theme with which the album deals. However, to appeal to the general market, sometimes the graphics become a showcase for the artist or overpower the recording's central Christian theme. Jesus should be the only "superstar" of Christian music.

Don't get legalistic, however, and ban any album simply because it pictures the artists involved. Try to discern the *spirit*, the emphasis, of the cover.

4. *Goals*. The goals of the artists are the most important element to check in Christian contemporary music. It's not enough simply to assume an artist's motives are pure. According to Jim Krupa:

> While we listen to the music, God is listening to the performer's motives (Proverbs 16:2). If the musician's motive is to please men rather than please God; or if a musician is more concerned with what people think than with what God thinks; or if the musician's heart is filled with selfishness and pride instead of humility and love, then his music will be an abomination to God regardless of the musical style he is playing.[14]

In every generation and in every culture, music has been used to worship because it is spiritual. As the language of the soul it is a powerful communicator of motives. Listen carefully to the music you choose and ask yourself if the artist's goal is to worship God. If not, you must ask, whom is he worshiping?

Are these standards too high? No, not really. After all, as Christians we are in a battle for our culture; and music is, as we have seen, an important part of that culture. As such, it should reflect the glory of God, but that doesn't mean it has to be Handel's *Messiah* in order to pass inspection. Christians must become, not spiritual snobs, but discriminating listeners.

In an interview with *Cornerstone*, Christian musician John Fischer said:

> There's a great truth in Colossians 3:16. It says, "Christ's message in all its richness must live in your hearts. Teach and instruct one another with all wisdom. Sing psalms, hymns, and sacred songs; sing to God with thanksgiving in your hearts. Everything you do or say, then, should be done in the name of the Lord Jesus, as you give thanks through him to God the Father" [GNB]. That became the cornerstone for what I wanted to build and continues to be so. . . . Talent isn't enough; there must be something filling the person.[15]

In addition to checking the goals of the artist, a Christian young person must scrutinize his own motives for listening to music. It's important to search and discover if you are listening to rock music—even if it is Christian rock music—purely out of rebelliousness.

If your parents have asked you to stop listening to all rock music, you have an obligation to obey. They are earthly representatives of God's authority and have been given responsibility for your life. Ultimately, it is their duty to govern your choice of music, as well as every other area in your life.

And it is your duty to obey. Obedience, however, is not without blessings. "Honor your father and your mother" is the only commandment with a promise attached: "that your days may be prolonged, and that it may go well with you" (Deut. 5:16, RSV). In other words, God grants you a long, joy-filled life for obeying your parents—which you should be doing anyway. It's a deal you can't refuse!

We hope this book, especially the next chapter, will help your parents deal with the issue of rock music, but your parents know best. If they believe rock music is harmful to you—even if it is contemporary Christian rock, abide by their rules. You'll never be sorry you did; God will richly bless you for laying down your desires in obedience.

The Christian Concert

Most rock concerts are filled with drugs, sex, violence, profanity and immorality. In comparison, any Christian concert would seem completely acceptable, and most are. However, as Christians we strive for *best*, not just better. We need to evaluate the concerts as well, to see that the atmosphere is wholesome and Christ is presented to the audience through the music.

Phil Keaggy, a Christian who is considered by both secular and Christian critics to be one of today's finest guitarists, says:

> In the context of a concert situation, the whole point is to lift up Jesus. I pray that the spirit of humility will come across in the performance, and that afterwards, if people were to meet me, they would sense that. I don't want to presume that I'm a humble person, but . . . I want them to know that I desire to lift whatever praise comes to me, to the Lord.[16]

Of course the spotlight is going to be on the artist, but when the star has this kind of attitude, it's easy to see the applause is really going to God.

Though an altar call is not always necessary, it is appropriate and has become an integral part of many bands' concerts. Paul Clark, a veteran Jesus musician with 10 albums to his credit, says:

> I've been renewed with a real heart for evangelism and we've seen a lot of young kids come to the Lord in the last six months. I've been ending our concerts with about a half hour of worship and then I've been preaching from the Word and making an appeal for decisions for Christ.[17]

Resurrection Band's concerts always end with an appeal as well. One concert was attended by a Jewish cameraman filming a news story. Later, he described his view of the scene to *Cornerstone* magazine: ". . . Kids were dancing, the band was rocking, but between songs they told you what they were thinking as Christians. Everyone was having a party as the band played; then suddenly Glenn Kaiser stopped singing and started preaching and 2,500 kids began listening to the gospel."[18] Such a scene probably seems bizarre to the average evangelical, but this kind of concert is much, much more than entertainment, and can offer a young person a personal challenge as well as a means to evangelize his unsaved friends.

If you are interested in finding some contemporary Christian artists whose music and lifestyles seem to reflect the principles we have been discussing, ask at a local Christian bookstore which sells tapes and records. Watch for notices of groups soon to appear in your area, and ask your youth group friends which artists they like. Christian radio stations, television stations and contemporary Christian music magazines are also helpful in making selections. For more sources, check the appendix.

To get you started, a few of the many current artists and groups are listed below. This list represents a wide variety of styles—from pop to heavy metal, and from easy listening to Christian "blues" (for lack of a better word). Of course, the list is not designed to be all-inclusive; that would be impossible since new artists enter the field every day, and many talented groups play to a very localized audience. However, the list is intended to let you know that there is a wide field of Christian artists with a zeal for the Lord, as well as a great deal of talent.

Contemporary Christian Music

ROCK*

Keith Green
De Garmo & Key Band
Alwyn Wall
Joe English Band
Phil Keaggy & Band
Bryn Haworth
David Meece & Band
Servant
Second Chapter of Acts
Mylon Le Fevre &
   BrokenHeart
Petra
Leslie Phillips
Bob Dylan
Barry Crompton
Rick Cua

Tom Franzak
Quickflight
Richie Furay
Shelter
Larry Norman
Resurrection Band
Reggie Vinson
Johnny Rivers
Randy Matthews
Loyd Thogmartin
William Harvey Jett
Isaac Air Freight
David & the Giants
Eternity Express
David Edwards Band
City Limits

HEAVY METAL

Resurrection Band
Daniel Band
the 77's
Servant
Undercover
Mylon Le Fevre &
   BrokenHeart

Prodigal
Petra
Sweet Comfort Band
Daniel Amos Band
Barnabus
Jerusalem
100% Proof
Edin-Adahl

NEW WAVE

Vector
Servant
Undercover

Phil Keaggy & Band
Steve Taylor & Band
Sheila Walsh

*Some artists are listed in more than one category.

JAZZ-ROCK FUSION

Koinonia
Thomas Goodlunas & Panacea
Will McFarlane
Beau McDougall

Glad
Phil Keaggy & Band
Kathy Hervie
Liberation Suite

SOUTHERN GOSPEL

Leon Patillo
Andrae Crouch
Jessy Dixon
Bobby Jones
Larnelle Harris
Edwin Hawkins
Paradise
Otis Skillings
Maria Muldaur

Shirley Caesar
Mighty Clouds of Joy
Bob Bailey
Garth Hewitt
Denny Correll
Tramaine Hawkins
Candi Stanton
Donna Summer
Carmen Licciardello

POP TOP-40 SOUND

The Imperials
Amy Grant
Dion
Kelly Willard
Mark Heard
Paul Clark Band
Chuck Girard
Dallas Holm & Praise
Michael & Stormie Omartian
Pat Terry Group
Chris Christian
The Archers
Leon Patillo
Randy Stonehill Band
Second Chapter of Acts
Keith Green
David Meece
Silverwind
Farrel & Farrel
Steve Camp & Band
Whiteheart
Michelle Pillar
Sandy Patti

Karen Voetglin
Benny Hester
Russ Taff
Debby Boone
Stephanie Boosahda
Scott Wesley Brown
Karen Lafferty
Lamb
Andrus Blackwood &
    Company
Marty McCall & Fireworks
Mickey & Becky Moore
Teri DeSario
The Cruse Family
Andrae Crouch
Tom Howard
Johnny Rivers
Bernie Leadon
John Fischer
Michael W. Smith
Noel Paul Stookey &
    Bodyworks
Al Green

222

MIDDLE OF THE ROAD (Easy Listening)

Nicholas	Rick Foster
Brown Bannister	Christine Wyrtzen
Evie & Pelle Karlsson	Harvest
Maranatha Singers	Twila Paris
Morning Star	Dino Kartsonakis
Dan Burgess Singers	Cynthia Clawson
Family	Michael Card
Don Francisco	Steve & Maria Gardner
Joni Eareckson Tada	Wendy & Mary
Joy Song	The New Gaither Vocal Band
Brush Arbor	Phil Driscoll
Andrew Culverwell	B. J. Thomas
Honeytree	Wayne Watson
Bonnie Bramlett	Found Free
Terri DeSario	Cam Floria
John Michael Talbot	Barry McGuire
Dave Boyer	Terry Talbot

Note: This listing is not an exhaustive one—there is a wide variety of Christian artists available. The preceding is just a sampling of that variety.

Remember also, we are not granting blanket approval for all the groups on this list. You still need to scrutinize the groups you listen to by the four criteria—lyrics, goals, graphics and lifestyles—and be the final judge of what you allow to enter your mind.

16

Between Rock and a Hard Place: A Message to Parents

"It took me a long time to discover that the key thing in acting is honesty," a young actor in television commercials once remarked. "Once you know how to fake that, you've got it made."[1] Faking it—it's the password for the plastic generation of the eighties. If you know how to "fake 'em out," you've got it made.

"Faking it" has no place in the Christian's life, however. In fact, Jesus spoke harshly against hypocrites who say one thing but do another, and who point out others' shortcomings while guilty of far worse offenses: "Why, then, do you look at the speck in your brother's eye and pay no attention to the log in your own eye?. . . You hypocrite! First take the log out of your own eye, and then you will be able to see clearly to take the speck out of your brother's eye" (Matt. 7:3, 5, GNB).

We parents hoping to confront our kids with the problems concerning rock music had better take Jesus' words seriously and look at our own lives first. Some of us have enough "logs" to build a Lincoln cabin, and yet we try to tell our kids, "Do as I say, not as I do." It might work with television commercials, but it won't with our youth. They can see through hypocrisy in an instant.

The underlying assumption of this book is that most teenagers, as well as parents, who read it know the Lord and have made a commitment to follow Him. Serving the Lord requires courage and faith, and is hard enough for an adult. But our children have an even tougher road with the pressures of society and their peers bearing down on them. They need, as role models, parents with a personal knowledge of the Lord and a conviction to live out a consistent Christian walk.

If you, Mom or Dad, have not accepted Jesus Christ into your life as your Lord and Savior, now is the time. Jesus stands at the door waiting for you to invite Him in (see Chapter 15).

The next step is to examine your lifestyle. If you are indiscriminate about the music to which you listen, and the TV programs or films you view, then you are between rock and a hard place. You are being a phony. No one is perfect, and your children don't expect perfection from you, but they are virtually allergic to phoniness.

An actor from generations ago, Charles Coburn, once told this story about his father: When Charles first fell in love with the theater, he spent much of his time seeing plays.

One day his father counseled him, "One thing, son, you must never do. Don't go to the burlesque house."

"Why not, Father?" the young man asked.

"Because you would see things you shouldn't," was his father's firm reply.

Sure enough, as soon as possible, young Coburn visited the burlesque house, and he did see something he shouldn't have—his father.[2] Naturally, the father's credibility was lost. In the same way, you as parents lose credibility if you are flawed role models. If you hope to challenge your youth on the rock issue, you'll first need to take a hard look at several key areas in your own lives.

If you spend hours a day watching television—even harmless programs— but spend little or no time in prayer, can you expect your children to view a personal relationship with God as top priority? Paul wrote, "Imitate me as I imitate Christ." Can you make the same declaration to your children?

In an article entitled "The Struggle for Our Children," the writer points out:

> In order for our youth to have the courage to resist the new morality, they must see their parents resist the double-standard morality of middle-class hedonism. If they see little difference between the lifestyle of their Christian parents and their friends' non-Christian parents, why should they suffer the social repercussions of being different?[3]

As parents, you should review your attitudes toward the secular standards of material possessions, social status and the pursuit of pleasure, to see if you are using them as yardsticks to measure happiness. If you are, how can you expect your own youth not to measure their self-worth by the secular standards of rock's pop culture?

Your living habits, as well, should come under scrutiny. If you use drugs merely to increase your comfort, alcohol to unwind, or cigarettes to keep weight off, how can you expect your children to fight the pressure to do the same? Albert Schweitzer once said, "Example is not the main thing in life. It is the only thing."[4] Perhaps it's still possible to discuss meaningfully the issue of rock music with your children without first breaking the nicotine habit or foregoing a nightly cocktail, but as Franklin P. Jones once said, "Children are unpredictable. You never know what inconsistency they're going to catch you at next."[5] You'll probably have to deal with it in your family discussions.

You will need to examine your own listening habits, too. A father approached Dan just as one Truth About Rock seminar was to begin, and urgently listed seven rock stars he wanted Dan to hit hard for his young daughter's benefit. Then he leaned over and whispered, "But don't say anything about Dolly Parton!"

That father probably already knew he was listening to music as compromising to his faith as his daughter's rock music was to hers. Country music, in fact, is notorious for lyrics about booze-filled nights spent at the local honkytonk, drowning out the sorrows of a good-love-gone-bad. So let's take a brief look at country music, using the criteria previously established for judging music, and see if it is as wholesome as it claims.

Thank God, I'm a Country Boy

Jerry Reed is the country fan's ideal—he's fun, plays a mean guitar, owns a passable singing voice, and possesses bushels of country charm. His tunes, however, leave something to be desired. In his song "I'm a Slave," an ode to smoking, gambling, drinking and adultery, he excuses his actions because he's "a poor helpless victim to the things my body craves." Perhaps the song is meant to be humorous, but sin is no laughing matter.

Another country ballad, recorded by Savannah, croons the same theme—sin is inevitable and we are helpless slaves to it. "Backstreet Ballet" first tells the sad tale of a starving young artist, then concludes, "Now her garter's filled with cash/And her daddy calls her trash . . ./Don't be ashamed girl, for what you had to do."

Sweet Loretta Lynn claims she'll always love a "Lyin', Cheatin', Woman Chasin', Honky Tonkin', Whiskey Drinkin' " man, and Grammy winner Janie Fricke praises the man she loves, who's "clever as the devil and just as wild/ He's crazy/But a little crazy's kinda nice."

Eastern mysticism in country western? Though you reckoned never the twain would meet, Willie Nelson brought them together with his song, "Little Old Fashioned Karma," and then paraphrased Ecclesiastes 3 for good measure: "A little bit of sowing/A little bit of reaping/A little bit of laughing/And a little bit of weeping. . . ."

Likewise, England Dan and John Ford Coley, known for their mellowsounding country rock tunes such as, "I'd Really Love to See You Tonight," have thrown out the East-is-East, West-is-West philosophy and now subscribe to the Baha'i faith. According to Bob Larson, they overtly use their concerts to evangelize, and Coley, who is a long-time member, admits he had "a strong Christian background."[6]

Country music is well-known for singing about religion—usually Christianity—out of one side of the mouth, and "boozin' " out of the other, but Tom T. Hall lyrically wedded the two in "Everything from Jesus to Jack Daniels," a tune describing a confrontation between a Valium-and-beer guzzler and a "youngster wearing robes and wanting money for his god who sits upon a plastic throne. . . ."

Billboard magazine said in October 1980, "Drugs are turning up in country songs with surprising frequency, along with frank references to sex."[7]

Country titles about drugs include, "Bombed, Boozed and Busted," "Caffeine, Nicotine and Benzedrine (and Wish Me Luck)," "Quaaludes Again," and "Drinkin' and Druggin' and Watchin' TV."

According to Dr. James M. Schaefer, director of the University of Minnesota's Office of Alcohol and Other Drug Abuse Programming, country western music can lead to alcoholism among listeners. "I used to be a heavy drinker," he confesses, "drinking my way from middle-class bars to Skid Row. I *always* listened to country music. And with that self-wallowing twang, it's a natural mood depressant. The correlation is there—country western music and drinking go hand in hand."[8]

Charlie Monk, head of April-Blackwood's Nashville division, told *Billboard*, ". . . country lyrics have always intimated sex and promiscuous affairs. The backstreets to romance have always been a part of country music."[9] Country's sex-filled titles include, "It's All Wrong, But It's All Right," "Holding Her and Loving You," "Why Do I Have to Choose," "I'd Love to Lay You Down," and "Take Me to Bed (and I'll Be Good)."

Billy "Crash" Craddock sings a crass little number called "Tell Me When I'm Hot": "Baby, won't you tell me when I'm gettin' there/I'll give you everything I've got. . . ." But Jerry Lee Lewis wins the award for country crude with his rendition of "My Fingers Do the Talkin' " which says, "I'll let my fingers do the walkin' when I get you alone/I'll let all ten do the talkin'/Across your erogenous zones. . . ."

As long ago as December 1975, Ron Thompson, the program director of Wheeling, West Virginia's, eminent 50,000-watt radio station, WWVA, printed an open letter to the music industry, chastising its leaders for their poor taste:

> Due to the profanity and distasteful lyrics we have been receiving on records by name artists, WWVA has initiated the following policy. WWVA AM/FM will not air suggestive or profane lyrics. We will delete questionable words and phrases before we play a record. Should the title fail to pass our code of ethics, or if an edit is impossible, the record will be not be aired. . . . It is not our policy to be moral crusaders, but we will not jeopardize our standing in the community.[10]

It would be wonderful if more radio stations took this commendable approach. However, what the station manager and others so indignant about country music's present condition often fail to recognize is that it has, as Charlie Monk implied, been even more sex-filled, vulgar and booze-sotted in the past. In fact, when *Billboard* first began to list country hits in March 1939, they noted that, for the sake of good taste, popular hillbilly tunes with double entendre had been "purposely omitted from this column."[11]

In the thirties and into the forties, singers now known as the grand old men of country, such as Jimmie Davis, Roy Acuff and Gene Autry, sang songs that would have melted WWVA's microphones—songs with titles such as, "Doin' It the Old Fashioned Way," "She's a Low-Down Mama," "Pistol Packin' Papa," and "High Behind Blues." The lyrics to such tunes reflect the vulgar, bawdy, beerhall ballads of colonial America and its motherland—ballads in which country music has its roots.

It's not just the songs which are immoral, though. Country music's heroes lead lifestyles that often surpass rock's raciest in their debauchery, and according to *Billboard*, "The artists' freewheeling personal lives . . . have played a role in stripping away some of the 'unspoken taboos' that once dominated country music."[12]

Country stars known as much for their liquor-filled, pill-popping lifestyles, as for their many country hits, are the late Hank Williams, Sr., and Jim Reeves, Johnny Cash and Jerry Lee Lewis. Although Cash has since been converted to the Lord and cleaned up his act, he recalls, "At that time, I was drinking a case of beer and taking up to 100 pills a day, uppers and downers. . . . If you had a picture of me then, you wouldn't believe it was me. I'm 6'2", but [at that time] I only weighed 150 pounds."[13]

Though country stars don't seem to flaunt their sexually promiscuous lifestyles as much as rock stars do, sex symbols such as Louise Mandrell, Dolly Parton and Tanya Tucker seem to be doing their utmost to knock down the barriers that have kept sex a supposedly taboo subject in country circles. Ironically, though country music may sing about the same subjects its kissin' cousin rock and roll does, and though Grand Ole Opry has its share of stars whose lives are odes to hedonism, the taboos still exist. Although something must be said for their efforts to maintain a moral atmosphere, it is often merely a hypocritical cover-up, something teenagers find revolting.

As Bob Larson notes in his book *Rock*:

> What disturbs young people the most is the veneer of religious hypocrisy that glosses over the country music scene. Such artists think nothing of singing praises of stolen love one minute and switching to "Amazing Grace" the next. Two of the biggest country hits of recent years, "Heaven's Just a Sin Away," and "It Don't Feel Like Sinnin' to Me," were recorded by singers who claim to be staunch church members.[14]

Louise Mandrell has even blamed her faith for her multiple marriages: "I've actually been married so often because of my Christian beliefs," Mandrell (whose first trip to the altar was at age 16) told *Us* magazine. "I just couldn't have sex with a man unless I was married to him."[15]

Aside from the whole hypocrisy issue, the most detrimental effect of country music is that its lyrics are its most essential and powerful element. As Steve Lawhead points out in *Rock Revisited*:

> . . . unlike rock 'n' roll—where studio arrangement, instrumental flamboyance and technical wizardry take priority over the words—country music is founded, formed and fashioned on the strengths of its lyrics. . . . Unquestionably, lyrics count as the single most important ingredient in a country hit.[16]

Because lyrics are country's most influential feature, radio commentator Paul Harvey's address to the 1980 Country Radio Seminar in Nashville as-

228

sumes added significance. The usually positive-minded broadcaster lamented country music's slide into what he labelled "pornography of the air waves."[17]

Likewise, country singer and songwriter, Conway Twitty, frankly comments on his 21-year history as a recording artist: "As a country artist, I'm not proud of a lot of things in my field. There is no doubt in my mind that we are contributing to the moral decline in America."[18]

Of course, it can be said country is most often enjoyed by adults who hopefully have their value systems set, not by impressionable youngsters; but that does not mesh with the scientific findings of research studying media's effect on value systems. Furthermore, what sort of example do parents set when they shun rock music for its questionable content, and yet plug into the local country station to sing along with such songs as, "I Loved 'Em Every One," or "Take This Job and Shove It"? How can we as parents expect our kids to stay true to their Christian convictions while watching Mom and Dad's inconsistent choice of music?

Other Heavyweight Offenders

While pointing fingers, in all fairness, it must be said that all styles of popular music need to be examined and critiqued. The so-called easy-listening pop music has had its share of stars with questionable lifestyles, and songs with dubious lyrical content. Soul, rhythm-and-blues, gospel, broadway, jazz and classical music have all been guilty of excesses and immorality at times. No matter what particular style a person prefers, it is important always to be a discriminating listener.

Shofar magazine says, "Each song, each piece of music should be judged on its own merit. No single artist can be accepted without thought. No single style can be accepted without thought. We are responsible to stop, listen and look at all that we hear."[19]

Another activity that needs inspection is television viewing. We can hardly speak to sons and daughters about the detrimental effects of hours spent plugged into earphones if we spend equal amounts of time flipping our remote channel selectors. In the same way that teens can be wooed by the slick, sexy message of Duran Duran, or the self-centered solution of Fixx, we can be indoctrinated as well by "All My Children," "Hillstreet Blues," or "Monday Night at the Movies."

Obviously, trends on television have, for some time, resolutely been moving in a direction away from God. Producers and studio executives repeatedly warn screenwriters to steer clear of moral themes if they wish to make a sale. "The current and very dominant trend," *Writer's Digest* says, "and likely to last according to many insiders, is sexual themes; both cheesecake and beefcake are currently on ample display in lurid storylines as the networks try desperately to compete with cable, video, etc."[20]

The professional writer's magazine went on to say an agent, who had recently attempted unsuccessfully to sell a very dramatic story with socially conscious undertones, was told that only sex is selling for network movies-of-the-week. "Everyone said the same thing," the agent reported, "that the networks are only buying 'commercial' ideas, which is another way of saying T & A."[21]

Though people claim to deplore the violence and sexual themes on television, ratings show they continue to watch as if mesmerized by the tube's glow. A study of western society's dependence on TV disclosed we are more dependent on our little electronic boxes than first imagined. According to Wilson Bryan Key, the study, conducted by the British Broadcasting Company, was created to test the viewers' ability to live without television for one year. One-hundred and eighty-four families were initially contracted to participate and were paid for not watching their "tellies." Families quickly began to drop out, though, and not one family lasted beyond five months. Other studies have met with similar results.

Researchers unanimously concluded the volunteers had "suffered withdrawal symptoms similar to those of drug addicts and alcoholics," and that the future would see an "increased dependence upon television among the general population."[22]

In light of the quickly advancing state of media technology, there is simply no accurate way to calculate the effects of constant media barrage, but the implications are serious. Key says Americans shouldn't underestimate the "media managed environment if they hope to survive as human beings."[23] As Christians, it's doubly important we heed that message.

What's a Mother (or Father) to Do?

1. *Get smart.* For starters, it's important that you get informed and stay informed. Your teenager will quickly spot a bluff. Of course, it takes time, but isn't that what child-rearing is all about? Too often parents become lax when their children get older, but just as it was important to read all the latest articles and books on the joys of toilet training when your offspring was a toddler, now it's time to be informed on subjects that can assist you as you attempt to guide that same child (who now stands three inches taller than you) into full, Christian adulthood. And even if you never quite mastered the toilet training techniques, you *can* learn about music and its effect on your child. It doesn't take talent, just time and concern.

We Christians are sometimes guilty of building ourselves "Christian ghettos." We don't attempt to communicate with or understand the world. Our kids, however, are immersed in the world—they need parents who have firsthand experience and can speak their language.

Your first stop in your teen's rock world should be the record department of your local variety store. Flipping through the album covers will make you feel as if you were flipping through the pages of *Playboy*. Along with sex, you'll see being peddled equal amounts of violence, drugs, hedonism and Satanism. Then take a look around you. You'll see young people not only flipping through but buying those same albums—some kids less than ten years old.

Once you're over the shock of the album covers, venture to a rock record store. More than likely you'll find drug paraphernalia for sale alongside the LP's. According to Marsha Manatt of the U.S. Department of Health, Education and Welfare, the paraphernalia industry offers preteen marijuana consumers "drug-related toys, games, and comic books. Though many of these items are purchased by adults, their commercial message to children—'Drugs are fun!'—is clear and effective."[24]

Dr. Mitchell Rosenthal, director of New York's Phoenix House Drug Rehabilitation Center, commented on the sale of these gadgets to teens and preteens:

> Here is a perfectly legal industry—a multi-million dollar one, we believe—based on the commercial exploitation and propagandizing of something that is illegal. . . . It's saying loud and clear, "Drug use is OK. Our culture expects you to get high."[25]

Since the album covers and lyrics of rock music often promote drug use, the sale of drug-related items in record shops is not surprising. Although many civic groups have been instrumental in preventing paraphernalia sales through legislation, the practice is still legal in most states. Manatt concludes:

> The practice of locating head shops . . . in record shops frequented by youngsters . . . makes it clear that children constitute the major growth market for the paraphernalia business. And the paraphernalia is already being marketed via the media that most influence adolescents—rock radio stations, record albums and popular magazines.[26]

Your third stop should be a magazine shop, bookstore or your local library. If the term "rock and roll" still conjures up images of the Shirelles, the Dave Clark Five or Herman's Hermits, you'll need to do some in-depth reading in order to get up-to-date. Browse through magazines used as source material for this book, such as *Rolling Stone*, *Hit Parader*, *Circus*, *Musician* and *Creem*. They will give you a feel for the rock music culture in which your teenagers are immersed. In addition, some magazines print lyrics to the latest hits.

Check out secular books on rock music history, biographies of rock celebrities and groups, and dictionaries of rock terms, as well as Christian sources on the subject. While you may find the secular sources sometimes offensive, be assured your children are exposed to this material every day. Watch for reviews in your local paper of the latest record releases, concert dates, and of rock-related movies.

Finally, turn on the music. Listen to your local rock radio station. If you've been listening only to inspirational music, you're in for an ear-opening experience. You will find the music not only loud, but pornographic. Similarly, much of the between-platter patter will be filled with sexual innuendo.

Whether or not you subscribe to cable TV, you should also tune in one of the rock video television programs, because for teens today, video *is* rock.

Finally, peruse your child's record collection. Note the artists he seems to prefer and the type of music those artists produce. Play the music and get familiar with the lyrics. Note how many songs deal with suicide, rebellion, violence, and the like.

2. *Get involved.* Let's face it, your teenager is probably not used to spending much time with you—if you are the average American family, both husband and wife involved with work, church and civic duties and the kids active in school, sports and other extracurricular activities and odd jobs. You maybe have allowed yourself to get so busy, you've forgotten your most important task: being a Christian family. It takes time to develop loving, trusting relationships, and that is what's needed in order to discuss any issue of importance, be it drug involvement, school problems, social situations or indiscriminate submersion in rock and roll music.

Before you give your child your views on life, you must first give him *yourself.* You'll never seem smarter to him than during the times you just sit and listen. He needs to see you are available when he needs you.

Teacher and writer Irene Primeau says:

> It has been said that values are caught not taught, and it is in the home that children catch the spiritual vision and emotional strength they need to cope with adverse social pressure. The best way for youth to see through the artificiality and emptiness of our hedonistic culture is to experience the opposite through good family relationships.[27]

Ask yourself what sort of impression your child has of you. Do you know how to carry on a quality conversation? Do you listen—or do you catch yourself saying, "Not now, I'm watching TV," or "Tell me later—I have to work late tonight"? Do you openly tell him of your own mistakes and problems. How often do you say, "I love you" and "I'm sorry"?

Learning to talk and listen to a teenager is a time-consuming task, but a rewarding one. A poem often given to new mothers says in essence, "Don't mind the dishes, and leave the cobwebs. They'll still be there tomorrow, but babies grow up quickly and soon are gone." Parents of teenagers need a similar reminder. Before you know it, your teen will be out the door and on his own. The time you have been given to mold his life is all too brief. There will be time later for the things you want to do and for working toward some of life's comforts—for now take time to love and listen. While your child is still with you, make sure *you* are with *him*, to support him in his struggles and be an effective role model.

3. *Get down on your knees.* God seems to be in the business of saving families. He saved Noah's family, He saved Lot's family, He saved the households of the Jews in ancient Egypt, and He saved the jailer in Philippi with his entire household. Paul, too, spoke of his "child in the Lord," Timothy, as having a sincere faith which lived first in his grandmother and was passed

on by God's grace through his mother.

As a parent, you can claim these examples as evidence that God wants each member of your family to experience Jesus as his Savior and to live a redeemed life. Remember, your child is His child too. But God wants you to bring your child to Him in prayer, to intercede for his needs and ask for God's gifts for him. Next, seek His answers for your teens, and pray that His peace would enter your discussions about rock music.

Then, spend time reading Scripture, your source of inspiration and instruction. Paul calls Scripture a two-edged sword—and with good reason. You'll be amazed how often a Bible-based answer will satisfy a defiant teenager!

Now you are ready for battle—and a battle it will be! Not necessarily with your teenager, but definitely against the "wiles of the devil." Remember, you are not fighting against simply the sloppy standards of some local deejay or the offensive behavior of the latest teen idol, or even against the would-be powers of corruption in corporate offices of the record-producing conglomerates.

You are "contending against the principalities, against the powers, against the world rulers of this present darkness, against the spiritual hosts of wickedness in the heavenly places" (Eph. 6:12, RSV). Rock music has become the devil's playground, and he's not going to allow you on his turf without a rumble.

Nothing New Under the Sun

Ecclesiastes says there is nothing new—nothing that hasn't happened before, but people seldom learn to profit from the past. They tackle a problem by breaking new ground instead of investigating past solutions. Is there evidence that music has affected young people in the past as it does today? Certainly the problem is not a new one, although today's electronic age has magnified it to staggering proportions.

Let's look to the past and apply some of the principles viewed then as solutions to the music issue.

In his preface to the *Wittenberg Gesangbuch* of 1524, Martin Luther voiced some thoughts that are applicable to our situation today:

> I wish that the young men might have something to rid them of their love ditties and wanton songs and might instead of these learn wholesome things and thus yield willingly to the good; also, because I am not of the opinion that all the arts shall be crushed to earth and perish through the Gospel, as some bigoted persons pretend, but would willingly see them all, and especially music, servants of Him who gave and created them.[28]

Five areas of action are suggested by Luther in this statement—actions which parents can readily use today to help free their young charges from the harmful effects of rock music. They are: (1) decide, (2) defer, (3) discern, (4) discard and (5) displace.

1. *Decide*. Luther said he hoped the young people of his day would "yield willingly to the good." In other words, if *they* make the decision, it has the most beneficial effect. As a parent, you need to take the time necessary to discuss the issue of rock music thoroughly and to explain *why* you have reached the conclusions you give your teen, rather than simply making ultimatums.

God commands parents, in Deut. 6:6–9, to teach their children godliness from morning to night, in the house and on the road, using every means available. It may take that much effort to guide a child to a decision to give up the rock music that is harmful to him, but it will be time well spent. The idea of teaching from morning until night indicates it will probably take more than one discussion—perhaps many.

And don't forget, listening is an important part of teaching. Your teenager is likely to have many objections and questions, as well as reasoning of his own. Don't mistakenly label such challenge as rebellion. From the time a child is old enough to speak, he asks "why." When he is little, it's merely amusing or irritating, but as he gets older, sometimes you find the "why's" threatening. An adolescent, though, needs to hear the reasoning you employ in reaching conclusions. It is the model he needs in learning to make value judgments of his own. You give him food, clothing and shelter; don't neglect to give the most important commodity of all—information.

Use materials from a variety of sources—books, tapes, seminars (such as the Truth About Rock seminars)—and of course listen with your teenager to his music and study album covers with him.

Should you actually forbid the playing of music you view as harmful? This is a very personal decision, one without a set answer. So much depends on the child as well as his age, his relationship with you and the depth of his involvement with rock.

Naturally, if your child is being persuaded through rock music to use drugs, consider suicide, or to rebel, or if your child is very young—seven to at least eleven—then more parental supervision is required and confiscation of record albums and tapes may be appropriate. Don't hesitate to do so.

Dr. Benjamin Spock says:

> In America more than in any other country, we parents, especially of the college-educated group, have lost a lot of our conviction about how much and what kind of guidance to give our children. . . . We seem to have become particularly fearful that we will make our children resent us or will distort their personalities if we exert too much authority over them. This parental hesitancy has been more marked in relation to adolescent children than to any other age group.[29]

This weakening of parental authority can confuse children who naturally desire boundaries set for them, even if they initially balk at them. Christian child psychologist Dr. James Dobson says that after years of working with children, he could not be more convinced that they derive security from knowing their limits.

There is security in defined limits. When the home atmosphere is as it should be, the child lives in utter safety. He never gets in trouble unless he deliberately asks for it, and as long as he stays within the limits, there is mirth and freedom and acceptance. If this is what is meant by "democracy" in the home, then I favor it. If it means the absence of boundaries, or that each child sets his own boundaries, then I'm inalterably opposed to it.[30]

One word of caution, however. If you feel you must confiscate records your teen has bought with his own money, pack them away until he or she leaves home. At that time, he can make his own decision to destroy the albums.

One more suggestion as you discuss this issue with your youngsters: Don't make God the fall guy. In other words, don't tell your teenager he has to throw out his music because "God says so"—it is a poor reason and will only lead to resentment. This is not to say you shouldn't make known God's desires and commands for our lives, only that you should not use Him as a wall to hide behind. Instead, provide explanation and teaching for your children. "Fathers," it says in Col. 3:21, "do not provoke your children, lest they become discouraged" (RSV). Ultimatums backed by "Because God says so" will provoke and discourage a child seeking to understand. Your teen needs principles he can live by.

2. *Defer.* Our tastes in music must yield to Jesus' lordship. Luther says he would like to see all the arts, especially music, "servants of Him who gave and created them." It was clear to Luther that all the arts can reflect God as extensions of His creativity. And to the extent they are submitted to the lordship of Jesus, they are good.

When you accept Jesus into your life, you are asking Him to be the Lord of its every square inch. However, the Lord is a gentleman and doesn't force you to yield to Him. He simply waits for you to release those areas you hold dear.

If rock music is one of the areas your teen is still clutching, he'll first need to defer it to God's authority. Once you and your child are in agreement that God desires changes in his listening habits, you need to pray together for the Lord to place in the child's heart the desire for a higher standard.

Before your teen does any "housecleaning," he needs to ask God to help him discern not only what is good, but what is the very best. He needs to pray for courage to follow through on his commitment to Him and his conviction to defer his desires to God's.

3. *Discern.* Luther challenged his young men to make certain not "all the arts shall be crushed to earth and perish . . . as some bigoted persons pretend." Even a cursory study of music demonstrates that not all secular music is bad, nor is all so-called religious music good. To super-spiritually condemn all rock music is to throw out the baby with the bath water.

Rock music is a cultural phenomenon and through it we can learn how and what our culture is thinking, as well as communicate to our culture. As Christians, we must not construct what evangelist Bob Mumford calls a "back to the fort" mentality. Christians are meant to be the salt of the earth— dissolving into the stew of society to give it the sweet flavor of the Lord—not a terrified mass huddled behind a Christian stockade till the Lord's return. We need not fear being "tainted" by the world; we can be in it and yet not of it.

What needs to occur, then, is a personal discernment process. Only you and your teenager know what particular music is appropriate for his age level, Christian maturity, environment, personality, etc. Obviously, some will find it necessary to fully clean out their record collections. Others should "fast" from all music for a time to help them see things clearly.

As you listen together to his albums, go beyond the beat and the sound to hear and discuss what is being said. Look at the album art and discern if it coincides with Christian values. Review the material you have gathered on your teenager's favorite rock celebrities. Discuss the way the music affects your child—what thoughts it conjures up, what mood it creates, whether it is positive or negative in nature.

As a word of caution, be certain your teen understands that you are condemning sexual perversion, not sex; rebellion, not honest questioning; hedonism, not wholesome fun. And be certain as well that you as a parent are teaching your child firm conviction, not legalism.

4. *Discard*. Luther says young men should have the courage to "rid them of their love ditties and wanton songs." When Jesus told the parable, that likened the kingdom of heaven to a net which gathers up great quantities of fish, He said the men on shore sorted the good fish into vessels, but threw out the inferior. Jesus didn't mention keeping the "not so bad" fish—only the very best. We need to be just as discriminating with the products of this world— saving the very best and discarding the rest.

Although a fire is a very graphic way to make a clean break and to seal one's agreement with the Lord, it is not the only means of disposal. Breaking and tossing the records in the trash is also fine. The important thing is to discard them in a way in which they can't bring harm to others. In other words, don't give them away, sell them, or leave them where others can pick them up.

5. *Displace*. Luther states, "I wish that young men might . . . instead of these, learn wholesome things." A vacuum cannot exist in nature; something will always rush in to fill it. Likewise, we can't exist with emptiness in our lives. If rock music formerly played a large part in your teenager's life and he now plans to discard it, a vacuum will develop that needs to be creatively filled.

Before your youngster has even made that decision, begin purchasing top-quality Christian contemporary and wholesome secular music. Although your young adolescent may not appreciate the music at first, start playing it occasionally to acquaint him with the variety of music available to help fill the gap.

Remember, too, that maintaining strong Christian convictions without the social support from fellowship with other Christians is almost impossible for all of us. For a teen, the burden is sometimes more heavy since he often has an intense fear of being different. For this reason, a church youth group is another positive displacement step. Once your child is more open, you might suggest he and his group attend a Christian concert by an artist you approve. Nothing will sell a kid on good music more than seeing an auditorium full of happy, "normal" looking kids, all having a great time. It will help him feel less a "misfit" in this music-oriented society.

As we have seen, however, music is only part of society's problem. Other influences—radio, television, films, magazines and books—all need to be discussed with your teenager. Remember, the standard for a Christian is "the very best." And also remember to provide alternatives. Support wholesome entertainment when it is available and let the promoters know how much you appreciate it.

Finally, see to it that family times displace some of the vacuum the trashing of rock music will create. Individual "dates" with your teen, family football games, and hot-dog roasts in the fireplace will all create memories to savor in the years ahead, as well as providing an alternative to the debilitating effects of much of rock music.

Ultimately, we have to ask ourselves what kind of society—what kind of culture—we want for ourselves and our children. More and more, our culture displays an irreconcilable pull away from the Judeo-Christian ethic, and our vulnerable youth are often too immature or too inexperienced in their faith to fight this irresistible force. If we Christian parents are contented doing nothing to help guide our children—as well as to struggle against the forces seeking to destroy our culture—then we are promoting the reign of the devil—the status quo.

In a *Cornerstone* excerpt from his book, *A Time for Anger*, Franky Schaeffer observes:

> To accept the idea that there is any part of life that Christianity should not affect, whether it be the family, politics, the law, the media, or the arts, is to make a tacit admission that Christianity is not true. We must act, and act now. We must dare to be human. We must dare to sacrifice in a selfish age. We must dare to be unfashionable. [We must] dare to live.[31]

The recommendations in this chapter are a big order. Life is hectic and already so full. But dare we not heed the call to steer our children from evil?

Our prayer should be that God would help us order our priorities and give us a new zeal for the care and training of our children, and that He would "turn the hearts of the fathers to the children, and the disobedient to the wisdom of the just, to make ready for the Lord a people prepared" (Luke 1:17, RSV).

Notes

References—Chapter 1
1. Jonathon Green, *The Book of Rock Quotes* (New York: Omnibus Press, 1982), p. 11.
2. *Ibid.*
3. David Pichaske, *A Generation In Motion* (New York: Schirmer Books, 1979), Preface.
4. Gary Herman, *Rock 'n' Roll Babylon* (Great Britain: Plexus Publishing Ltd., 1982), p. 22.
5. Jonathon Green, *The Book of Rock Quotes* (New York: Omnibus Press, 1982), p. 34.
6. Gary Herman, *Rock 'n' Roll Babylon* (Great Britain: Plexus Publishing Ltd., 1982), p. 26.
7. Ray Bonds, editor, *The Harmony Illustrated Encyclopedia of Rock,* 3rd Ed. (New York: Crown Publishers, Inc., 1982), pp. 30–32.
8. Gary Herman, *Rock 'n' Roll Babylon* (Great Britain: Plexus Publishing Ltd., 1982), p. 25.
9. Jonathon Green, *The Book of Rock Quotes* (New York: Omnibus Press, 1982), p. 14.
10. Arnold Shaw, *Dictionary of American Pop/Rock* (New York: Macmillan, 1982), p. 287.
11. Gary Herman, *Rock 'n' Roll Babylon* (Great Britain: Plexus Publishing Ltd., 1982), p. 16.
12. Albert Goldman, *Elvis* (New York: Avon Books, 1981), p. 227.
13. Gary Herman, *Rock 'n' Roll Babylon* (Great Britain: Plexus Publishing Ltd., 1982), p. 19.
14. Arnold Shaw, *Dictionary of American Pop/Rock* (New York: Macmillan, 1982), p. 287.
15. Albert Goldman, *Elvis* (New York: Avon Books, 1981), pp. 700, 701.
16. *Ibid.,* p. 701.

References—Chapter 2
1. Jonathon Green, *The Book of Rock Quotes* (New York: Omnibus Press, 1982), p. 21
2. David Pichaske, *A Generation In Motion* (New York: Schirmer Books, 1979), p. 159.
3. Michael Lydon, "Rock For Sale," as it appeared in *The Age of Communication,*

240

William Lutz, editor (California: Goodyear Publishing Company, Inc., 1974), p. 407. (Copyright 1969 by Michael Lydon, from *Rock Folk,* by Michael Lydon, The Dial Press.)

4. David Pichaske, *A Generation In Motion* (New York: Schirmer Books, 1979), p. 160.
5. *Ibid.*
6. *Ibid.*
7. Dave Marsh and Kevin Stein, *The Book of Rock Lists* (New York: Dell Publishing Co., Inc., 1981), pp. 152, 153; Carl Belz, "Television Shows and Rock Music," as it appeared in *The Age of Commication,* William Lutz, editor (California: Goodyear Publishing Company, Inc., 1974), pp. 401–404. (Copyright 1969, Oxford University Press, Inc., from *The Story of Rock.*)
8. Jonathon Green, *The Book of Rock Quotes* (New York: Omnibus Press, 1982), p. 32.
9. David Pichaske, *A Generation In Motion* (New York: Schirmer Books, 1979), p. 58.
10. Bruce Pollock, *When Rock Was Young* (New York: Holt, Rinehart & Winston, 1981), p. 133.
11. Michael Lydon, "Rock For Sale," as it appeared in *The Age of Communication,* William Lutz, editor (California: Goodyear Publishing Company, Inc., 1974), p. 408. (Copyright 1969, by Michael Lydon, from *Rock Folk,* by Michael Lydon, The Dial Press.)
12. *San Francisco Chronicle* (April 13, 1966), p. 26.
13. Wilson Bryan Key, *Media Sexploitation* (New Jersey: Prentice-Hall, Inc., 1976), p. 132.
14. Gary Herman, *Rock 'n' Roll Babylon* (Great Britain: Plexus Publishing Ltd., 1982), p. 138.
15. *Time* magazine (January 18, 1971).
16. *People* magazine (January 16, 1984).
17. Jann Wenner, *Lennon Remembers* (New York: Fawcett Popular Library, 1971), pp. 84–86.
18. *Time* magazine (January 18, 1971).
19. *Time* magazine (September 22, 1967), p. 62.
20. Wilson Bryan Key, *Media Sexploitation* (New Jersey: Prentice-Hall, Inc., 1976), p. 131.
21. Peter Brown and Steven Gaines, *The Love You Make: An Insider's Story of the Beatles* (New York: McGraw-Hill, 1983).
22. Bryan Wilson Key, *Media Sexploitation* (New Jersey: Prentice-Hall, 1976), p. 136.
23. David Pichaske, *A Generation In Motion* (New York: Schirmer Books, 1979), p. 97.
24. *Ibid.,* p. 96.
25. Gary Herman, *Rock 'n' Roll Babylon* (Great Britain: Plexus Publishing Ltd., 1982), p. 157.
26. Wilson Bryan Key, *Media Sexploitation* (New Jersey: Prentice-Hall, 1976), p. 135.
27. Ray Bonds, editor, *The Harmony Illustrated Encyclopedia of Rock,* 3rd ed. (New York: Crown Publishers, Inc., 1982), p. 14, as published in *Time* magazine (April 25, 1967).
28. David Dalton, *The Rolling Stones: The First Twenty Years* (New York: Alfred A. Knopf, 1981), p. 53.

29. David Pichaske, *A Generation In Motion* (New York: Schirmer Books, 1979).
30. Ray Bonds, editor, *The Harmony Illustrated Encyclopedia of Rock,* 3rd ed. (New York: Crown Publishers, Inc., 1982), p. 197.
31. Gary Herman, *Rock 'n' Roll Babylon* (Great Britain: Plexus Publishing Ltd., 1982), p. 143.
32. "Death at the Coliseum: The Night That Shook the World of Rock," *Families* magazine (October 1981), p. 108.
33. David Pichaske, *A Generation In Motion* (New York: Schirmer Books, 1979), p. 76.
34. Gary Herman, *Rock 'n' Roll Babylon* (Great Britain: Plexus Publishing Ltd., 1982), p. 7.
35. Michael Lydon, "Rock For Sale," as it appeared in *The Age of Communication,* William Lutz, editor (California: Goodyear Publishing Company, Inc., 1974), p. 408. (Copyright 1969 by Michael Lydon, from *Rock Folk,* by Michael Lydon, The Dial Press.)
36. Gary Herman, *Rock 'n' Roll Babylon* (Great Britain: Plexus Publishing Ltd., 1982), p. 63.
37. "The History of Heavy Metal," *Hit Parader* magazine (Fall 1983), p. 7.
38. "KISS Removes the Lipstick," *St. Paul Pioneer Press* (October 23, 1983), p. 3E.
39. *Ibid.*
40. "Not the Sound of Silence," *Newsweek* magazine (November 14, 1983), p. 102.
41. "The History of Heavy Metal," *Hit Parader* magazine (Fall 1983), p. 8.
42 *Circus* magazine (December 30, 1976), p. 61.
43. "Punk Rock Bands Seen Inspiring New Wave of Violent Behavior," *St. Paul Pioneer Press/Dispatch* (July 19, 1980), p. 2B.
44. *Newsweek* magazine (January 23, 1984), p. 56.
45. Arnold Shaw, *Dictionary of American Pop/Rock* (New York: Macmillan, 1982), p. 293.
46. *Ibid.*
47. *Ibid.*, p. 294.
48. *Newsweek* magazine (January 23, 1984), p. 56.
49. David A. Noebel, *The Legacy of John Lennon* (Nashville, TN: Thomas Nelson Publishers, 1982), p. 92.
50. *Ibid.*

References—Chapter 3

1. Rev. Kenneth E. Parker, "Music, the Cultural Frontier of the Church," *Windstorm Christian Music* magazine (July/August, 1983), p. 10.
2. *The American Journal of Psychiatry,* vol. 99, p. 317.
3. *New York Times* magazine (May 8, 1983), p. 55.
4. Rev. Kenneth E. Parker, "Music, the Cultural Frontier of the Church," *Windstorm Christian Music* magazine (July/August, 1983), p. 10.
5. Michael Lydon, "Rock For Sale," as it appeared in *The Age of Communication,* William Lutz, editor (California: Goodyear Publishing Company, Inc., 1974), p. 413. (Copyright 1969 by Michael Lydon, from *Rock Folk,* by Michael Lydon, The Dial Press.)
6. "Teen Media Use," *USA Today* (November 30, 1983), p. D1.
7. Statistics courtesy of WCCO radio, Mpls., MN, figures for January 1983.
8. Albert Goldman, *Elvis* (New York: Avon Books, 1981), p. 243.

9. *Ibid.,* p. 387.
10. Vance Packard, *Hidden Persuaders* (New York: McKay, 1957), p. 165, as quoted from *Tide* magazine, journal of merchandisers.
11. *Circus* magazine (August 3, 1978), p. 41.
12. *Circus* magazine (August 31, 1978), p. 30.
13. Dave Marsh and Kevin Stein, *The Book of Rock Lists* (New York: Dell Publishing Company, Inc., 1981), p. 130.
14. Richard Corliss, "Manufacturing a Multimedia Hit," *Time* magazine (May 9, 1983).
15. Steven Levy, "Ad Nauseam, How MTV Sells Out Rock & Roll," *Rolling Stone* magazine (December 8, 1983), p. 74.
16. Richard Corliss, "Manufacturing a Multimedia Hit," *Time* magazine (May 9, 1983).
17. *TV Guide* (March 27, 1981), p. A-67; figures from Television Bureau of Advertising.
18. *USA Today* (December 22, 1983), p. D5.
19. Carl Belz, "Television Shows and Rock Music," as it appeared in *The Age of Communication,* William Lutz, editor (California: Goodyear Publishing Company, Inc., 1974), p. 398. (Copyright 1969 by Carl Belz, from *The Story of Rock,* by Carl Belz, Oxford University Press.)
20. Albert Goldman, *Elvis* (New York: Avon Books, 1981), p. 241.
21. Wilson Bryan Key, *Media Sexploitation* (New Jersey: Prentice-Hall, 1976), p. 209.
22. *The New York Times* magazine (May 8, 1983), Section 6.
23. "Rock 'n' Roll Video: MTV's Music Revolution," *People Weekly* magazine (October 17, 1983), p. 96.
24. Steven Levy, "Ad Nauseam, How MTV Sells Out Rock & Roll," *Rolling Stone* magazine (December 8, 1983), p. 33.
25. "Rock TV Channel Grabs Us Over Time," *USA Today* (November 30, 1983), p. D1.
26. Steven Levy, "Ad Nauseam: How MTV Sells Out Rock & Roll," *Rolling Stone* magazine (December 8, 1983), p. 34.
27. *Ibid.*
28. *Ibid.,* p. 79.
29. *Ibid.,* p. 33.
30. *Ibid.,* p. 76.
31. *Campus Life* (March 1984), p. 61.
32. Steven Levy, "Ad Nauseam: How MTV Sells Out Rock & Roll," *Rolling Stone* magazine (December 8, 1983), p. 76.
33. *Campus Life,* (March 1984), p. 61.
34. "Video Retailers are Dancing to Tune of Hot New Releases," *Ramsey County Review* (September 28, 1983).
35. Dianne Noel, "Videoview," *Hit Parader* magazine (September 1983), p. 39.
36. Noe Goldwasser, "Music on Video: Selling a Sight for Sore Eyes," *USA Today* (November 17, 1983), p. 6D.
37. "Rock 'n' Roll Video: MTV's Music Revolution," *People Weekly* magazine (October 17, 1983), p. 99.
38. Steven Levy, "Ad Nauseam: How MTV Sells Out Rock & Roll," *Rolling Stone* magazine (December 8, 1983), p. 34.
39. Dan Sperling, "Students Rock Along," *USA Today* (February 10, 1984), p. 5D.
40. Noe Goldwasser, "Music on Video," *USA Today* (November 17, 1983), p. 6D.

41. *Newsweek* magazine (April 2, 1979), p. 58.
42. *The New York Times* magazine (May 8, 1983), p. 56.

References—Chapter 6
 1. Steve Lawhead, *Rock Reconsidered* (Downers Grove, IL: InterVarsity Press, 1981), pp. 106, 107.
 2. Jerry Solomon, "Between Rock and a Hard Place," *Shofar* magazine (Fall 1983), p. 9.
 3. *Super Rock* magazine (June 1978), p. 94.
 4. *Rolling Stone* magazine (September 16, 1982), p. 14.
 5. *Us* magazine (July 21, 1981), p. 73.
 6. Roy Trakin, "Record Reviews," *Hit Parader* magazine (September 1983), p. 24.
 7. Francis Schaeffer, "The Battle For Our Culture," *New Wine* magazine (February 1982), p. 7.
 8. *Newsweek* (December 21, 1981), p. 75.
 9. Bob Larson, *Contemporary Christian Music* magazine (April 1983), p. 51.
10. Roy Trakin, "Record Reviews," *Hit Parader* magazine (September 1983), p. 25.
11. Steve Lawhead, *Rock Reconsidered* (Downers Grove, IL: InterVarsity Press, 1981), p. 46.
12. Bob Larson, *Rock* (Wheaton, IL: Tyndale House, 1982), p. 27.
13. Jerry Solomon, "Between Rock and a Hard Place," *Shofar* magazine (Fall 1983), p. 11.
14. Jerry Solomon, "Between Rock and a Hard Place," *Shofar* magazine (Fall 1983), p. 11.
15. *Rolling Stone* magazine (December 8, 1983), p. 58.
16. *U.S. News and World Report* (October 31, 1977).
17. *Time* magazine (April 28, 1967), p. 54.
18. *Circus* magazine (October 17, 1978), p. 34.
19. *Circus* (July 7, 1977), p. 40.
20. *Hard Rock* magazine (June 1978).
21. Jonathon Green, *The Book of Rock Quotes* (New York: Omnibus Press, 1982), p. 81.
22. *Circus* magazine (April 27, 1980).
23. *Circus* magazine (June 17, 1976).
24. *Circus* magazine (June 23, 1977).
25. Bob Larson, *Rock* (Wheaton, IL: Tyndale House, 1982), p. 160.
26. *Ibid.*, pp. 141, 142.
27. Stephan Demorest, *Hit Parader* magazine (July 1978), p. 60.
28. *Circus* magazine (June 23, 1977).
29. Craig Harrington Rock Seminar as cited in *Rolling Stone* interview).
30. *Circus* magazine (June 23, 1977), p. 31.
31. *Hard Rock* magazine (June 1978), p. 62.
32. *Circus* magazine (March 31, 1981), p. 43.
33. *Ibid.*
34. *Circus* magazine (January 30, 1980), p. 34.
35. *Hit Parader* magazine (September 1983).
36. *Circus* magazine (February 28, 1977).
37. *Us* magazine (August 5, 1980), p. 64.

38. *Us* magazine (September 30, 1980).
39. *Circus* magazine (February 10, 1976), pp. 35, 36.
40. *Ibid.*
41. *Us* magazine (January 6, 1981).
42. *Us* magazine (October 26, 1980), p. 38.
43. Dave Marsh and Kevin Stein, *The Book of Rock Lists* (New York: Dell Publishing Co., Inc., 1981), p. 82.
44. *Rolling Stone* magazine (February 19, 1981), pp. 54, 55.
45. *Ibid.*, p. 55.
46. *Us* magazine (December 8, 1981), p. 51.
47. David Gleman, with others, *Newsweek* magazine (September 1, 1980), pp. 49–53.
48. Wilson Bryan Key, *The Clam Plate Orgy* (New Jersey: Prentice-Hall, Inc., 1976), pp. 92, 93.
49. Hal Lindsey, with C. C. Carlson, *The Late Great Planet Earth* (New York: Bantam Books, 1970), p. 6.
50. *Us* magazine (August 4, 1981), p. 68.
51. *Circus* magazine (January 20, 1976).
52. Bob Larson, *Rock* (Wheaton, IL: Tyndale House, 1983), p. 33.
53. *Ibid.* (1982), p. 41.
54. *Circus* magazine (March 17, 1977), p. 34.
55. *Ibid.*, p. 31.
56. *People* magazine (June 23, 1980).
57. Barry, Robin and Maurice Gibb, as told to David Leaf, *Bee Gees, the Authorized Biography* (New York: Dell, 1979), pp. 75–81.
58. *Rolling Stone* magazine (May 17, 1979).
59. *USA Today* (December 19, 1983), p. 3A.
60. *Circus* magazine (June 1, 1976).
61. *Ibid.*
62. *Hit Parader* magazine, "AC/DC—Past, Present and Future" (August 1982), p. 58.
63. *Circus* (December 1971), p. 46.
64. *Rolling Stone* magazine (October 28, 1971), p. 41.
65. *Hit Parader* magazine (July 1975), p. 64, as recorded in Bob Larson, *Rock* (Wheaton, IL: Tyndale House, 1983), p. 135.
66. Ray Bonds, editor, *The Harmony Encyclopedia of Rock,* 3rd ed. (New York: Crown Publishers, Inc., 1982), p. 235.
67. *Circus* magazine (December 22, 1977), p. 12.
68. *Us* magazine (September 29, 1981), p. 45.
69. *Circus* magazine (September 30, 1982), p. 61.
70. *Circus* magazine (July 31, 1983), p. 39.
71. *Billboard* magazine (December 10, 1977), p. 38.
72. *Circus* magazine (November 1974), p. 64.
73. Jerry Solomon, "Between Rock and a Hard Place," *Shofar* magazine (Fall 1983), p. 11.
74. Bob Larson, *Rock* (Wheaton, IL: Tyndale House, 1983), p. 33.
75. *Circus* magazine (April 14, 1977).
76. *Life* magazine (October 3, 1969).
77. Chris Ramsey, "Rx for the 80's," *Cornerstone* magazine (Volume 10: Issue 54), p. 6.
78. *Ibid.*, p. 7.

79. *Ibid.*
80. *Ibid.*
81. Marsha Manatt, Ph.D., *Parents, Peers and Pot* (Rockville, MD: US Department of Health), p. 33.
82. *Ibid.*, p. 24.
83. *Ibid.*, p. 24.
84. *Circus* magazine (December 30, 1976), p. 30.
85. Several of the songs listed in the drug reference section were compiled by David Pichaske, *A Generation In Motion* (New York: Schirmer Books, 1979), p. 117.
86. Jerry Solomon, "Between Rock and a Hard Place," *Shofar* magazine (Fall 1983), p. 10.

References—Chapter 7
1. Miles White, "Our Heroes Can Make Us Heroic, Too," *USA Today* (November 14, 1983), p. 5D.
2. *USA Today* (November 31, 1983), p. 6D.
3. *People* magazine (October 1982).
4. "The Facts. . . ," *Cornerstone* magazine (Volume 9: Issue 51), p. 20.
5. Chris Ramsey and Diana Pavlac, "Teenage Wasteland: The Suicide Fantasy," *Cornerstone* magazine (Volume 11: Issue 62), p. 5.
6. *Newsweek* magazine (November 6, 1967), p. 101.
7. Gary Herman, *Rock 'n' Roll Babylon* (Great Britain: Plexus Publishing Ltd., 1982).
8. Dave Marsh and Kevin Stein, *The Book of Rock Lists* (New York: Dell Publishing Co., Inc., 1981), p. 5.
9. *Circus* magazine (March 17, 1977).
10. "Rockers recall the '60s," *USA Today* (December 15, 1983), p. 2D.
11. *People* magazine (September 7, 1981), p. 60.
12. *Us* magazine (August 3, 1982).
13. *Rolling Stone* magazine (October 20, 1977).
14. "In the Spotlight," *Seventeen* magazine (October 1983), p. 170.
15. *Time* magazine (December 17, 1979), p. 94.
16. Dave Marsh and Kevin Stein, *The Book of Rock Lists* (New York: Dell Publishing Co., Inc., 1981), p. 48.
17. Jim Miller, "Britain Rocks America—Again," *Newsweek* magazine (January 23, 1984), p. 56.
18. *Ibid.*, p. 53.
19. *Circus* magazine (October 1982).
20. *People* magazine (September 1, 1981), p. 60
21. *Minneapolis Star and Tribune* (May 24, 1982), p. 2A.
22. *Hit Parader* magazine (March 1981), p. 27.
23. *Hit Parader* magazine (February 1982), p. 25.
24. *Circus* magazine (July 31, 1981), p. 45.
25. *Circus* magazine (October 10, 1978), p. 26.
26. *Circus* magazine (July 31, 1981), p. 33.
27. *Circus* magazine (March 31, 1981), p. 47.
28. *Rolling Stone* (April 26, 1984), p. 19.
29. *Us* magazine (November 25, 1980), p. 64.
30. *Circus* magazine (March 17, 1977).

246

31. *Circus* magazine (August 24, 1976), pp. 24–27.
32. Chris Ramsey, "Rx for the 80's," *Cornerstone* magazine (Volume 10: Issue 54), p. 7.
33. Lisa Robinson, *Creem* magazine (October 1975).
34. Hunter Davis, *The Beatles* (New York: McGraw Hill, 1968).
35. *Rolling Stone* (January 7, 1971).
36. Bob Larson, *Babylon Reborn* (Carol Stream, IL: Creation House, 1977), p. 126.
37. *People* magazine (December 13, 1975).
38. "People," *USA Today* (January 16, 1984), p. 2D.
39. Ekland Britt, *True Britt*, excerpts as taken from *Us* magazine (May 26, 1981), pp. 61–71.
40. Gary Herman, *Rock 'n' Roll Babylon* (Great Britain: Plexus Publishing Ltd., 1982), p. 44.
41. *Esquire* magazine (June 1972), p. 186.
42. Bob Larson, *Babylon Reborn* (Carol Stream, IL: Creation House, 1977), p. 121.
43. *Circus* magazine (January 5, 1978), p. 42.
44. *Circus* magazine (January 20, 1976), p. 36.
45. *Rolling Stone* magazine (February 2, 1984), p. 28.
46. *Hit Parader* magazine (March 1982), p. 28.
47. *Circus* magazine (March 4, 1980), p. 40.
48. *Circus* magazine (September 30, 1981), p. 18.
49. Bob Larson, *Babylon Reborn* (Carol Stream, IL: Creation House, 1977), p. 71.
50. Jonathon Green, *The Book of Rock Quotes* (New York: Omnibus Press, 1982), p. 80.
51. *Rolling Stone* magazine (May 12, 1983), p. 25.
52. *Rolling Stone* magazine (April 21, 1977).
53. *Rolling Stone* magazine (February 19, 1981), p. 54.
54. *Rolling Stone* magazine (May 31, 1982), p. 72.
55. *Circus* magazine (May 27, 1980), pp. 31–33.
56. Jonathon Green, *The Book of Rock Quotes* (New York: Omnibus Press, 1982), p. 80.
57. *Circus* magazine (October 10, 1978), p. 35.
58. *Ibid.*
59. *Circus* magazine (February 20, 1976), p. 24.
60. Ray Bonds, editor, *The Harmony Encyclopedia of Rock,* 3rd ed. (New York: Crown Publishers, Inc., 1982), p. 234.
61. *Circus* magazine (October 31, 1982), p. 22.
62. Bob Larson, *Rock* (Wheaton, IL: Tyndale House, 1983), p. 156.
63. *Circus* magazine (February 10, 1976), pp. 35–37.
64. *Us* magazine (January 6, 1981).
65. *Rolling Stone* magazine (September 15, 1980), p. 14.
66. *Rolling Stone* magazine (March 4, 1981), p. 33.
67. David A. Noebel, *Rock 'n' Roll: A Prerevolutionary Form of Cultural Subversion* (Manitou Springs, CO: Summit Press, 1980), p. 5.
68. Dave Breese, "The Marks of a Cult" (Wheaton, IL: Christian Destiny), p. 1.
69. *Ibid.*, p. 2.
70. Bruce Pollock, *When Rock Was Young* (New York: Holt, Rinehart & Winston, 1981), p. 142.

71. *Saturday Evening Post* (August 8, 1964).
72. Walter Scott, *Personality Parade* (July 26, 1981), p. 2.
73. John Lennon, *A Spaniard in the Works* (New York: Simon & Schuster, 1965), p. 14.
74. *Circus* magazine (June 17, 1976), pp. 45, 46.
75. *St. Paul Pioneer Press* (March 20, 1983), pp. 3E, 4E.
76. *Rolling Stone* magazine (July 9, 1981), p. 49.
77. *Rolling Stone* magazine (September 3, 1981), p. 18.
78. *Us* magazine (August 5, 1980).
79. *Circus* magazine (June 22, 1978).
80. *Us* magazine (January 5, 1982), pp. 48, 49.
81. *Circus* magazine (January 19, 1978), p. 22.
82. "Black Magic Blackmore," *Circus* magazine (April 30, 1981).
83. *Ibid.*
84. *Cornerstone* magazine (Volume 9: Issue 52), p. 41.
85. *Circus* magazine (March 23, 1976), p. 29.
86. "In the Spotlight," *Seventeen* magazine, (January 1984), pp. 56, 112.
87. Bob Larson, *Rock* (Wheaton, IL: Tyndale House, 1983), p. 41.
88. *Circus* magazine (October 13, 1977), p. 28.
89. *Hit Parader Yearbook* (1981), p. 4.
90. *Hit Parader* magazine (July 1975), p. 64.
91. Tony Sanchez, *Up and Down with the Rolling Stones* (New York: William Morrow & Co., Inc., 1979), pp. 147, 148.
92. *Circus* magazine (March 17, 1977), p. 58.
93. David Noebel, *The Legacy of John Lennon* (Nashville, TN: Thomas Nelson Publishers, 1982), p. 102.
94. *Hard Rock* magazine (June 1978), pp. 23, 24, 61, 62.
95. Jonathon Green, *The Book of Rock Quotes* (New York: Omnibus Press, 1982, p. 61, taken from an article in *Newsweek,* March 21, 1966).
96. "A Doctor Speaks Out," *Cornerstone* magazine (Volume 10: Issue 54), p. 9.
97. "Close-Up: Teenage Alcoholics, *USA Today* (November 3, 1983), p. 3D.
98. Chris Ramsey, "Rx for the 80's," *Cornerstone* magazine (Volume 10: Issue 54), p. 7.
99. Gary Herman, *Rock 'n' Roll Babylon* (Great Britain: Plexus Publishing Ltd., 1982), p. 52.
100. *People* magazine (August 29, 1983), p. 22.
101. Ray Allen, *Rolling Stone Interviews* (Volume 1), p. 410, as cited in *They're Out to Steal Your Children,* Ray Allen (Granbury, TX: American Research Press, 1979).
102. Christopher Connelly and Parke Puterbaugh, "Dennis Wilson's Last Wave," *Rolling Stone* magazine (February 2, 1984), p. 36.
103. "The Close of an Endless Summer," *People* magazine (January 16, 1984), p. 27.
104. *Ibid.*
105. "Pink Floyd Off the Wall," *Hit Parader* magazine (September 1983), p. 61.
106. *Rolling Stone* magazine (July 18, 1974), p. 54.
107. "People," *USA Today* (January 18, 1984), p. 2D.
108. *Time* magazine (September 10, 1979).
109. Jonathon Green, *The Book of Rock Quotes* (New York: Omnibus Press, 1982), p. 64.
110. *Rolling Stone* magazine (February 2, 1984), p. 14.

248

111. *Rolling Stone* magazine (August 20, 1981), p. 10.
112. *Rolling Stone* magazine (December 8, 1983), p. 56.
113. Bob Larson, *Babylon Reborn* (Carol Stream, IL: Creation House, 1977), p. 63.
114. *Ibid.*, p. 70.
115. Jonathon Green, *The Book of Rock Quotes* (New York: Omnibus Press, 1982).
116. *Rolling Stone* magazine (January 12, 1978), p. 13.
117. Jonathon Green, *The Book of Rock Quotes* (New York: Omnibus Press, 1982), pp. 62, 65.
118. Ray Bonds, editor, *The Harmony Encyclopedia of Rock,* 3rd ed. (New York: Crown Publishers, Inc.), p. 96.
119. *Time* magazine (August 9, 1969), p. 76.
120. *Us* magazine (June 10, 1980).
121. *People* magazine (August 28, 1978), p. 72.
122. *Us* magazine (April 14, 1981), p. 71.
123. *People* magazine (March 16, 1981), p. 91.
124. Bob Gilbert and Gary Theroux, *The Top Ten* (New York: Simon & Schuster, 1982), p. 166.
125. Bob Larson, *Rock* (Wheaton, IL: Tyndale House, 1983), p. 142.
126. *Circus* magazine (August 3, 1978), pp. 36–38.
127. "Word of Faith," Kenneth Hagin Ministeries, pp. 6, 7.
128. Los Angeles *Herald Examiner* (March 28, 1981), Section A, p. 12.
129. Bob Larson, "Perspectives," *Contemporary Christian Music* magazine (April 1983), p. 51.

References—Chapter 8
1. John Camp, "Ministers Try to Shake 'Devil Rock'," *St. Paul Pioneer Press* (November 27, 1979).
2. "Youthquake," *Look* magazine (1967), p. 67.
3. "Grandmaster Flash and the Furious Five," *New Sounds* magazine (April 1984), p. 14.
4. *Ibid.*
5. "Sex Pistols, Anarchy in the 70's," *New Sounds* magazine (April 1984), p. 26.
6. *Ibid.*
7. "Interview: BowWowWow," *Cornerstone* magazine (Volume 11: Issue 64), p. 41.
8. "Peter Schilling: Nobody's Perfect," *New Sounds* magazine (April 1984), p. 10.
9. "Michael Jackson, Miracle Man," *New Sounds* magazine (April 1984), p. 28.
10. "Michael Jackson, Superstar," *USA Today* (December 2, 1983), p. 2A.
11. "Michael Jackson, Miracle Man," *New Sounds* magazine (April 1984), p. 28.
12. "The Peter Pan of Pop," *Newsweek* magazine (January 10, 1983), p. 53.
13. *Ibid.*, p. 54.
14. *Ibid.*
15. "Picks and Pans," *People* magazine ((January 16, 1984), p. 16.
16. "In the Spotlight," *Seventeen* magazine (October 1983), p. 90.
17. *Rock* magazine (August 1983), p. 60.
18. *Us* magazine (April 14, 1981), p. 72.
19. *Newsweek* magazine (April 2, 1979).
20. Jonathon Green, *The Book of Rock Quotes* (New York: Omnibus Press, 1982), p. 44.

21. *Circus* magazine (August 31, 1981), p. 38.
22. "Future Pop Boy George," *New Sounds* magazine (April 1984), p. 19.
23. *Bay Area* magazine (February 1, 1977).
24. *Rolling Stone* magazine (December 2, 1970), p. 35.
25. "In the Spotlight," *Seventeen* magazine (January 1984), p. 112.
26. *USA Today* (January 27, 1984), p. 2D.
27. James Taylor, *Today's Music*.
28. *St. Paul Dispatch* (October 28, 1982), p. 12B.
29. *Circus* magazine (February 1972), p. 61.
30. *Circus* magazine (April 1974), p. 41.
31. "Not the Sound of Silence," *Newsweek* magazine (November 14, 1983), p. 102.
32. *Super Rock* magazine (June 1978).
33. Edwin Miller, "Brian Setzer, of the Stray Cats," *Seventeen* magazine (April 1973), pp. 167, 193.
34. Jonathon Green, *The Book of Rock Quotes* (New York: Omnibus Press, 1982), p. 19.
35. "Van Halen Cashes in on Rock Rebel Image," *USA Today* (January 16, 1984), p. 4D.
36. *Time* magazine (July 10, 1968), p. 57.
37. *Newsweek* magazine (November 6, 1967), p. 101.
38. *Rock* magazine (August 1983), p. 60
39. *Circus* magazine (April 14, 1977).
40. *Circus* magazine (February 10, 1976).
41. *Billboard* magazine (December 11, 1976), p. 39.
42. *Us* magazine (February 3, 1981).
43. *People* magazine (May 21, 1979), p. 53.
44. *Circus* magazine (October 1978), p. 22.
45. Jonathon Green, *The Book of Rock Quotes* (New York: Omnibus Press, 1982), p. 14.
46. *Rolling Stone* magazine (October 18, 1979), p. 37.
47. Tony Scaduto, *Mick Jagger: Everybody's Lucifer* (New York: D. McKay & Co., 1974).
48. *Newsweek* magazine (April 2, 1979), p. 64.
49. *Circus* magazine (April 1974), p. 41.
50. Bob Larson, *Babylon Reborn* (Carol Stream, IL: Creation House, 1977), p. 72.
51. *People* magazine (July 13, 1981), p. 104.
52. *Circus* magazine (January 31, 1976), p. 39.
53. *Creem* magazine (Autust 1977).
54. "Sexuality Slips Into Neutral Gear," *USA Today* (February 3, 1984), p. 1D.
55. Arnold Shaw, *Dictionary of American Pop/Rock* (New York: Macmillan, 1982), p. 308.
56. "On the Beat," *New Sounds* magazine (April 1984), p. 22.
57. *Truth About Rock* Report (December 1982), p. 2.
58. Albert Goldman, *Elvis* (New York: Avon Books, 1981), pp. 438, 439.
59. *Ibid.,* p. 436.
60. *Newsweek* magazine (December 20, 1976).
61. *Circus* magazine (January 19, 1978), p. 22.
62. "Rock Music! What Is Spiritual Adultery?" *Onward Christian Courier* (November 1983), p. 14.
63. *Circus* magazine (December 17, 1978), p. 23.
64. *Rolling Stone* magazine (April 7, 1977), p. 49.

65. *Circus* magazine (August 3, 1978), p. 23.
66. Bob Larson, *Rock* (Wheaton, IL: Tyndale House, 1982), p. 35.
67. *Ibid.*
68. *Rolling Stone* magazine (June 25, 1981), p. 37.
69. Bob Larson *Rock* (Wheaton, IL: Tyndale House, 1982), p. 34.
70. "Strange Days, Iron Maiden," *Hit Parader* magazine (August 1982), p. 14.
71. "Rock Music! What Is Spiritual Adultery?" *Onward Christian Courier* (November 1983), p. 14.
72. *Newsweek* magazine (January 4, 1971).
73. *Time* magazine (December 16, 1974), p. 39.
74. Bob Larson, *Rock and the Church* (Carol Stream, IL: Creation House, 1971), p. 66.
75. *Circus* magazine (April 14, 1971).
76. "Heavy Metal Happenings," *Hit Parader* magazine (September 1983), p. 12.
77. "Cult Update," *Cornerstone* magazine (Volume 9: Issue 53), p. 44.
78. *Bread For Children* (January/February 1984), p. 1.
79. *Circus* magazine (April 17, 1979), p. 16.
80. *Rolling Stone* magazine (November 22, 1973), p. 32.
81. Albert Goldman, *Freakshow* (New York: Atheneum, 1971), pp. 164, 165.

References—Chapter 9

The following sources were used to compile the list of rock and roll obituaries:

Rolling Stone magazine
The Legacy of John Lennon by David A. Noebel
Rock 'n' Roll Babylon by Gary Herman
Los Angeles Times
A Generation In Motion by David Pichaske
Who's Who In Rock Music, edited by William York
Freak Show by Albert Goldman
Rock 'n' Roll Rip-Off! by Emmett Barnard
The Book of Rock Quotes, by Jonathon Green
Encyclopedia of Rock, edited by Phil Hardy and Dave Lang
The Book of Rock Lists by Dave Marsh and Kevin Stein
Billboard magazine
The Jackson County Livewire
People magazine
Record magazine
Rock by Bob Larson
Loving John by May Pang
Word of Faith by the Kenneth Hagin Ministries
Rock Record by Terry Hounsome and Tim Chambre
Top Pop Artists & Singles 1955–1978 by Joel Whitburn
The Top Ten by Bob Gilbert and Gary Theroux
Elvis by Albert Goldman
New Sounds magazine
USA Today
The Beach Boys by Byron Preiss
Rock magazine

References—Chapter 10
1. Charley Crespo, "Pick Hit," *Hit Parader* (September 1983), p. 28.
2. Aurora Mackey, "The Frightening Facts About Teen Suicide," *Teen* (October 1983), p. 10.
3. *Rolling Stone* magazine (June 28, 1979).
4. *Ibid.*
5. *Sound and Music Output* (December 1982).
6. Brock Helander, *The Rock Who's Who* (New York: Schirmer Books, 1982), p. 312.
7. *Circus* magazine (August 24, 1976), p. 27.
8. *Rock* magazine (February 1984).
9. *Ibid.*
10. *St. Paul Pioneer Press* (June 4, 1983), p. 8B.
11. *Rock* magazine (February 1984), p. 59.
12. *Hit Parader* magazine (November 1982), p. 58.
13. Bill McAllister, St. Cloud *Daily Times* (January 27, 1983).
14. *Circus* magazine (March 31, 1981), p. 44.
15. *Ibid.*, p. 43.
16. *Circus* magazine (June 23, 1977), p. 31.
17. *Rolling Stone* magazine (February 19, 1981), p. 54.
18. *Rock* magazine (February 1984), p. 39.
19. *Ibid.*, p. 36.
20. Brock Helander, *The Rock Who's Who* (New York: Schirmer Books, 1982), p. 103.
21. Jon Trott, "Pornography," *Cornerstone* magazine (Volume 11: Issue 62), p. 20.
22. *Ibid.*
23. *People* magazine (October 3, 1977), p. 108.
24. *Ibid.*
25. "Vinyl Exam," *Rock* magazine (February 1984), p. 58.
26. *Ibid.*
27. United Press International (February 1982).
28. *Newsweek* magazine (December 19, 1983), p. 92.
29. *People* magazine (September 7, 1981), p. 60.
30. Michael Bane, *Who's Who in Rock* (New York: Facts on File, Inc., 1981), p. 121.
31. *Rolling Stone* magazine (January 4, 1973), p. 16.
32. Dave Marsh and Kevin Stein, *The Book of Rock Lists* (New York: Dell Publishing Co., Inc., 1981), p. 81.
33. *Us* magazine (February 3, 1981), p. 46.
34. Michael Bane, *Who's Who in Rock* (New York: Facts on File, Inc., 1981), p. 46.

References—Chapter 11
1. Michael Peck, "Youth Suicide," *Death Education*, 1982, p. 32, as taken from *Cornerstone* magazine (Volume 11: Issue 62), p. 4.
2. *Ibid.*
3. *Circus* magazine (Volume 11: Issue 62), p. 6.
4. U. Bronfenbenner, "Nobody Home: The Erosion of the American Family," *Psychology Today* (October 1977), p. 41.
5. *Ibid.*

252

6. *Newsweek* magazine (August 15, 1983), p. 72.
7. *Ibid.*, p. 74.
8. Jerry Solomon, "Between Rock and a Hard Place," *Shofar* magazine (Fall 1983), p. 11.
9. *Cornerstone* magazine (Volume 11: Issue 62), p. 6.
10. Emmett Barnard, *Rock 'n' Roll Rip-Off!* (New York: Carlton Press, 1982), p. 37.
11. *Rock Yearbook, 1982* (New York: Saint Martins Press, 1982), p. 189, as quoted by Michael Haynes, *The god of Rock* (Lindale, TX: Priority Ministries, 1982), p. 198.
12. *Cornerstone* magazine (Volume 11: Issue 62), p. 6.
13. William V. Rauscher, *The Case Against Suicide*, as quoted by *Cornerstone* magazine (Volume 11: Issue 62), p. 7.
Special Note: *Cornerstone* magazine's poignant, informative article on teenage suicide was very helpful in the writing of this chapter.

References—Chapter 12
1. Wilson Bryan Key, *Media Sexploitation* (New York: Signet, 1977), p. 7.
2. Art Athens, "Beware Here Come the Mind Manipulators," *Family Health* magazine (December 1978), p. 40.
3. "Secret Voices," *Time* magazine (September 10, 1979), p. 71.
4. R.C. Morse and David Stoller, "The Hidden Message That Breaks Habits," *Science Digest* (September 1982), p. 28.
5. Vance Packard, *The People Shapers* (Boston: Little, Brown & Co., 1977), p. 135.
6. *Ibid.*, p. 136.
7. R.C. Morse and David Stoller, "The Hidden Message That Breaks Habits," *Science Digest* (September 1982), p. 28.
8. Vance Packard, *The People Shapers* (Boston: Little, Brown & Co., 1977), p. 136.
9. *Ibid.*, p. 137.
10. Art Athens, "Beware Here Come the Mind Manipulators," *Family Health* magazine (December 1978), p. 34.
11. Wilson Bryan Key, *Clam Plate Orgy* (New Jersey: Prentice-Hall, Inc., 1980), p. 175.
12. "Secret Voices," *Time* magazine (September 10, 1979), p. 71.
13. *Ibid.*
14. Felicia Lee, "Whispering Messages to the Mind," *USA Today* (November 4, 1983), pp. 1D & 2D.
15. "Secret Voices," *Time* magazine (September 10, 1979), p. 71.
16. *New Times* magazine (May 13, 1977), p. 62.
17. Wilson Bryan Key, *Media Sexploitation* (New York: Signet, 1977), p. 117.
18. Michael Bane, *Who's Who in Rock* (New York: Facts on File, Inc., 1981), p. 23.
19. Wilson Bryan Key, *Media Sexploitation* (New York: Signet, 1977), p. 117.
20. Brock Helander, *The Rock Who's Who* (New York: Schirmer Books, 1982), p. 162.
21. Mike Warnke, *The Satan Seller* (Plainfield, NJ: Bridge Publishing, Inc.).
22. *New Times* magazine (August 7, 1978), p. 19.
23. *Circus* magazine (July 1975).

24. David A. Noebel, *The Legacy of John Lennon* (Nashville, TN: Thomas Nelson Publishers, 1982), p. 103.
25. Ross Pavlac, "Backward Masking, Satanic Plot or Red Herring," *Cornerstone* magazine (Volume 11: Issue 62), p. 40.
26. *Newsweek* magazine (May 17, 1982), p. 61.
27. Wilson Bryan Key, *Clam Plate Orgy* (New Jersey: Prentice-Hall, Inc., 1980), p. 95.
28. Tony Sanchez, *Up and Down With the Rolling Stones* (New York: William Morrow & Company, 1979), p. 150.
29. Vance Packard, *The People Shapers* (Boston: Little, Brown & Co., 1977), p. 137.
30. Wilson Bryan Key, *Clam Plate Orgy* (New Jersey: Prentice-Hall, Inc., 1980).
31. Vance Packard, "The New (and Still Hidden) Persuaders," *Reader's Digest* (February 1981), p. 122.
32. *Ibid.*
33. Wilson Bryan Key, *Media Sexploitation* (New York: Signet, 1977), p. 117.
34. Art Athens, "Beware Here Come the Mind Manipulators," *Family Health* magazine (December 1978), p. 39.
35. R.C. Morse and David Stoller, "The Hidden Message That Breaks Habits," *Science Digest* (September 1982), p. 28.
36. "Return of the Hidden Persuaders," *Psychology Today* magazine (May 1982).
37. Michael Haynes, *The god of Rock* (Lindale, TX: Priority Publications, 1982), p. 64.
38. Ross Pavlac, "Backwards Masking, Satanic Plot or Red Herring," *Cornerstone* magazine (Volume 11: Issue 62), p. 41.
39. *St. Paul Dispatch* (May 24, 1982).
40. *Newsweek* magazine (May 17, 1982), p. 61.
41. *Saturday Review* magazine editorial, as cited in "Sneaky Stimuli and How to Avoid Them," *Christianity Today* (January 31, 1975), p. 9.
42. *Ibid.*, p. 10.

References—Chapter 13

1. John Waddey, "Were Your Kids at This Rock Concert?" *Christian Family* magazine (August 1983), p. 18.
2. *Rolling Stone* magazine (June 26, 1980), p. 38.
3. *Circus* magazine (April 28, 1977).
4. *Newsweek* magazine (November 14, 1983), p. 102.
5. *Ibid.*
6. Lowell Hart, *Satan's Music Exposed* (Huntington Valley, PA: Salem Kirban, Inc., 1980), p. 102.
7. *People* magazine (February 9, 1981), p. 86.
8. *Creem* magazine (September 1981), p. 33.
9. *Future Life* magazine (December 1980), p. 23.
10. Martin Keller, "Tube-Tied," *City Pages* (October 12, 1983), p. 29.
11. *Circus* magazine (June 30, 1981), pp. 21, 22.
12. Lowell Hart, *Satan's Music Exposed* (Huntington Valley, PA: Salem Kirban, Inc., 1980), pp. 101, 102.
13. *Circus* magazine (August 24, 1976).
14. *Hit Parader* magazine (Fall 1983), p. 37.
15. *Rock* magazine (February 1984), p. 29.

254

16. *Minneapolis Tribune* (October 9, 1983), p. 10F.
17. David Pichaske, *A Generation In Motion* (New York: Schirmer Books, 1979), p. 207.
18. *USA Today* (January 13, 1984), p. 1D.
19. *Minneapolis Tribune* (December 18, 1983), p. 1G.
20. *Contemporary Christian Music* magazine (August 1983), pp. 23–25.
21. *Rock* magazine (February 1984).
22. *Rolling Stone* magazine (October 28, 1982), p. 39.
23. *Circus* magazine (January 23, 1979), p. 19.
24. *Circus* magazine (December 11, 1979), p 21.
25. *Circus* magazine (March 17, 1977).
26. *Newsweek* magazine (March 10, 1980), p. 101.
27. *Circus* magazine (May 4, 1980), pp. 30, 31.
28. *Circus* magazine (May 27, 1980), p. 18.
29. *St. Paul Pioneer Press* (March 6, 1983).
30. *Minneapolis Tribune* (February 19, 1981), p. 3A.
31. *Time* magazine (December 17, 1979), p. 89.
32. *Circus* magazine (March 31, 1981), p. 30.
33. *Ibid.*
34. *USA Today* (February 17, 1984), p. 1D.
35. *Hit Parader* magazine (Fall 1983), p. 37.
36. *Circus* magazine (March 31, 1981), p. 30.
37. Bob Larson, *Babylon Reborn* (Carol Stream, IL: Creation House, 1977), p. 112.
38. *Rolling Stone* magazine (March 15, 1984), p. 28.
39. *Ibid.*
40. *Hit Parader* magazine (June 1982), pp. 5, 7, 8.
41. *Hit Parader* magazine (February 1982), p. 41.
42. Michael Bane, *Who's Who in Rock* (New York: Facts on File, Inc., 1981), p. 88.
43. *Rolling Stone* magazine (August 19, 1971).
44. *Circus* magazine (February 28, 1981).
45. *Rock* magazine (February 1984), p. 51.
46. *Us* magazine (January 6, 1981), p. 34.
47. *Hit Parader* magazine (September 1979), p. 31.
48. *Circus* magazine (July 7, 1977), p. 40.
49. *St. Paul Pioneer Press* (March 20, 1983), p. 3E.
50. *Circus* magazine (July 7, 1977).
51. *Us* magazine (December 9, 1980).
52. *Creem* magazine (September 1981), p. 33.
53. *Rolling Stone* magazine (April 14, 1983), p.   55.
54. *Sound* magazine (March 31, 1983).
55. *USA Today* (January 13, 1984), p. 5D.
56. *Rolling Stone* magazine (May 11, 1972), p. 39.
57. *Circus* magazine (October 10, 1978). p. 22.
58. *Hit Parader* magazine (February 1982), p. 59.
59. *Us* magazine (December 8, 1981), p. 51.
60. *Circus* magazine (February 28, 1982), p. 21.
61. *Hit Parader* magazine (February 1982), p. 59.
62. *Us* magazine (February 3, 1981), p. 47.
63. *Pittsburgh Press* (November 2, 1982), p. A-ll.

255

64. *Newsweek* magazine (April 7, 1969), p. 31.
65. Brock Helander, *The Rock Who's Who* (New York: Schirmer Books, 1982), p. 142.
66. Bob Larson, *Rock* (Wheaton, IL: Tyndale House, 1982), p. 156.
67. Jonathon Green, *The Book of Rock Quotes* (New York: Omnibus Press, 1982), p. 83.
68. *Rolling Stone* magazine (July 22, 1971), p. 24.
69. *Rolling Stone* magazine (February 1981).
70. Brock Helander, *The Rock Who's Who* (New York: Schirmer Books, 1982), pp. 576, 577.
71. Michael Bane, *Who's Who in Rock* (New York: Facts on File, Inc., 1981), p. 139.
72. *Time* magazine (September 11, 1978).
73. United Press International (March 5, 1983).
74. *Circus* magazine (March 31, 1981), pp. 58, 59.
75. *Rolling Stone* magazine (March 25, 1976), p. 9.
76. Bob Larson, *Rock* (Wheaton, IL: Tyndale House, 1982), p. 132.
77. *Circus* magazine (January 20, 1976).
78. Bob Larson, *Rock and the Church* (Carol Stream, IL: Creation House, 1971), p. 66.
79. *The Sweet Potato* (September 1980), pp. 23, 24, 43, 44.
80. Bob Larson, *Rock* (Wheaton, IL: Tyndale House, 1982), p. 41.
81. *Circus* magazine (August 16, 1976), p. 30.
82. Brock Helander, *The Rock Who's Who* (New York: Schirmer Books, 1982), p. 378.
83. *Newsweek* magazine (March 27, 1972), p. 77.
84. *Circus* magazine (April 1972), p. 38.
85. *USA Today* (Feburary 13, 1984), p. 1D.
86. *Rolling Stone* magazine (February 3, 1972), p. 30.
87. *Us* magazine (August 5, 1980).
88. *Circus* magazine (September 28, 1976), p. 37.
89. *Us* magazine (February 3, 1981).
90. *USA Today* (January 16, 1984), p. 4D.
91. *Rolling Stone* magazine (November 12, 1981), p. 56.
92. *War on Drugs* (March/April 1981), p. 10.
93. *Hard Rock* magazine (June 1978), p. 59.
94. Michael Haynes, *The god of Rock* (Lindale, TX: Priority Ministries Publications, 1982), pp. 130, 131.
95. *People* magazine (January 16, 1984), p. 86.
96. *Ibid.*
97. *Circus* magazine (May 4, 1978).
98. *Us* magazine (June 24, 1980).
99. *Circus* magazine (May 11, 1978).
100. Michael Haynes, *The god of Rock* (Lindale, TX: Priority Ministries, 1982), p. 16–19.

References—Chapter 14
1. Steve Lawhead, *Rock Revisited* (Downers Grove, IL: InterVarsity Press, 1981), pp. 59, 60.
2. Mark Bego, excerpted from the book *Michael!* (New York: Pinnacle Books, 1984), as distributed by the *Los Angeles Times* Syndicate, and published in

 Minneapolis Tribune (March 4, 1984), p. 1G.
 3. *Ibid.*
 4. *Ibid.*
 5. Phillip Schewe, "Sensory Thresholds," *Physics Today* (January 1984), p. S-38.
 6. *Hit Parader* magazine (February 1982), p. 41.
 7. *Circus* magazine (April 10, 1979), p. 27.
 8. *Hit Parader* magazine (February 1982), p. 41.
 9. George Forell, *Corporation Ethics: The Quest for Moral Authority* (Philadelphia, PA: Fortress Press, 1980), pp. 62–63.
 10. Wilson Bryan Key, *Media Sexploitation* (New Jersey: Prentice-Hall, 1976), p. 190.

References—Chapter 15
 1. *Circus* magazine (September 13, 1976).
 2. *Ibid.*
 3. *Ibid.*
 4. *Ibid.*
 5. *Ibid.*
 6. Kenneth Boa, *Seeds of Change* (Westchester, IL: Crossways Books), as quoted in *Contemporary Christian Music* magazine (April 1983), p. 52.
 7. *Cornerstone* magazine (Volume 9: Issue 53), p. 39.
 8. *Ibid.* p. 41.
 9. "Resurrection Band: Uptempo 1980's Heavy Metal, New Wave and Power Pop," *Christian Contemporary Music* magazine (February 1982), p. 28.
 10. *Truth About Rock* Report (June 1983), p. 1.
 11. "Word of Faith," Kenneth Hagin Ministries, pp. 6, 7.
 12. Foster Braun, "Dallas Holm & Praise," *Windstorm* magazine (July/August 1983), p. 28.
 13. "Steve Taylor: New Wave, Satire & Sparrow," *Cornerstone* magazine (Volume 12: Issue 66), p. 41.
 14. Jim Krupa, "Principles for Evaluating Christian Contemporary 'Rock' Music" (Open Door Fellowship Church), p. 5.
 15. *Cornerstone* magazine (Volume 12: Issue 65), p. 38.
 16. Foster Braun, "The Inside Story: Phil Keaggy The Master's Musician," *Windstorm* magazine (July/August 1983), p. 46.
 17. Chris Ramsey, "Paul Clark," *Cornerstone* magazine (Volume 11: Issue 63), p. 41.
 18. *Cornerstone* magazine (Volume 11: Issue 64), p. 43.

References—Chapter 16
 1. Wilson Bryan Key, *Clam Plate Orgy* (New Jersey: Prentice-Hall, Inc., 1980), p. 118.
 2. *The Lookout* magazine (June 19, 1983), p. 14.
 3. "The Struggle for Our Children," *New Covenant* magazine (September 1982), p. 7.
 4. Paul Lewis, "Let's Sharpen Your Fathering Focus," *Dads Only* (June 1983).
 5. *Ibid.*
 6. Bob Larson, *Rock* (Wheaton, IL: Tyndale House, 1982), p. 33, and originally in: *Rolling Stone* magazine (April 7, 1977), p. 23.
 7. *Billboard* magazine (October 11, 1980), p. 3.
 8. *Us* magazine (March 31, 1981), p. 12.

9. *Billboard* magazine (October 11, 1980), p. 32.
10. Nick Tosches, *Country—The Biggest Music in America* (New York: Stein & Day, 1977), p. 117.
11. *Ibid.*, p. 118.
12. *Billboard* magazine (October 11, 1980), p. 65.
13. Cher Merrill, "Man In Black: The Inner Holocaust."
14. Bob Larson, *Rock* (Wheaton, IL: Tyndale House, 1982), p. 83.
15. John Reggero, "Breaking Away," *Us* magazine (May 23, 1983), p. 23.
16. Steve Lawhead, *Rock Reconsidered* (Downers Grove, IL: InterVarsity Press, 1981), p. 32.
17. *Billboard* magazine (October 11, 1980), p. 32.
18. *People* magazine (September 3, 1979), p. 82.
19. Jerry Solomon, "Between Rock and a Hard Place," *Shofar* magazine (Fall 1983), p. 12.
20. *Writer's Digest* magazine (March 1984), p. 58.
21. *Ibid.*
22. Wilson Bryan Key, *Media Sexploitation* (New Jersey: Prentice-Hall, Inc., 1976), p. 207.
23. *Ibid.*, p. 207.
24. Marsha Manatt, *Parents, Peers and Pot* (U.S. Dept. Health, Education & Welfare), p. 27.
25. L. Johnston, "Children in Test Buy Drug Trappings Freely at Head Shops," *New York Times* (March 30, 1978).
26. Marsha Manatt, *Parent's Peers and Pot* (U.S. Dept. Health, Education & Welfare), p. 27.
27. Irene Primeau, "The Struggle for Our Children," *New Covenant* magazine (September 1982), p. 7.
28. Jerry Solomon, "Between Rock and a Hard Place," *Shofar* magazine (Fall 1983), p. 8.
29. Dr. Benjamin Spock, *Raising Children in a Difficult Time* (New York, NY: W. W. Norton, 1974).
30. Dr. James Dobson, *Dare to Discipline* (Wheaton IL: Tyndale House Publishers, 1980), p. 56.
31. Franky Schaeffer, *A Time for Anger* (Crossways Books), as cited in *Cornerstone* magazine (Volume 11: Issue 63), p. 29.

Appendix 1: May the Source Be with You

Magazines

There are a number of Christian magazines every bit as fun to read, and full of information on the latest music news, as *Rolling Stone* or *Circus*. These magazines give facts about Christian music artists and their styles of music, their latest releases and their concert dates. There are interviews, record reviews, and articles on issues of interest to young adults.

1. *Contemporary Christian* (formerly *Contemporary Christian Music*), a monthly magazine, covers issues vital to contemporary Christians, reviews music and arts from a Christian perspective, and discusses current issues to help readers better understand their faith and how it relates to the world around them. Address: CCM Publications Inc., Box 6300, Laguna Hills, CA 92653.

2. *Cornerstone*, a bimonthly magazine published by Jesus People, USA, a nonprofit community, presents a Christian worldview on a variety of issues of interest to young adults and teens, including music. Of special interest are reviews of records and interviews with Christian artists in both secular and Christian contemporary music. Address: Cornerstone, Jesus People USA, 4707 North Malden, Chicago, IL 60640.

3. *Windstorm,* a comprehensive monthly magazine, studies the world of Christian music and features articles dealing with issues and answers confronting today's Christian. Address: Windstorm, 15160 West 8 Mile Road, Suite 309, Oak Park, MI 48237.

4. *New Christian Music* magazine, published in England, but covering the contemporary Christian music scene both here and in Europe, provides record reviews, interviews with the stars, and more. Address: New Christian Music Magazine, 7 Hounslow Avenue, Hounslow, Middlesex, England.

Secular Books on Rock Music

The Harmony Illustrated Encyclopedia of Rock, Ray Bonds, editor (New York, Crown Publishers, Inc.).

Dictionary of American Pop/Rock, Arnold Shaw (New York: Macmillan).

Who's Who in Rock, Michael Bane (New York: Facts on File).

The Rock Who's Who, Brock Helander (New York: Schirmer Books).

Elvis, Albert Goldman (New York: Avon Books).

The Beatles, Davis Hunter (New York: McGraw Hill).

Up and Down with the Rolling Stones, Tony Sanchez (New York: William Morrow & Co.).

Loving John, May Pang and Henry Edwards (New York: Warner Books).

The Beach Boys, Byron Preiss (New York: St. Martin's Press).

The Love You Make: An Insider's Story of the Beatles, Peter Brown and Steven Gaines.

Michael!, Mark Bego (New York: Pinnacle Books).

Books on Christian Contemporary Music

Why Should the Devil Have All the Good Music?, Paul Baker (CCM Publications, P.O. Box 6300, Laguna Hills, CA 92653). Also available is a three-hour film documentary on "Jesus Music" and its history.

Christian Books on Rock Music

The Legacy of John Lennon, David A. Noebel (Nashville, TN: Thomas Nelson).

Rock, Bob Larson (Wheaton, IL: Tyndale House).

Babylon Reborn, Bob Larson (Carol Stream, IL: Creation House).

Rock 'n' Roll: A Prerevolutionary Form of Cultural Subversion, David A. Noebel (Manitou Springs, CO: Summit Press).

Rock and the Church, Bob Larson (Carol Stream, IL: Creation House).

The god of Rock, Michael Haynes (Lindale, TX: Priority Publications).

Rock Revisited, Steve Lawhead (Downers Grove, IL: InterVarsity Press).

Peters Brothers Hit Rock's Bottom (St. Paul, MN: Truth About Rock Ministries).

Books on the Media

Media Sexploitation, Wilson Bryan Key (New York: Signet).

The People Shapers, Vance Packard (Boston: Little, Brown & Co.).

Clam Plate Orgy, Wilson Bryan Key (New Jersey: Prentice-Hall).

Books on Drugs and Cults

Parents, Peers and Pot, Marsha Manatt (Washington, DC: US Dept. of HEW).

Kingdom of the Cults, Walter Martin (Minneapolis, MN: Bethany House).
Larson's Book of Cults, Bob Larson (Wheaton, IL: Tyndale House).

Reference Materials from Truth About Rock Ministries

Tapes

Rock Seminar Tape: A cassette of the original seminar that made national headlines. This revealing tape details 90 minutes of facts and figures on rock music's threat to young people.

Glossary of Rock Groups: A 60-minute cassette with excerpts from America's top 40, with running commentary.

Backward Masking: Hear messages deliberately placed on rock songs backward or through other subliminal techniques. Includes Queen, Led Zeppelin, Cheap Trick, ELO, Styx and more.

Documentation

Documentation I—What the Devil's Wrong With Rock Music?: Quotes, interviews, song lyrics and facts about rock stars presented in no-nonsense form.

Documentation II—Rock Music Research: Updated facts, figures and information on rock stars' lifestyles, intentions, lyrics and album covers.

Backward Masking: A look at the controversial subject of subliminals, with documentation of subliminal messages in rock music as well as advertising. Also includes more information about lyrics and lifestyles, and quotes of today's rock groups.

The Peters Brothers Hit Rock's Bottom: Documentation in book form with all the latest information on the groups, including Boy George, Billy Joel, David Bowie, Hall & Oates, BowWowWow, and more.

Other Items

Truth About Rock Report!: Monthly updates on the ministry, as well as in-depth reporting on the activities of rock groups, the latest in Christian contemporary music news, helpful information and dates of upcoming seminars around the country.

Slides of the Rock Music Seminar: Duplicates of the visuals used by the Peters brothers, including album covers, lyrics, title slides, and Scripture verses. Literally hundreds of hours of production time and thousands of dollars were invested in this material so you can present your own "rock talk."

Why Knock Rock Video: A one-hour, made-for-TV video featuring the Peters brothers in an actual seminar setting. Available on ½- or ¾-inch tape for sale or rent.

Truth About Rock Seminars: If you are interested in having the Peters brothers in a rock music informational seminar to minister to both teens and adults in your area, or a cooperative city-wide rally with several other congregations, write us. Information about the seminars, as well as all Truth About Rock materials, are available by writing: **Truth About Rock, P.O. Box 9222, St. Paul, MN 55109.**

Parent's Action Groups for Drug Abuse

Parents working with other parents can help fight drug and alcohol abuse and its promotion through head shops in record stores and similar establishments. For more information on successful campaigns, write: National Federation of Parents for Drug-Free Youth (NFP), P.O. Box 722, Silver Spring, MD 20901. Enclose $10 and you will receive a Parents' Group Starter Kit, including parent/youth brochures, a list of parents' groups in your area, and a subscription to NFP's newletter.

Teen Phone Line for Help

Dial-A-Teen, 624 Indiana Avenue, N.W., Washington, DC 20004. If you need help—any kind of help—or just want someone to lend an ear, dial **(202) 738-TEEN.**

Radio Programs

If we were to list all the radio programs throughout the U.S. and Canada that play Christian contemporary music, we would probably fill another book. There are so many and each has a distinctive style or format, and variety of music.

One near-nationwide radio program is available: the two-hour *Larry Black Show* originating in Nashville, at top-rated WKDF. The show is syndicated for play on at least 110 radio stations. Check your local listings for this long-standing evangelistic show mixing the best in Christian and secular top-40 hits.

Also worth mentioning is the conversion of the former XERF—the "border-blaster" that sent Wolfman Jack's legendary voice across the country in the fifties with the latest in rock and roll—to the new LOVE 16. The station is still as powerful—sending 250,000 watts of clear channel sound into the heavenlies—but now the broadcasts contain, for the most part, contemporary Christian music. Plans for the station include broadcast of a Christian Grand Ole Opry, live from Denver, to the world every Saturday night. The station can be heard in all the states and many other countries as it beams contemporary Christian hits around the clock. A license is pending to increase the station's output to 500,000 watts (*Contemporary Christian* magazine, April 1983, p. 26).

The Ten Most Wanted List

Each year rock and roll produces new artists who add to the overwhelming list of veterans already promoting, through their lyrics and lifestyles, graphics and goals, ideas which defy the Christian ethic. While we know it is important to continue to fight against those who promote the offensive material permeating much of rock music today, we are not condemning the rock stars themselves. In fact, we pray for them every day.

In hope that, through prayer and open dialogue, many of rock music's most notorious stars can come to know Christ and thus change their music and their motives, we have compiled a list of Ten Most Wanted. If you would like to change the future of rock music, and of one of American culture's most pervasive influences, please pray for the artists on this list on a daily basis. You might also consider writing to them. Tell them about Jesus and let them know you love them and are praying for them—but also that you cannot tolerate their behavior and recorded material. Give them an opportunity to meet the Lord through you!

Rock and Roll's Ten Most Wanted

1. **Angus Young** (AC/DC)
   ATI, 888 Seventh Avenue, New York, NY 10106
2. **Rob Halford** (Judas Priest)
   Great Southern Co., 560 Arlington Place, Macon, GA 31201
3. **Prince**
   Cavallo, Ruffalo, Fargnoli Management; 11340 West Olympic Boulevard; West Los Angeles, CA 90064
4. **Joe Elliot** (Def Leppard)
   Polygram Records, 810 Seventh Avenue, New York, NY 10019
5. **Gene Simmons** (KISS)
   The KISS Army, P.O. Box 840, Westbury, NY 11590
6. **Mick Jagger** (Rolling Stones)
   8335 Sunset Boulevard, Los Angeles, CA 90069
7. **David Bowie**
   c/o William Morris Agency, 151 El Camino, Beverly Hills, CA 90212
8. **Ozzy Osbourne**
   ATI, 888 Seventh Avenue, New York, New York 10106
9. **David Lee Roth** (Van Halen)
   The Van Halen Fan Club, P.O. Box 2128, North Hollywood, CA 91602
10. **Steve Perry** (Journey)
    Journey International Fan Club, P.O. Box 404, San Francisco, CA 94101

Appendix 2: Writing to Washington

The next time you hear a song on your local radio station which you find offensive, send a letter to your representative or senator. As noted in the petition on the following page, obscene and indecent language *is* prohibited by law, and so is the sale of drugs.

Each time you send a letter to one of your congressmen, send a carbon copy to the Chairman of the FCC, Washington, D.C. 20554. If these people receive enough letters, eventually they'll begin to listen. For added clout, send another copy to the owner/manager of the radio station. Believe it or not, he is swayed by letters. Here is a sample letter:

Representative or Senator
Washington, D.C. 20515

Dear Congressman————:
It is my understanding that federal law prohibits pornography (or drug sales) via the nation's airwaves. I recently heard a song entitled ————— on radio station (call letters) in (city, state). The song described (or stated) —————. In your opinion, is this pornographic (or obscene or does it promote drug abuse, etc.)?

I urgently request your assurance that: (1) You are investigating the scope of this problem; (2) You are searching for legal relief for all of us and will give me details when your plan is formulated; (3) You are as interested as I am in insuring a wholesome musical atmosphere for our children.

Thank you for your concern.

Sincerely,

—————

NATIONAL PETITION

To Stop Pornographic Music
From Being Sold to or Played on the Public Airwaves in the Presence of Minors.

Mr. President, Members of Congress and Chairman of the F.C.C.:

We, the undersigned, are hereby petitioning all federal branches of government involved and all honorable men concerned to stop innocent children from being immorally influenced by pornography disseminated through music sold to minors or played over the public airwaves in violation of existing law which states,

"Whoever utters any obscene, indecent or profane language by means of radio communication, shall be fined not more than $10,000 or imprisoned not more than two years or both."

U.S. Code Title 18, Section 1464

We demand the establishment of the following:

(1) A record rating system that will aid parents in monitoring the music to which their children listen—a system similar to that used in motion picture ratings;

(2) The banning of all obscene, indecent, or profane records (or records so rated) from play over the public airwaves via radio or television;

(3) Prohibition of sale of any obscene, indecent or profane records (or records so rated) to any minor under the age of 17, except by consent of parent or guardian.

(Print address, city, state and zip)

Name

Address

City   State   Zip

Name

Address

City   State   Zip

Name

Address

City   State   Zip

Name

Address

City   State   Zip

Name

Address

City   State   Zip

Name

Address

City   State   Zip

Name

Address

City   State   Zip

Name

Address

City   State   Zip

Name

Address

City   State   Zip

Name

Address

City   State   Zip

Name

Address

City   State   Zip

Name

Address

City   State   Zip

Name

Address

City   State   Zip

Name

Address

City   State   Zip

Name

Address

City   State   Zip

Name

Address

City   State   Zip

Feel free to make copies of this petition. When they are filled, send to:

Truth About Rock, P.O. Box 9222, St. Paul, MN 55109.

How to Contact the Peters Brothers

Seven countries, 40 states, 1,000 seminars, 1,000,000 attenders—the Peters Brothers will go anywhere to expose youth to the TRUTH ABOUT ROCK.

To schedule a "Why Knock Rock?" seminar in your area or for information on other documentation on rock music in books, slides, video and audio cassettes, write or call

The Peters Brothers
Truth About Rock
Box 9222
North Saint Paul, MN 55109
(612) 770-8114